SELECTIVE TROUT

The Last Word on Stream Entomology
and
Aquatic Insect Imitation

DOUG SWISHER AND CARL RICHARDS

ILLUSTRATED BY DAVE WHITLOCK
FOREWORD BY NICK LYONS

SKYHORSE PUBLISHING

Skyhorse Publishing books may be purchased in bulk at special discounts for sales promotion, corporate gifts, fund-raising, or educational purposes. Special editions can also be created to specifications. For details, contact the Special Sales Department, Skyhorse Publishing, 307 West 36th Street, 11th Floor, New York, NY 10018 or info@skyhorsepublishing.com.

Skyhorse® and Skyhorse Publishing® are registered trademarks of Skyhorse Publishing, Inc.®, a Delaware corporation.

Visit our website at www.skyhorsepublishing.com.

10 9 8 7 6 5 4 3 2

Library of Congress Cataloging-in-Publication Data is available on file.

Cover design by Tom Lau
Cover photo credit: Doug and Sharon Swisher

Print ISBN: 978-1-5107-2985-8
Ebook ISBN: 978-1-5107-2986-5

Printed in China

Table of Contents

Acknowledgments

WE WISH TO THANK the following persons, each of whom contributed so generously to our work:

Joe Brooks, truly the world's number-one fly-fisherman, for his insistence upon perfection;

Art Flick for the inspiration provided not only by his angling accomplishments and contributions, but also by being Art Flick;

Ernie Schwiebert for the identification of some Eastern species and the inspiration provided by his many contributions to the world of fly-fishing;

Vince Marinaro for his pioneer work in terrestrial fishing and in new-pattern innovations;

Justin Leonard, George Edmunds, and Steven Jensen for their invaluable assistance in identifying species of aquatic insects across the entire country;

Dr. Brian Armitage of the Ohio Biological Survey, for identifying many caddisfly specimens;

Dr. Richard Merritt of Michigan State University, coeditor of *Aquatic Insects of North America;*

Jeff Cooper of the Michigan Water Resources Commission, for help in identifying specimens;

Larry Solomon and Eric Leiser, authors of *Caddis and the Angler;*

Gary LaFontaine, author of *Caddisflies;*

John Juracek and Craig Mathews, authors of *Fishing the Yellowstone Hatches,* for advice;

John Shewey, author of *Mastering the Spring Creeks;*

Bob Braendle, coauthor of *Caddis Super Hatches;*

Steve Hiner of Virginia Tech for collecting and identifying aquatic insects of Southern Appalachia;

Brett Billings of Eastern Kentucky for collecting and identifying aquatic insects of Southern Appalachia;

John Doty of Trout South Magazine for collecting and identifying aquatic insects of Southern Appalachia;

Terry Chilcoat of the TVA for collecting and identifying aquatic insects of Southern Appalachia.

Foreword to the 2018 Edition

I CONFESS TO UTTER confusion when the proposal for *Selective Trout* reached me at Crown Publishers in 1970. I had begun the "Sportsmen's Classics" series, reprints of older fly-fishing titles that warranted new lives; these constituted, at the time, most of what I knew about the ample tradition of fly-fishing literature. My fortunate first choice had been *Art Flick's New Streamside Guide to Naturals and Their Imitations* and I had on my list of others, either already in production or in my sights, Vince Marinaro's *A Modern Dry-Fly Code*, Jim Leisenring's little book on the wet fly, Preston Jennings's *A Book of Trout Flies*, Sparse Grey Hackle's *Fishless Days, Angling Nights*, and three or four others. There was little work to be done on these books—their value established, their form fixed.

Art Flick's book promptly sold out its first printing of 7,500 copies and thus persuaded the editor-in-chief of the error in his dogmatic assertion that "fishing books never sell." Emboldened when he told me to sign up a whole lot more Flicks, I advised him that first he should endorse my earlier request to add a water-resistant binding because the identification of trout-stream insects usually took place streamside. He suggested instead a *lead* binding so the book would sink and require a new copy.

What confused me first about the proposal were the many line drawings of the new patterns Doug and Carl had developed. They looked weird, like futuristic fantasies, and I had no idea they could possibly catch trout.

Selective Trout came to me after the authors had fished with Art Flick and at his recommendation; Joe Brooks had introduced them to Art and had already agreed to write an introduction to the book. My skeptical turn of brain rarely accepts endorsements as final so I studied the manuscript with care and especially matched words and the logic for them to the odd images. Frankly, I was scared. It was one thing to find and publish acknowledged "classics," another to pick a new book of worth. What I first saw was that the removal of hackle beneath the fly made perfect sense since hackle obscured the silhouette that had to be a major trigger for trout to strike. And then it all began to add up, so in the end I contracted for the book and worked to put all the elements together—a larger format to accommodate drawings in the border, directly supporting the text, and the book for the home not hauled to the stream.

That was more than forty-five years ago and the book became the most successful of any fly-fishing title I published; more, it dramatically changed our views about the construction of trout flies, led to dozens of invaluable developments by others, and made all fly-tying practice much more flexible and inventive. And the flies took more trout.

With later invaluable changes and additions, especially the color artwork by Dave Whitlock and some important tweaking, the book is now better than ever and it is a great pleasure to think it will continue to inspire and encourage fly tyers for generations to come. This is one of the most important, timeless, and genuinely helpful fly-fishing books and has a place in every fly-fisher's library.

NICK LYONS
WOODSTOCK, NEW YORK
JUNE 2017

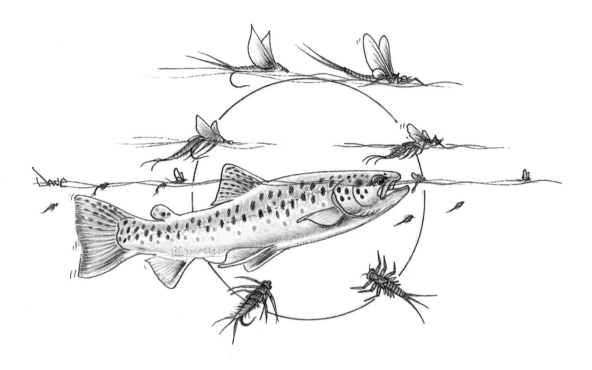

CHAPTER 1

Science and Selectivity

THE SELECTIVITY OF trout has always been the most difficult and challenging of the numerous problems that confront the fly fisherman. With fishing pressure increasing at a tremendous rate, the problem will become even more acute. The growing popularity of fly fishing, combined with the activities of the great dam builders, will increase this pressure in the coming years. Each season we find more and more fishermen wading our favorite pools, and paralleling this trend, we find our friend the trout becoming more and more selective. With the advent of special fishing regulations and an increase in the number of no-kill areas, trout that are caught more than once become even more selective and leader shy.

Even before the recent deluge of fishermen, however, there was a need for new patterns and techniques to fool those selective risers. How many times have you been involved in that typical situation of dozens of fish feeding all around, but you get nothing but refusals? At almost all of these frustrating times the problem is having the wrong fly—a fly that is probably too large, too bushy, and obviously very unrealistic in appearance.

For us, having the *right* fly for a given hatch is 100 percent more effective and much more satisfying than fumbling along with something "fairly close." The *right* fly is the one that resembles the natural so closely that the fish *seem* to prefer it over the real thing. A good imitation can mean the difference between thirty fish and no fish on a given day. Many of the old standard patterns just do not work well during these selective situations. If the fish move for them at all, they drift up, take a long leisurely look, and then turn disdainfully away.

Anglers are eager to blame their inability to take fish on a variety of factors. Some excuses include, "My tippet was too heavy," "My casting was bad today," or "I couldn't get a drag-free float." In most cases, the real reason was having the wrong fly. Since one of the most common is the tippet excuse, we did some experimenting in this area, using tippets that were much larger and stiffer than recommended. We scored just as well as we did with the smaller tippets—*when* we had the right fly on. For example, on the tiny *Tricorythodes* spinner, we've used 4X and 5X tippets without *any* drop-off in success.

But before even a realistic imitation will raise a trout, it is necessary to know which fly the fish are feeding on. The Au Sable River in Michigan and other even-flowing rivers like it all over the country have many different species of aquatic insects hatching every day of the season. These rich rivers have high lime content that results in tremendous hatches. In fact, two or three different species will often be on the water at the same time. On these prolific waters, the fisherman must not only match the hatch but also discover *which* hatch the fish are taking. It can be difficult, but it is certainly never dull.

To make matters even more complicated, individual fish may exhibit an individual preference during a multiple hatch. This phenomenon is due to the varying character of the stream below the lines of drift. Correspondingly, each nymphal type requires its own kind of water habitat, and, as a result, higher concentrations of specific species occur in specific areas.

An observant and creative angler should be able to conquer these selective situations. During peak emergence periods, the trout usually throw caution to the wind by boldly coming out from their hiding places and feeding voraciously. This is the fulfillment of every fly fisherman's "dream"—his magic moment—and he should make the most of it. It is also the moment of truth. For at this point, with the stream pocketed with feeding trout, an angler's skill is given its sternest test.

After experiencing many of these frustrating slack-line episodes, we decided to attempt a logical and scientific approach to the problem by making a closer study of the trout's food and its feeding habits. We were aware of the aquatic insects that trout feed on and the standard patterns used to imitate those insects, but since standard dressings were so consistently ineffective during periods of heavy feeding and high selectivity, we wanted to look at the situation more closely.

The average fly fisherman is a fairly observant and creative fellow. He is aware of the floating and flying creatures around him, and he is also conscious of the relationship between these graceful winged creatures and the trout's diet. He is even able to create or purchase an imitation that closely resembles the size, color, and shape of the natural he observed—or *thought* he observed! However, observation is where the trouble usually begins. To "observe" sounds like a very simple and basic process. But when it comes to observing aquatic insects, more than a casual glance is required.

Most fishermen who claim to know "what the hatch is" have merely watched an insect fly or float by at a distance of at least 3 or 4 feet. In many cases, when an insect is caught and observed at close range, preferably with some magnification, it will look much different than when it is floating past your rod tip or flying overhead. The first step in our quest for a solution to the problem, then, was to begin collecting aquatic insects—mostly mayflies, caddisflies, and stoneflies—and then to observe them under magnification.

Each of us interprets color differently, so we decided the best way to accumulate the desired information was through close-up photography, or to be more specific, photomicrography. Our goal was to produce true color photographs of each stage of all the most important aquatic insects. And, just as important, we wanted to magnify these photographs enough to obtain a trout's-eye view of each insect. The reason for wanting a magnified view is quite simple. If we hold a fly, or any object, for that matter, at a distance of only 3 or 4 inches from our eyes, it is completely out of focus. It will be blurred and appear as a very dim and indistinct form. In order to bring it into focus and see it clearly, a magnifying lens of 2 to 3 power is required. Since trout inspect drifting flies at this same close range, it would thus seem obvious that we must use similar magnification factors in our photography.

Not only did we obtain ideas for improved patterns from the pictures, but we also accumulated much valuable data and experience while collecting the specimens. We automatically found out how, when, and where each insect emerges during the collection process. This information, in turn, was used to develop hatching calendars, and it provided many new ideas about technique. By using the hatching calendar, the new patterns, and the how, when, and where information, it became possible to apply an orderly scientific approach to fly fishing. We expected to increase our catch per hour and reduce sharply the number of those baffling moments of "unmatched hatches." The plan worked for us—and it can for you.

For the expert, we offer new and interesting changes in some of the old standard patterns that have supposedly withstood the test of time. For the beginner, we offer a simplified and logical introduction into the world of fly fishing. In these pages you will find an examination of the principal aquatic and terrestrial insects forming the trout's diet, emergence calendars that can be adapted for use in any section of the country, full instructions for tying the new patterns, and large full-color photographs to help identify and imitate the insects.

We have only scratched the surface of this sport that deals with the whims and fancies of the trout. Many chapters and volumes have yet to be written, but we hope we have opened up a new avenue of thinking and have created a fresh, systematic, and scientific approach.

CHAPTER 2

Collecting,
Photographing, Identifying

THE EQUIPMENT USED in our study falls into three general categories: collection, photographic, and identification. However, the methods and equipment needed to collect specimens do not have to be complicated or expensive; what can be done is limited only by your ingenuity.

Many nymphs and winged insects can be collected by hand, whereas others must be obtained with the aid of various kinds of seines and nets. For the collection of underwater specimens, a simple hand seine can be used. This device consists of a strip of window screen connected to two wooden handles. A piece of screen 30 inches long by 20 inches wide attached to 3-foot handles is quite functional and easy to carry in a car.

To use this seine, the collector stands in the water facing downstream, holding the screen at arm's length, tight against the bottom of the stream. When the bottom material is disturbed and dislodged, usually by digging with the feet, both specimens and debris will flow into the seine. The nymphs can then be either picked off by hand or washed into a suitable container. Many other types of seines can be devised, depending on the

A simple kitchen strainer

whims of the collector. For example, a simple kitchen strainer attached to the end of a long handle is useful for catching some of the free-swimming nymphs that occupy the deeper runs, whereas a screen-wire scap net of rugged construction is helpful in obtaining the muck-burrowing nymphs.

Collection of the winged stages (duns and spinners) can be more varied and difficult, partly because of the short period that they are available. The ideal time to capture freshly hatched duns is immediately after they've emerged and are floating along on the surface. This is when we all want to be on the stream anyway. It is usually a simple task to scoop up a few floating duns with the aid of a small aquarium hand net. In fact, one of these

8-inch aquarium hand net

nets should be a permanent part of the equipment carried in any fishing vest. It may look easy to snatch a floating fly from the water's surface with the bare hand, but at least for the smaller specimens, it is very difficult.

Spinners can be captured in the same manner as the duns when they fall into the water after mating. Both duns and spinners can be found in such places as bushes and trees along the streamside, on bridge abutments and docks, on weeds growing along the bank, and on cabin walls. (One of our favorite spots is at a service station near the banks of the Au Sable River in Grayling, where duns and spinners are attracted by the bright lights.) Spinners can also be caught with long-handled butterfly nets as they swarm overhead.

Caddisflies can be collected by using a long-handled sweep net passed over bushes, grasses, and trees near a river. With good populations of caddisflies and a recent hatch, you can quickly capture many insects this way. The easiest method for collecting adult caddisflies is to place a light trap near a river just before dark. This consists of a white pan with some rubbing alcohol in the bottom and a portable fluorescent light placed nearby. Caddisflies will be attracted to the light, crawl into the alcohol, and then become trapped. Unlike mayfly nymphs, caddis larvae and pupae are difficult to capture in a seine. They are best collected by picking the cases off rocks and logs.

Originally, all of our collecting was done at the stream, usually during a fishing expedition. However, it soon became evident that something more was required to facilitate the study. We could not possibly be on the stream during each emergence to sample all of the hatches, so we decided to transport nymphs from the stream to our homes, where they were put into aquariums to complete their growth. This allowed us to keep track of most of the major hatches every day, not just during periodic fishing trips.

Long-handled butterfly nets

Of even greater importance was the tremendous advantage gained for our photographic efforts. It is much easier to keep the camera ready in the one spot it is needed than to tote it along on each fishing excursion, where constantly varying light and weather conditions exist. A freshly hatched dun can be quickly removed from the aquarium and placed on the miniature photographing stage before color changes begin. There is no wind or rain to contend with, the light source can remain constant, and much of the guesswork is eliminated. Nymphs can be photographed right through the aquarium walls and their habits thoroughly observed.

Other advantages provided by the aquarium are faster growth of the insect and, perhaps most important, more fishing time for the fisherman. By being indoors during the winter months, nymphal growth is greatly accelerated, thereby producing hatches 2 to 3 months early. Hendricksons, for example, which normally hatch in the stream during late April and May, will come as early as February in the aquarium. This means that picture taking and identification can be concluded far in advance of the natural time schedule, and this, of course, results in more fishing time.

A few of the aquariums used by the authors

Microscopes, cameras, and other equipment in the authors' lab

Some nymphs, such as *Siphlonurus* and *Isonychia,* have difficulty in adapting to aquarium life, but most of the important species can be reared very well in standard tropical fish aquariums with filters. Our aquariums range from 5 to 40 gallons in size, and we maintain a water temperature of approximately 65 degrees F. We seine nymphs from many locations around the state and country so that we can identify as many species as possible. To date, we have obtained insects from most of the important trout states, including Michigan, Montana, New York, Idaho, Wyoming, Colorado, Vermont, New Jersey, and Pennsylvania. Some of the more important rivers we have studied include the Beaverkill and Esopus of New York; the Paulinskill and Pequest of New Jersey; Paradise Creek of Pennsylvania; the Madison, Yellowstone, and Big Hole of Montana; Henry's Fork of the Snake in Idaho; and the Au Sable in Michigan.

In order to produce the pictures we desired, we had to obtain equipment that would enable us to make photomicrographs. The pictures produced by photomicrography permit detailed and precise study of minute objects. In our case, the minute objects are aquatic insects. Generally speaking, photomicrography is a process by which we can record on film any subjects that are smaller than the resulting film image. Specifically, for our study, we can say that images recorded from actual size to approximately four times actual size are regarded as photomicrographs. An additional requirement is that a camera lens is used instead of supplementary optics, such as those of a microscope.

Good close-up photographs of naturals to be imitated are invaluable to the fly tier. This is especially true when designing a new pattern that is intended to be more effective than existing ones. Memory is not reliable, and details the eye does not catch will show up in the photographs.

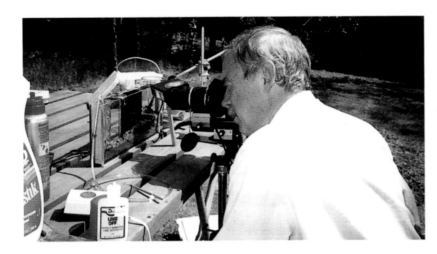

35-mm single-lens reflex camera
with a 55-mm macro lens

Here are some of the techniques we use to photograph live insects both in water and on land. Some can be used for other prey forms, such as minnows and crayfish. These are reliable methods that can be counted on for good results even in the field; some require very little set-up time.

You will need the following equipment: a 35-mm single-lens reflex camera with a 55-mm macro lens (or a set of simple macro lenses that fit on a bellows); an extension bellows and a sturdy tripod; an electronic flash with a power mount for reliable lighting; a light box to diffuse the light so the subject is clearly visible on all sides; a glass aquarium for immature aquatic insects; a glass petri dish to hold immature aquatic insects; and a set of eyeglass blanks to place over the insects so they will hold still.

Most of this equipment can be purchased at a camera shop, along with the instructions for using it. Light boxes of various dimensions (depending on the size of the subject) can be easily constructed from inexpensive materials at home. Aquariums can be made at a glass shop from window glass, or you can buy the glass and put it together yourself. Pet shops stock 5-gallon aquariums, but smaller ones are more convenient. You can obtain eyeglass blanks from an optometrist and petri dishes from a scientific equipment supply house.

The two most important but difficult aspects of any type of photography are good lighting and proper exposure. These are even more challenging in microphotography. A light box and electronic flash will provide the proper lighting for most situations. The light box consists of a balsa-wood base (available from a hobby shop) with a simple box frame glued together. Natural vellum (from an art supply store) is glued over, around, and in front of the frame, and a hole is cut in front of the light box to accept the lens. The subject is cemented (with a tiny dot of superglue) to a twig or other suitable mount and placed in the light box. The lens is then adjusted for focus, and the shot is taken at the proper exposure with the camera set for manual operation.

To determine the proper exposure (*f*-stop), load a roll of slide film into the camera. Using the flash and light box, take one shot of a neutral-colored subject (such as a Kodak gray card) at each *f*-stop (*f*/22 to *f*/3.5). Instruct the photofinisher to develop the roll but not cut the film; leave it on the roll. By examining the continuously numbered frames you will discover which is the correct exposure for that particular film for a neutral-colored subject. If your electronic flash is fairly powerful, it will probably be between *f*/22 and *f*/16—which is ideal because these apertures provide good depth of field. If you are not getting enough light at *f*/22 or *f*/16, use a higher-speed film (ISO 100, 200, or 400).

When shooting an actual subject, you must *bracket* the exposures with at least three lens settings: the *f*-stop you think is correct, one over, and one under. This is because not all subjects are a neutral color; lighter subjects need less light (a smaller opening) and darker ones need more (a larger opening). Slide film is better slightly underexposed, and print film is better slightly overexposed. The correct setting differs with the size of the subject and its distance from the lens. If you are using a bellows for greater magnification, the bellows extension will cause a variation in exposure; the more the bellows is extended, the more light is needed (a larger lens opening). With all of these variables it is critical to take a test roll of a subject and bracket the shots. Then the correct setting for a subject is generally known, and when you get into the field you will be able to set up quickly and take your shots with confidence.

For our shots of adult insects we hold the subject with a simple stand. It consists of a small plastic base with a hole drilled in it, and a nail that fits the hole which has been glued into the base of an alligator clip. This will hold a twig from a tree or bush and can be moved up and down. We glue the insect to the twig by placing a very small amount of superglue on the twig. Then we place the light box over the stand and take the shot. With this setup, good and reliable pictures of adult insects, such as mayflies and caddisflies, can be taken quickly in the field.

An alternate setup is a glass aquarium without water. Place some leaves in the aquarium, introduce the insects, and give them time to settle down. When they have stopped moving around, the shots can be taken using the method we will describe for subjects in water (below). This setup can produce very natural-looking shots, but it takes more time and equipment, so it is not as convenient in the field.

We always try to fill as much of the frame with the subject as possible. When you are using a photograph and dress an imitation, the more detail the better. A shot of a small caddisfly on a big leaf may be artistic, but it is not much use to fly tiers for designing an imitation.

Some subjects photograph much better using backlighting. Examples are insects with some translucence in their anatomy, such as mayflies, which seem to glow when backlit. Even though caddisfly wings are translucent, they are folded back over the opaque body and do not appear translucent in photographs even when backlit.

When we require backlighting we do not use the light box. We mount the subject in the normal manner using the stand, camera, and electronic flash used for the front light. Above and behind the subject we place another electronic flash that has a slave unit attached to it. This picks up light from the front light and fires the backlight. As with all techniques, make a test roll and bracket the subject.

Shooting fish, crustaceans, and immature forms of aquatic insects in water requires a very different staging than shooting mature insects in the air. We use a small aquarium made from window glass cemented together with waterproof cement purchased at a tropical fish store. Any glass shop can easily make this setup for you, or you can have them cut the glass pieces and cement them together yourself. Gravel or sand is placed on the bottom, water from the subject's area is poured into the aquarium, and the creature or creatures are introduced. The camera is positioned and adjusted, and the shots are taken. All things being equal, more light is needed when photographing a subject in water, as the liquid will absorb some light. You can eliminate the light box and still get good results. The light from the flash should hit the glass at a 45-degree angle. This eliminates light bouncing back into the lens.

When shooting overhead pictures of small insects such as mayfly nymphs, we put them into a glass petri dish filled with water (filtered to eliminate dust) and place a curved eyeglass blank over the insect. Feeling the top of the glass on its back, the insect thinks it is hidden under something and stays still. These blanks come in different sizes and curves suitable for different sizes of insect. You can obtain them from any store that sells prescription eyeglasses.

The lighting for this setup is one flash overhead and one underneath for backlighting. Backlighting is very important when photographing nymphs, as it makes them glow on the body parts that are translucent. Both flash units are aimed so that the light strikes the water at a 45-degree angle. The camera is aimed straight down, and the petri dish is placed on a glass table or a stand with a hole cut in the middle so the light from underneath illuminates the petri dish from the bottom. The light box is not used in this setup.

The identification of aquatic insects is a highly interesting process, but it can also be very challenging. Identification at the family and genus levels is usually quite routine, but determination of the final species can be puzzling and uncertain. There are so many similarities among closely related species that it can be extremely difficult to recognize the differences. Some of the basic equipment needed for the identification process includes a low-power wide-field microscope, scalpel, forceps, dissecting needles, eyedroppers, glass slides, storage vials and racks, various hand magnifiers, and a variety of reference books.

Our equipment is mostly uncomplicated and inexpensive. Much of it, such as nets, seines, and stages, can be designed and fashioned by anyone. Other items, such as cameras and microscopes, may be quite expensive, and their techniques can be mastered only with practice. It is especially important that you be familiar with the camera and photography techniques. Nothing is as disappointing as arriving home from some exotic and expensive location with important shots only to discover the lighting or exposure was incorrect.

CHAPTER 3

The Need for Realistic Imitation

THE SINGLE MOST overriding problem the fly fisherman must deal with is procuring an artificial fly that will gull the trout into thinking the fly is a natural insect. And the single most difficult period for accomplishing this deception is during the rise to a hatch of naturals. During this period the fish become familiar with a specific insect after feeding on it over and over. The finest leader, the smoothest casts, and the most beautiful drag-free floats are all useless if the trout is not duped into thinking that the artificial is the real thing.

Most anglers experience real success only when the fish are not selective, at those times when rise activity is sparse or nonexistent. During heavy feeding activity, however, some anglers are virtually helpless. Their predicament is usually due to the unrealistic appearance of the standard patterns of trout flies. These patterns simply do not simulate, to the trout, their view of the naturals. But realistic and effective patterns for specific hatches make it possible to hook and release many more trout, even during the most selective rises.

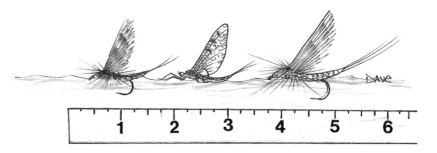

The mayfly natural, middle, is adequately imitated by the fly on the left. The imitation on the right does not match the size or color of the natural.

Trout feeding habits vary greatly depending on the velocity of water and type of stream that the fish inhabit. All very small trout feed mainly on aquatic insects. As they grow larger, however, other fish—such as minnows and even smaller trout—become increasingly important to their diet. This cannibalistic tendency is accelerated on rapid rivers, such as the lower Madison, and on streams with little insect life. Much energy is required to chase food through fast, heavy currents, so the prey must be large enough to be worthwhile. On these swift streams, larger trout may not feed heavily on small insects. Thus, the dry-fly angler will generally profit more if he concentrates on those rivers where the hatch produces consistent and reliable feeding activity.

The types of streams that are conducive to the dry fly and to selective rising trout are:

1. *Slow pools, interspersed with riffles or rapids.* Examples include the Beaverkill and the Neversink in the East; and Rock Creek, the Yellowstone, the North and South Forks of the Platte, and the upper Madison in the West.

2. *Uniform flow, unbroken water.* Examples include the limestone rivers of the East, such as the Letort and Big Springs in Pennsylvania; the Au Sable in Michigan; and the spring creeks of Idaho and Montana, such as Henry's Fork of the Snake and the numerous Gallatin River Valley spring creeks.

These types of waters are quite common, and it is in them that we find our extraordinarily selective trout. On these sleek rivers, large trout will remain "insect eaters" much longer because they can hover and sip small bites without expending large amounts of energy in the slow, easy flow. The more rapid the current, the larger the insect must be to lure the fish up to the surface. Many rivers have fine hatches of very small mayflies all season long, but if the water is too fast they are not usually of prime importance. On the more ideal fly water, such as the placid limestone and spring creeks, large fish can and do feed well on even the smallest mayflies. In these waters, the fish get a more leisurely look at their food and have good "close vision." This enables them to differentiate between the tremendous variety of flotsam and jetsam blown and washed into a river, and the small, live, naturally camouflaged aquatic insects floating by them. Therefore, fish in these slower and more fertile waters become ultraselective during a hatch because of the long observation time available to them.

On quiet rivers, trout often seem to prefer very small insects, ignoring much larger ones that may be hatching simultaneously. This is usually because the small flies are much more numerous. Since tiny mayflies are more difficult for the angler to see than large ones, he may erroneously believe the larger fly to be more prevalent and important. Occasionally, when trout are feeding on very large naturals, they seem to lose their native caution and hit almost any concoction. This phenomenon may account for some individual opinions that realistic patterns are not important or necessary. However, we feel that as the size of the natural decreases, the selectivity of the trout actually appears to increase and become more critical.

When fishing a #28 hatch, for example, a 1-mm variation from the natural means at least a 30 percent dimensional error—which is disastrous and results in nothing but refusals from the trout. Good fish often gorge on these very tiny naturals, and we've found that realistic imitation is essential in these critical situations for any consistent success. Also, it is important to bear in mind that on fertile rivers these small flies comprise the real bulk of the trout's diet. The minute species hatch in far greater numbers and with much more consistency than the larger mayflies.

The major aquatic insects that trout feed on, in their usual order of importance, are:

1. Mayflies—upwings, Ephemeroptera
2. Caddisflies—downwings, tentwings, Tricoptera
3. Stoneflies—downwings, flat wings, Plecoptera
4. Midges—downwings, glassy wings, aquatic Diptera

Mayflies have wings that, when folded at rest, are upright. They are the only aquatic insects with upright wings and, as such, are easily recognized. Mayflies are by far the most important aquatic insects. They come in all sizes, from #4 to #28.

On some rivers, especially below impoundments, caddisflies surpass mayflies for numbers and availability. Caddisflies have wings that are folded down and "tentlike" in an inverted V when the insect is at rest. Most caddisflies are size #14 to #20. It is usually difficult for the angler to identify the type of insect hatching by watching them fly over the river. *You must catch one and examine it at rest, in your hand.* We cannot overemphasize this point. Examine it closely, or the chances are you will be fooled. A fluttering caddis can easily resemble a stonefly at a distance.

Stoneflies are next in importance. Most species prefer fast, rocky water and hatch by crawling onto some object such as a rock or a log. They are taken by trout mainly on their egg-laying flights. Stoneflies have flat wings when at rest. They vary in size from the exceedingly large salmonfly of the western rivers to tiny #20s, although the most prevalent size is #14 to #20. Yellow is their most common color.

On many quiet waters, midges are of prime interest and are equally as important as caddisflies. They are very small, ranging from #18 to #28, often much smaller, but fish do feed on them enthusiastically, and these periods offer exciting, light-tackle fishing. Midges have flat, glassy wings and are true flies.

The fly fisherman who knows what is hatching and has realistic imitations will consistently be more effective than the angler relying on trial-and-error methods. In the following chapters we will delve into the detailed life cycle of these insects and their emergence characteristics, and explain how to imitate them successfully.

CHAPTER 4

Mayflies: The Upwings

THE UPWINGS, OR mayflies, form the group of aquatic insects that make up the order Ephemeroptera. More than five hundred different species exist on the North American continent. Four stages—egg, nymph, subimago (dun), and imago (spinner)—comprise the complete life cycle of the mayfly. Nymphs are the immature forms that live on the river bottom, in weeds, under rocks, in sand and gravel, and in muck banks along the stream's edge. Subimagoes are the winged form that emerges from the nymphal case; they float along on the water's surface, inflating their wings, and then fly away to a sheltered resting place. The imagoes are the second winged stage that results from the final molt. After shedding, they return to the stream where mating, egg laying, and death complete the cycle.

In some species, this cycle can be as short as 5 or 6 weeks, whereas some of the large ephemerids, such as *Hexagenia*, require a period of 2 years before maturity is reached. Some of the small *Baetis* flies mature from egg to adult in 4 or 5 months, which allows two broods per year of the same species. Still other flies, such as *Baetis tricaudatus*, have an overlapping se-

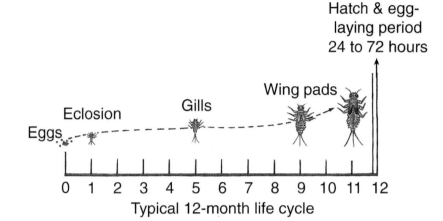

Isonychia mayfly

ries of broods: a 6-month cycle during the warmer part of the year and a 9-month cycle during the winter. In general, however, most species have a 1-year cycle. Depending on water temperature and conditions, most mayfly eggs hatch within a period of 1 to 4 weeks.

Immediately after eclosion, when the nymph hatches from the egg, the nymphal evolution begins. At the conclusion of each stage of development, the nymph molts or sheds its outer skin, which is composed mainly of chitin (a chemical relative of cellulose). The period between any two consecutive molts is called an instar. During nymphal life, most mayflies pass through an average of twenty to thirty instars, which range from only a few days apart, at first, to as long as 2 weeks toward the end. Usually, after ten instars, the gills begin to develop, and at fifteen instars, the wing cases become visible. The later instars give evidence of the developing adult characteristics such as the wings, eggs, and genitalia. Practically all species of mayfly nymphs use microscopic algae and aquatic vegetation as their food source. Only a few, such as *Isonychia* and *Metreturus*, are either partially or completely predacious on other insect forms.

The body of the mayfly nymph is made up of three main parts: head, thorax, and abdomen. Main features of the head include compound eyes, situated on each side; three simple eyes (or ocelli) arranged in a triangle between the compound eyes; the antennae, which lie on top and toward the front of the head; and the complicated mouthparts below. The thorax is made up of three elements: the prothorax, the mesothorax, and the metathorax. The prothorax lies directly behind the head and bears the front pair of legs. The mesothorax is the middle and largest segment of the thorax; it bears the middle pair of legs and the forewing pads. Both the hind pair of legs and hindwing pads are borne by the metathorax. Ten segments comprise the abdomen, of which from four to seven bear gills at their posterolateral corners. All mayfly nymphs are strictly aquatic and respire by means of gills that can vary immensely in shape and size. Gills are either threadlike (filiform), platelike (lamelliform), or some combination of the two. The tenth or terminal segment of the abdomen bears either two or three slender tails.

The various types of mayfly nymphs are each well adapted to specific aquatic habitat, as illustrated by the following list.

Hexagenia limbata,
from underwater

1. Burrowing—sand and gravel, mud	*Ephemera*
	Litobrancha
	Hexagenia
2. Gravel and rubble	*Ephemerella*
	Paraleptophlebia
	Baetis
	Epeorus
	Plauditus (Pseudocloeon)
3. Underside of stones	*Stenonema*
	Rhithrogena
	Heptagenia
4. Submerged plant beds	*Baetis*
	Callibaetis
5. Leaf drift and detritus (nonburrowing)	*Ephemerella*
	Stenonema
	Heptagenia
6. Detritus (little or no current)	*Tricorythodes*
	Brachycercus
	Caenis
	Ephemerella
	Baetisca
	Leptophlebia
	Stenonema
7. Free swimming (quiet water)	*Siphlonurus*
8. Free swimming (moderate to fast water)	*Isonychia*
	Siphloplecton

The nymphs of each species have their own time and method of emergence. For example, *Siphlonurus* and *Isonychia* nymphs usually (but not always) leave the water by crawling onto sticks, stems of plants, logs, or stones, where the nymphal skin is shed and left behind. This process is fairly slow, requiring 4 or 5 minutes. *Hexagenia* nymphs, on the other hand, come to the surface of the water, split their nymphal skin, and then the subimago emerges quickly. After a short rest on the shed epicuticle, it is ready for flight. This entire sequence takes only about 2 minutes. Some species cast off their nymphal integument underwater and struggle to the surface where bedraggled wings must be inflated before flight can occur. In general, however, the nymphs of most species rise to the surface, where the nymphal skin splits and the dun emerges. As soon as the wings are dried sufficiently, the newly hatched subimago takes to the air and finds a resting place for the final molt.

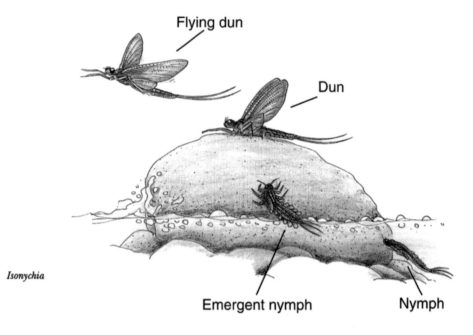

Flying dun

Dun

Isonychia

Emergent nymph

Nymph

Hex nymphs

Epeorus nymphs underwater

Ephemerella subvaria

In this first winged stage, the typical mayfly has two pairs of upright wings, with the anterior pair being much larger than the hind pair. A few species—*Plauditus, Tricorythodes, Brachycercus,* and *Caenis*—lack these hindwings. Wings in the dun stage are semiopaque and display underdeveloped venation (veins), while the bodies tend to be dull in appearance as compared with the imago stage. The adult characteristics, such as eyes, tails, and legs, can be observed—constricted and compressed—under the subimaginal skin. This condition can last from only a few minutes to several days, depending on the species and weather conditions. *Hexagenia,* for example, takes 3 days or more to transform into the spinner stage, whereas *Tricorythodes* usually makes the final molt within several minutes after emergence. For most species, the time between emergence and the final molt is about 24 hours. Ephemeroptera is the only order of insects that undergoes this second stage of development between nymph and final adult.

The imago, or spinner, is usually quite different in appearance from the subimago. The true mayfly has a smooth and shiny body and often displays coloration that varies radically from the dun. It is difficult to believe that dun and spinner belong to the same species. Tails of the imago often become much longer and the wings become clear and hyaline (chitinlike) with fully developed venation. Legs and eyes generally become longer and larger, especially in the male.

The reproduction process normally occurs soon after the final molt has been completed. Mating swarms are composed of male spinners, with an occasional female that flies into the multitude to secure a mate. Once paired, the male uses his long forelegs to hold the thorax of the female and also curls his abdomen into position to make contact with the eggs. In this position, with the larger female supporting both insects, they fly away from the swarm to complete copulation. After the fertilization process has been finished, the female deposits her eggs and dies shortly thereafter.

The females deposit their eggs in a number of distinct ways. Females of *Heptagenia* land on the water, and while riding the current for a short distance, extrude part of their eggs into the stream. They then fly over the water for a few minutes and return again to deposit more eggs. This process is repeated until all of the eggs are extruded. The females finally float downstream in the spent position.

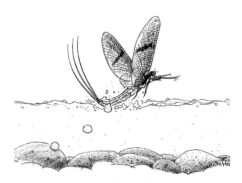

Stenonema depositing eggs

The females of such genera as *Ephemerella* form their eggs in a round mass beneath the tip of the abdomen. Then they fly close to the water and suddenly dip down to break the surface film and release the entire sac into the stream. The eggs sink rapidly to the bottom, where they stick to stones or other objects.

Females of the *Baetis* species land on a stone, log, or some other object protruding from the stream and crawl beneath the surface to deposit their eggs. In some species of *Stenonema*, *Leptophlebia*, and *Siphlonurus*, the females dip the end of their abdomen into the surface of the water at intervals as they fly low over the stream. The dipping action allows a few eggs to be washed off each time until they are all deposited. Females of the Ephemeridae family, such as *Ephemera simulans* and *Hexagenia limbata*, merely land on the water's surface and extrude all of their eggs at once. They remain on the surface with their wings flush in the film until they drown or are eaten by fish.

Stenonema nymph

Knowledge of the life cycle of mayflies can obviously be of tremendous value to the angler. For example, it is clear that the trout have four good opportunities to feed on the various stages of most mayflies: as a nymph on the bottom or on the way up; as an emerging dun slightly under or in the surface film; as a dun drifting on the surface; and as a spinner after it falls back into the water. This requires at least four patterns of artificials for many species, and sometimes more if the males and females are very dissimilar.

The life cycle varies among the Ephemeroptera, and these differences are extremely important. For example, knowing that the subimagoes of *Tricorythodes* quickly molt into spinners indicates the simultaneous presence of both duns and spinners—which, in turn, means that you have to determine which stage the fish are feeding on.

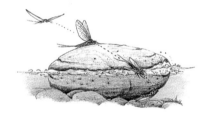

Baetis find suitable rocks for ovipositing, crawl under, and lay their eggs.

The various types of mayflies have a wide range of requirements in relation to the kind of water they need. Some mayflies like fast gravel runs (*Ephemerella subvaria*); some like submerged plant beds (*Baetis* species); some like detritus with little or no current (*Tricorythodes* species); some like to burrow in sand and gravel (*Ephemera simulans*); and some like to burrow in mud (*Hexagenia limbata*). Others, such as *Siphlonurus*, are quiet-water free swimmers, and some, such as *Isonychia*, are fast-water free swimmers.

Most types of mayflies actually must have their particular type of water to survive. It is evident that a river with most or all of the different environ-

Heptagenia depositing eggs

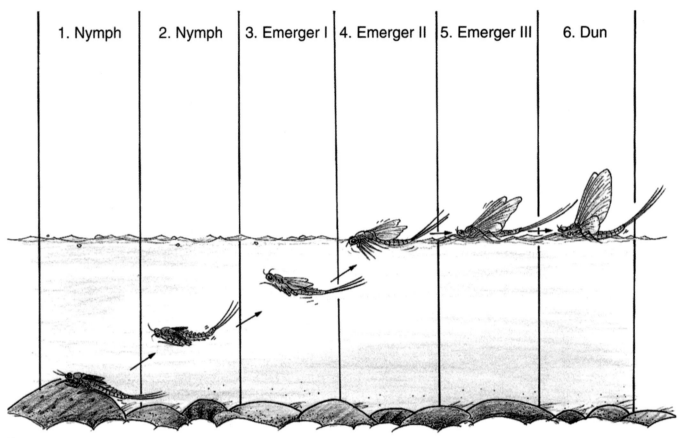

| 1. Nymph | 2. Nymph | 3. Emerger I | 4. Emerger II | 5. Emerger III | 6. Dun |

Emergence

ments will have a larger variety of species than a fast, rocky stream with no weed beds, mud banks, or quiet waters. The latter stream would be lacking entire families of mayflies, and this would reduce the variety of hatches considerably. A fly fisherman who likes to cast over rising trout would obviously be much better off choosing a river with a wide variety of water bottoms.

CHAPTER 5

Patterns Evolved:
No-Hackle Duns, Paraduns,
Emerging Patterns,
Stillborns, and Spinners

WHEN WE LOOKED at our first photographic efforts, we were even more convinced about the need for better patterns. Countless failures with "standard" dressings had built up a strong desire to alter and improve them. These initial photographs may have been lacking in clarity and quality, but they were certainly good enough to get us started in the right direction. No more than a casual glance was needed to spin the wheels of creativity. It became obvious that we had uncovered a new concept and a fresh approach.

Probably the most exciting aspect was the challenge of creating new flies based on what we saw in these fascinating photomicrographs. As most fly tiers know, there is nothing more satisfying than to contrive a new idea for a fly, assemble it at the bench, and then discover that it achieves at least some degree of success in the stream. Such auspicious episodes, however, usually expand your ego but often overestimate the effectiveness of the fly. It is satisfying to concoct a new pattern and doggedly declare it to be the best and only pattern you will cast upon the water. However, pursuing this methodology is neither sensible nor productive.

Standard-hackle dry fly coming into the window

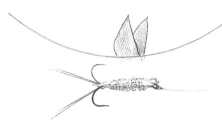

No-Hackle Dun coming into the window

Hen Spinner not yet in window

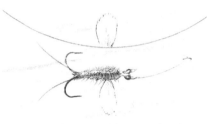

Hen Spinner with one wing in film and out of window, the other wing slightly off surface of water and in the window

Front view of No-Hackle Dun coming into window

Paradun coming into window

Unfortunately, most flies designed in this manner are merely created in accordance with the whims and fancies of the fly tier. Assuredly, these creations will be effective in taking fish *part* of the time, but let's be realistic. There are times when almost *anything* will work. These are the *easy* periods when trout can be taken without much effort or difficulty. *Everyone* should be experiencing action during this time of low selectivity. Such periods should scarcely be ignored or thought of as offering little or no sport. On the contrary, it's always a pleasure to be in the stream and doing "business," no matter what degree of angling prevails. In fact, these are probably the best periods for the neophyte to get acclimated to the sport and to catch a few fish; they will certainly whet his interest. In addition, the expert can sharpen his casting, work on new techniques, test the durability and floatability of new flies, and also increase his score in the process.

The real challenge, however, comes when the trout become *selective*. Steady feeders that zero in on a certain fly can be extremely difficult to fool, especially with some of the "shaving brush" patterns that probably look like gigantic monstrosities to the fish. Close-up views of these unnatural-looking, bristlelike artificials must make the trout wonder what strange new creature is invading his domain.

Many of the standard patterns are so ridiculous that we fishermen, 30 feet away, could easily see our artificial stand out like a sore thumb as it drifts with a group of naturals. Most of you have probably had this experience. But *stop and think.* If you can tell the difference from 30 feet away, the trout that is 3 inches away must be having hysterics. At any rate, he can be very reluctant to take our offering unless it is a fairly accurate simulation of the real thing. Thus, when the fish become highly selective, we must make every effort to reproduce the outstanding features of the natural. This includes not only characteristics of size, shape, and color, but also such peculiarities as how the fly floats on the water and how it behaves in its environment.

Probably the most important aspect of our approach in developing new patterns was maintaining an open mind. We more or less had to pretend that standard dressings and techniques never existed, so that our thinking

THE WINDOW

Rays of light that strike the surface of water at an angle of less than 10 degrees are reflected upward. Unless an object actually penetrates the surface of the water, trout cannot see surface objects when the light the objects reflect is at an angle of less than 10 degrees; this creates a cone of vision commonly referred to as the window. As a mayfly dun floats in the current it will be almost invisible until it floats into the window. The first part of a mayfly that a trout can see clearly is the tips of the wings. We believe that this triggers the first part of the rise, and that this is why realistic wings are the most important part of an imitation.

would not be influenced or affected by precedent or habit. In this modern era of super-selective trout and heavily fished streams, we needed to keep an open and inquiring mind if we hoped to create the patterns needed for selective situations. The lore and heritage of our "sport of sports" are vital to the complete enjoyment and appreciation of fly fishing. But true inventiveness and originality are also part of the fly fisherman's heritage, for many patterns that are now considered "traditional" were once dramatic innovations themselves.

Ideas for new patterns resulted mainly from the observation of our color photographs. Depending on the size of the insect, most of these pictures, or photomicrographs, were shot anywhere from one to four times life size. Probably the great majority, flies that ranged from 5 to 10 mm in length, were taken at magnifications between 2X and 3X. The main objective was to fill the viewing area of the lens as much as possible without cutting off any of the important features. This procedure provided pictures that gave us detailed studies of the characteristics of each species. Critical features such as size, shape, proportion, and color could then be easily observed and examined.

Colors as seen under these magnifications are the ones the trout seem to prefer. Many naturals appear to be one color when held in the hand or seen floating *on* the water, but when viewed under magnification are another color entirely. We have experimented many times using both colors and have found that the artificial using the color revealed in our photographs is normally much more effective.

This was vividly illustrated in our search for a better *Ephemerella dorothea* imitation. The standard yellow-bellied pattern worked well on occasion, but it was not consistent. Looking at the handheld specimens seemed to suggest that this dressing was valid, but an examination of magnified color pictures revealed the presence of either an orange or olive cast, depending on the locality. Addition of either the orange or olive element to the pattern has increased its effectiveness tremendously. Another example of this color phenomenon was seen in certain members of the Baetidae family. Many of these minute species are more popularly known as blue-winged olives, supposedly because they exhibit wings that appear blue and bodies that appear olive in color. However, under magnification, some of these "olive" bodies surprisingly turn out to be brownish and the wings more grayish than blue.

Proper shape and proportion are extremely important in the construction of effective patterns. Most mayfly duns and spinners have slender, delicate bodies, so the imitations should be dressed accordingly. However, few current artificials exhibit this quality. Nymphal bodies, on the other hand, are generally more varied in shape and can be round, flat, oval, slender, or robust. These exact shapes and proportions can easily be determined from close examination of our photographs. This information can then be applied to the tying process to produce more realistic flies. Body silhouette is probably more critical in the construction of nymphs than dry flies, mainly because the body is the most outstanding feature of the nymph.

1. Natural mayfly approaching window: only abdomen, tails, and parts of legs visible

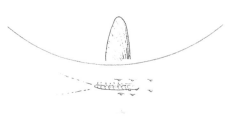

2. First glimpse of wing in window

3. Body now half in, half out of window

4. Mayfly completely in window

In considering the dry fly, however, we must be equally concerned with the shape of *both* body and wings. When the freshly hatched dun approaches the "window," the first elements to be seen *clearly* and *completely* by the trout are the wings. This visual contact is important, as the rise is initiated or triggered at this time. The wings of our artificial must provide a close representation of the wings of the natural so the trout will respond and begin the rise. The body, however, is just as important. Even though the wings have been accepted and the rise has been triggered, the final decision as to the authenticity of the offering has yet to be made. At this point, before contact is accomplished, the entire fly enters the window, allowing close examination by the trout. During this final critical observation both wings and body must be right or a refusal will result. This reasoning can be used to explain the so-called short strikes we often encounter and also those times when the trout comes up, looks at the fly, and then drops back into feeding position.

Duck or turkey feather segment
No-Hackle Dun

Duck-shoulder or turkey-wing Gray-and-Tan No-Hackle Dun

One of the most difficult problems of fly tying is to procure suitable wing materials that will hold their shape when wet. More research is required in this critical area but, for the present, some of the better wing materials include duck-shoulder feathers, turkey-body feathers, shaped hackles, hackle fibers, and various types of hair. Legs and tails normally show up very little in most species and can hardly be considered as outstanding physical features. The tails of the artificial fly, however, have an extremely important function in the positioning of the fly on the water. Stiff high-quality fibers should be used and then spread, or split, at a wide angle. Fibers attached in this manner form outriggers, or stabilizers, that keep the fly in an upright position. This is absolutely necessary for the effective simulation of a newly hatched dun. Hackle or hackle fibers can be used to represent legs but they are not necessary for this purpose. Depending on individual preference, hackle may be used for flotation but should be kept as sparse as possible. Actually, if proper material and techniques are used, hackle is not normally required.

One of the most important discoveries we made for dry flies, which we cannot emphasize enough, is that *flies with high-quality dubbing on light-wire hooks need no hackle to float them.* In fact, when properly treated with flotant, it is almost impossible to sink them—even if you try.

One of the most essential yet seemingly simple aspects of creating a deadly pattern is size. This is especially true for the smaller flies, those less than 7 or 8 mm in length. If, for example, we are trying to imitate a natural that is 5 mm long and our artificial ends up being 6 mm long, we are a whopping 20 percent too large. One millimeter does not sound like much, but it can mean the difference between success and failure, particularly when diminutive patterns are used. The best procedure is to measure the natural accurately and then tie the artificial on a hook bearing a shank of the proper length. At streamside, it is helpful to use a small hand magnifier to obtain an accurate comparison of artificial to natural. This identification part of our study requires precise measurement of each specimen, and this information is then put to use in the tying process. It is far better to use actual measurements than hook size when describing patterns. Hook specifications differ greatly and are therefore unreliable for our purpose, other than as a general denotation of size.

Another factor that affected the development of new patterns was the action, or lack of action, of each species both in, on, and above the water. Most of this information was gained through observations made at streamside or at the aquarium. The majority of in-water activity was observed in the home aquariums, where nymphal life could easily be inspected on a day-to-day basis. Watching the nymphs move about and emerge into adults provided valuable knowledge for designing new subsurface and in-the-film patterns. Streamside observations offered us criteria for new adult dressings and corresponding techniques for their effective application.

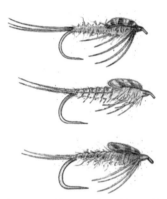

Extended-body wiggle nymph with quill segment wing case

NYMPHS

Probably the most basic requirement of a nymphal pattern is that some type of dubbing should be used for the body. Other materials such as quills, floss, wool, thread, and plastics may look enticing on the vise, but they take on a distinctly unnatural appearance when they are wet. Our nymphs have bodies constructed from such furs as rabbit, muskrat, opossum, fox, mole, and beaver. Fine-textured furs or dubbing should be utilized for small flies, size #20 and smaller—not only for appearance but also for ease of spinning. White domestic rabbit (or synthetic) is an excellent dubbing material because it can be readily dyed to the proper color and it is usually fine grained. Tails from wild rabbits have the added advantage of providing many light-to-dark shades when dyed a certain color. Legs and tails are normally best imitated with such feathers as wood duck, mallard, or partridge tinted to the proper shade. Some of the better wing case materials include ostrich herl, quill segments, breast feathers, fur, and foam.

Three mayfly nymphs with quill segment wing cases

Nymphs tied without wing cases

Ostrich herl or CDC wing case mayfly nymphs

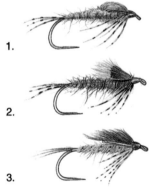

Fur wing case nymphs:
1. Fur tied down on both ends
2. Tuft of fur tied down at head
3. Leather strip of fur tied down at head

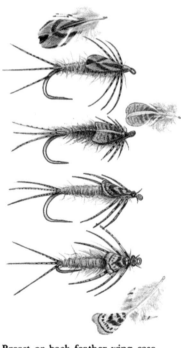

Breast or back feather wing case nymphs. Top and bottom: cock pheasant back and neck feathers; middle: partridge-shoulder feather.

1. Duck wing shoulder feather

2. Trim tips to web. Cut stem.

3. Rooster neck hackle trimmed to form a shaped wing.

4. Hen hackle tip for wing.

Epeorus Nymph with quill segment wing case and gills picked out from abdomen dubbing

Preparation for wings.

Here is our recommended procedure for tying an extended-body wiggle nymph.

1. Make a loop from a thin strand of piano wire in the length you require for the abdomen of the nymph.

2. Put the loop in a fly-tying vise and tie on the tails and fur so that just the loop sticks out from the body.

3. Make another loop of piano wire and insert it in the first loop. The abdomen is then tied on through the second loop to form a hinge. Then tie the second hinge on top of a 5X short-shank hook.

4. Tie the thorax, wing cases, and hackle on the hook part of the nymph and finish as usual.

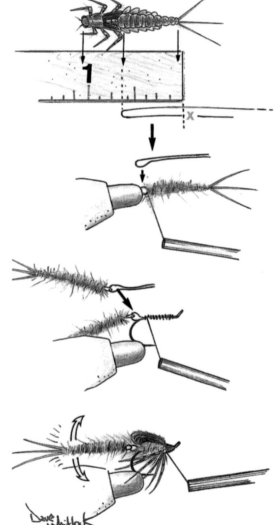

Our observation of nymphs swimming about in the aquarium revealed possibilities for several different patterns. We noticed that all species swim with a distinct undulating movement of the abdomen. Attempts to imitate this situation resulted in extended-body and "wiggle" nymphs.

The extended-body nymph has the abdomen tied on a piece of wire or hook that can be bent in any direction. This makes the nymph look more realistic and is simple to tie. The wiggle nymph, however, carries the idea a step farther by adding a hinge between the thorax and abdomen. This allows the rear part of the fly to move freely, and it more closely simulates the movement of the real nymph. The wiggle nymph is somewhat more difficult to tie but it can be mastered with a little practice. Many methods can be used, but probably the best one involves very fine wire or monofilament for the hinge. Use a short-shank hook for the thorax and leave a small loop of wire extended from the bend. Loop another piece of wire through the first loop and then construct the abdomen and tails on the doubled-back piece.

An easier method is to tie the back part of the fly on a small hook first, and then cut off the bend. Attach this part (the abdomen) to the thorax with a fine wire or monofilament loop. We have also used rubber bands and plain tying thread for the hinge. As for the legs, let most of the fibers extend backward conventionally, but a tie a few of them forward. Sometimes stiffer materials, such as deer or porcupine, are necessary for the front legs. These extended-body and wiggle nymphs have proven themselves to be very effective, not only in matching the hatch, but also when used as attractors.

Pale Morning Dun Duck Segment No-Hackle Emerger

The most important nymphal pattern may be the floating nymph. Our extensive use of the stomach pump over the past 25 years has shown that a huge part of the trout's diet consists of nymphs that are drifting in or on the surface film. These are very difficult for the angler to see because of their typically dark coloration and low profile. The fish, however, have the advantage of backlighting and can pick them off with ease. We tie these patterns on light-wire hooks and use materials that promote good flotation. For the all-important wing case, spin a large ball of dubbing or use one of the commonly available foam materials. These flies are more difficult to see than a high-floating dun, but they are quite often the key to fooling a selective riser.

Pale Morning Dun Hackle Tip Emerger

EMERGERS

Imitations of the emerging nymph are probably the most deadly and effective patterns of all, and many fish are fooled throughout the season by this breed of artificial. There are many ways to explain the effectiveness of the emerging pattern. When tied with short wings and on heavy hooks, it is an excellent nymphal imitation that can be fished deep. When tied on medium-weight hooks and dressed with longer wings, it is deadly during the initial stages of the hatch. On fine-wire hooks, it can often be fished very effectively throughout the entire hatch. In fact, it can be treated with a flotant and will often produce more strikes than the subimago imitation. In general, emerging patterns are identical to standard nymphal patterns, except that wings replace wing cases. Hackle points do a good job of simulating the newly sprouted wings, but duck-shoulder feathers, hackle fibers, hair, fur, and shaped feathers are also recommended.

These emergers can be even more effective if a shuck is added. This imitates the most vulnerable stage of a mayfly, a dun struggling out of its nymphal shuck. The pattern also simulates a dun that has become entangled in its shuck. There are many more of these crippled or stillborn duns than you might imagine.

TYING THE MAYFLY EMERGER

A mayfly's shuck is opaque, unlike the shuck of a caddis pupa, which is translucent. Mayfly shucks are the exoskeleton of the nymph, and they are almost always darker than the body of the dun that emerges from it. The easy way to imitate the shuck is to tie in a piece of dark, shiny, synthetic yarn so that it trails behind the body. There is also a more time-consuming but accurate way to create a shuck. With a piece of transparent thread (monofilament), make an overhand knot around the yarn shuck and two or three tail fibers so that the tails trail the body of the shuck. Trim and cement the knot with superglue, then tie this in at the bend of the hook. This will produce a shuck with the correct shape.

The body of the emerging dun should be spun fur, the color of the dun, and the wing should be of short hair or feather fibers. A few turns of hackle can be wound either just before or behind the wing. These should be clipped off at the top.

STILLBORNS AND CRIPPLED DUNS

After our original development of the no-hackle dry fly, the discovery of the "stillborn phenomenon" in 1972 was undoubtedly one of the most exciting events in our angling careers. In looking back, it is amazing that it took us so long to figure out this common occurrence. Obviously the "stuck in the shuck" part of the hatch had been going on right under our noses for many years. Now everyone is aware of this situation, and dozens of patterns are tied to simulate stillborns.

In this stage of the hatch, the dun is struggling to get out of its nymphal skin and is very vulnerable to feeding trout. Rises are usually quiet and unhurried. An effective stillborn pattern, called by some a "captive or crippled dun," should imitate the dun up front and the trailing case in the rear. Originally we used hen-hackle tips to simulate the shuck, but now we use shiny, synthetic yarn. The shuck of natural mayflies is opaque, so it is important to use a dark shade of yarn. Realism is also increased if tails are added to the trailing case.

There are many variations that can be used to imitate the dun part of the fly. One of the most deadly involves duck-quill segments, mounted Sidewinder style, for the wings. You can have both wings up or both trapped

Stillborn Pale Morning Dun

down, or one up and one trapped down. Deer hair, either clumped or fanned from waterline to waterline, makes an extremely durable wing. A clump of fur—such as the short gray fibers of a snowshoe rabbit—along with parachute hackle is also deadly.

DUNS

Our imitations of freshly hatched subimagoes are tied with materials and techniques similar to those used for nymphal patterns—with a few exceptions. Tails, for example, should be fashioned from stiff, top-quality hackle fibers or Chinese boar bristles and spread as far as possible. As we mentioned earlier, it is very important to follow this procedure to ensure proper positioning of the fly on the water. Stiff fibers spread in this manner act as stabilizers to keep the fly in an upright position. Legs, when imitated, should likewise be constructed of top-quality hackle since this will provide better flotation than the breast or body feathers used in nymphal construction. The use of fur for dun bodies affords the same advantages obtained in the underwater dressings; it also floats beautifully when treated with dry-fly solution. Next to fur, some of the synthetic dubbing, because of its low moisture absorption and color availability, can be made into attractive high-floating bodies. Furs, synthetics, and blends—when treated with flotant—are vastly superior to any other materials. They are available in a variety of colors, are easy to work with and durable, and look realistic on the finished fly.

The greatest variable found in the construction of the floating dun undoubtedly lies in the wing construction, both in materials and techniques. Some of these materials include quill segments, hair, breast feathers, fur, hackle fibers, body feathers, synthetics, hackle points, CDC, and shaped feathers. These can be mounted in a single clump, divided, or fanned from waterline to waterline. Duck quill segments are the most realistic and delicate, whereas hair is probably the most durable. Body feathers, such as duck or goose shoulder, display an excellent combination of delicacy and durability.

Natural crippled dun,
Drunella lata

Parachute patterns have been very effective when duns are on the water, probably because this type of fly can hardly help but land right-side up on every cast. We have used parachutes for a long time to imitate the large Ephemeridae duns, but we had never tried them for small flies. Initial attempts with #18s and #20s were successful, and now we tie them all the way down to #28s. The hackle is mainly to position the fly properly on water; it is *not* for flotation and should be kept as sparse as possible. Hackle that is too heavy will only obscure the delicate outline so necessary for success with these small patterns. Hair, shaped feathers, and hackle fibers can all be used to make excellent wings for these flies.

The most deadly pattern to evolve from our study is the no-hackle fly. We observed from our photographs that legs play a very insignificant role in the outline of most mayflies. This fact prompted a close-up study of standard artificials, in which we noticed that *hackle was a ridiculous imitation of legs*. It was not only too bushy, but it also obscured the outline of both the

Paradun with hen-hackle feathers

Extended-body Paradun with elk
wings and deer-hair body

body and wings. Instead of being the least significant feature, as it should have been, it was by far the *most* significant feature. The obvious solution was to cut down or eliminate the hackle altogether. This we did, and when we combined the new design with fur bodies, split tails, and various wings, the new no-hackle flies produced results far superior to those of any flies we had ever tied.

Our first no-hackle flies were tied in late May 1964 and were designed for the sulphur dun on the Au Sable River. The originals had a clump of honey-dun hackle fibers for the tails, an orangish-yellow spun-fur body, and a single clump of yellowish-tipped deer hair for the wings. The first test of these new creations produced some fantastic fishing. As long as the presentation was good and the fly landed upright, there were very few refusals, even when peak numbers of naturals were on the water and the fish had become super-selective. We were ecstatic. The new flies provided by far our best performance ever during a heavy hatch of sulphur duns.

The only disturbing fact was that the flies did not always land upright. Some fish would still take the fly even though it was lying on its side, but most made a false rise and refused it. Our first attempt at rectifying this problem was to fan out the deer hair wing 180 degrees from waterline to waterline. Returning to the same pool the following night, we found that the fan style landed upright much more often but was not quite as deadly as the original clump wing. The reason for the difference in effectiveness becomes obvious when you inspect both flies from underneath, which is, after all, the trout's point of view. The single clump of deer hair certainly looks more like the upright wings of a freshly hatched dun than does a bunch of hair fanned halfway around the body.

Unhappy with the results of the fan-wing fly, even though it worked better than standard flies, we went back to the drawing board for a better way to make the fly float upright and yet retain a realistic wing silhouette. This is when we came up with the split-tail idea. Spinning a tiny ball of fur at the rear of the shank makes it very easy to crimp the tail fibers into the ball and get a 90-degree split. If done properly, the fly not only will land upright but will also float better and look more like a natural.

Armed with two types of split-tail no-hackles—clump wing and fan wing—we again attacked the sulphur dun hatch. Both types landed upright, floated well, were very durable, and caught lots of fish. When the trout got really finicky during the peak of the emergence, however, the clump wing outscored the fan wing. Looking at both floating on the water, it's easy to see that the clump wing looks more like the real thing. The fan-wing no-hackle, known as a Comparadun to some anglers, may not fool as many fish, but it is probably a good choice for less experienced anglers. Having a wing with more volume or hair in contact with the water, it is naturally a better floater. Until a caster develops that quick snap of the wrist to pop the water out of a sodden fly, an extra-buoyant imitation is well appreciated. (A really good caster can usually make a fly land upright whenever he wants.)

The next step in developing the no-hackle fly was to come up with a practical pattern for the really tiny hatches. Shortly after the sulphurs stopped hatching in the middle of the 1964 season, the emergence of the tiny blue-winged olives began. These diminutive little rascals are 4.5 to 5 mm in length, a true #24, and had always seemed impossible to imitate. We tried to tie some of our newly developed deer-hair no-hackles in this size, but the coarseness of the hair resulted in some really crude-looking monstrosities. To match the delicacy of the very small flies, we used hen hackle fibers for the clump wings on our original flies. Later we found that turkey flats, CDC, fur, and extra-fine hair such as snowshoe rabbit also worked well.

Toward the end of that 1964 season, during our annual trip to the spring creeks of Montana, we developed another type of no-hackle—the Duck-Quill Sidewinder. Even though this is just one of our many styles, the Sidewinder is the pattern most anglers associate with us. The wings are constructed of a pair of matched quill segments (goose is fine for larger flies). The wings are mounted so that they radiate from the sides of the body. Protruding from the waterline they create a "wedge effect," and coupled with widely split tails they ensure that the fly lands upright. A properly tied Sidewinder is definitely our choice for selective trout when an imitation of the fully hatched dun is needed. Nothing imitates the wings of a mayfly better than duck-quill segments.

The difficult part of tying the Sidewinder is mounting the wings so that they look natural and come out of the sides of the body. Like anything else, if you want to master the technique, you must be willing to spend some time at the vise. The key is holding or pinching the wings properly with your thumb and index finger. Then, when you tighten the thread, the butts of the feathers crimp evenly without bunching.

The unquestioned expert in tying the Sidewinder is Bill Monahan of Michigan. Most tyers get the wings too long, too narrow, and too upright because it is easier to do that way. It is much more difficult to make the wings short, wide, and sloping back as in a real mayfly. One look at Bill's flies and you know they are both realistic and durable.

TYING THE SIDEWINDER NO-HACKLE DUN (DUCK FEATHER SECTION WING)

Begin by tying in the widely spread tails and bodies. The wings are made from a section of duck primary or secondary feathers and tied in so they come from the side of the body. This V-effect of the wings, as well as the widespread tails, allows the fly to land and float upright. When placing the wings, the tier holds the feather sections between the thumb and forefinger so they straddle the hook on both sides and slope back at a 45-degree angle. A bit of pressure will hold the feathers in place. The tying thread is then slipped between the thumb and forefinger around the feathers and pulled tight. When the wings are in place, a small thorax is dubbed and the head is tied off. The winging process is difficult to explain, but with some practice it becomes easy. Here is our method. First tie in the tails and abdomen. Hold the wings in position, with the thumb and forefinger applying only light pressure. This enables you to slip the thread between these two fingers while still holding the wings in position. The thread is wrapped around the wings between the thumb and forefinger one and a half times, taking the thread underneath and over top of the hook. The butts are then tied in alongside the hook. A small thorax is dubbed, tied in front of the wings, and the head is tied off. Some pliable cement may now be painted on the base of the wings for durability.

TYING THE SIDEWINDER NO-HACKLE DUN (SHAPED DUCK SHOULDER FEATHER WING)

This pattern is tied exactly like the first except that the wings are duck-shoulder feathers, which can be tied in without shaping them—or they can be shaped with a wing burner or with scissors. Once the wings have been shaped, they are held in place and a few wraps are tied around the base of the wings—not on the stems but on the first few fibers of the feather, and not too tightly. At this point the wings can be adjusted so they are even. Place a drop of glue on the wraps and let them dry. Now wrap the stems tightly, spin a small thorax, and tie the ends off.

THE V-HACKLE DUN (THE ALMOST NO-HACKLE)

The original Sidewinder No-Hackle is still the imitation that selective trout will take at hatch time when they will take no other fly—*except one.* The Sidewinder is an imitation of a mayfly dun with the wings coming off the sides of the thorax. Placing the wings on the sides acts as a wedge when the fly lands on the water. Along with the split tails, this helps the fly float upright. The Sidewinder is the pattern of choice during a heavy emergence in all but very fast, broken water. The problem with the pattern is that it works so well, the angler enjoys many more strikes than he is used to with traditional patterns, and after three or four fish the wings become disheveled.

The truth is, the angler usually messes up the wings simply by unhooking the fish. Barbless hooks will eliminate or at least minimize this tendency. An angler who releases fish should probably use a barbless hook anyway. A case in point is Michigan's Muskegon River, which is full of browns and rainbows from 8 to 18 inches and some much larger. The Muskegon is heavily fished by anglers who practice no-kill. At the end of the season, these fish have been caught and released many times, and most have jaws that are injured and bleeding. The use of barbless hooks would eliminate these injuries and make it much easier to retrieve flies without mangling them.

We realized that the Sidewinder could be fragile if care is not taken when unhooking fish, and also that some people were having trouble tying in the duck-shoulder wings. So we began looking for a version that would incorporate the pattern's imitative qualities but be easier to tie and also more durable. We briefly mentioned a fly in the original edition of *Selective Trout* that we called the V-Hackle. It is tied like the no-hackle except that the wings are constructed out of small shoulder feathers from the base of mallard duck wings or other game birds. Pigeon wings are one of our favorites for smaller patterns. These wing feathers can be burned to shape using a wing burner or cut to shape with scissors. This produces an extremely natural-looking wing shape. The wings can also be tied in without shaping them (this takes less time) and are almost as effective as the burned wings because they slim down when wet.

The only other difference in the tie is that one cock hackle is wound on two turns behind the wing and two turns in front of the wings, then trimmed off at the bottom and top, leaving only the side barbules. This pattern works as well as the Sidewinder and is certainly easier for most people to tie. It has an excellent silhouette and is easier to balance. It almost never lands upside down or on its side. The three wide-split tails and the hackle on the sides provide a triple outrigger effect that is unbeatable for floating the fly in an upright position. The pattern is more effective than regular parachutes because it has no hackle sticking out the front and back, and the hackle it does have is very sparse and in the correct position to represent legs.

We recently fished a tailwater river in Tennessee with pale afternoon duns *(Ephemerella rotunda)* that start emerging in April and continue through November. This water is gin clear, fairly slow, and the fish see the naturals almost all day for 8 months. By fall they really know what to look for and are more selective than any fish we have seen. In the spring the angler can get away with 5X tippets, but by fall 8X became necessary. The wings of the V-Hackle do not twist 8X tippets when the pattern is tied correctly. The only patterns that will take these fish consistently are No-Hackles and V-Hackles.

The colors of the bodies of these duns (and many other mayfly species) can vary greatly. The model for this pattern came from Tennessee's South Holston River and features a lot of orange coloring. The same species on other rivers can be mostly yellow with brown markings on the dorsal area, and some may have a bit of olive in them. Here is our step-by-step methodology for tying them.

Pale afternoon dun *(Ephemerella invaria* and *Ephemerella rotunda)*

1. Tie in three straw-colored tail fibers using yellow tying thread. We like mink-tail guard hairs or Chinese boar for durability.

2. Place your thumbnail under the tails and press upward to split them. When the tails are positioned correctly, place a touch of superglue on the base of the tails to lock them permanently in position.

3. Dub the abdomen using fine yellow dubbing with a touch of orange.

4. Take a pair of suitable shoulder feathers and trim the butts, but do not strip them or they will be weakened. Shape them by using a wing burner, then trim them with scissors, or leave them natural.

5. Tie in the wing feathers at the middle of the thorax so they slope back at a 45-degree angle and are slightly divided. Remember that *natural mayfly*

Extended-body Green Drake Paradun with cut wings

Pale Morning Dun No-Hackle Dun with duck quill segment wings

No-Hackle Dun with wings mounted on sides, gray/yellow, duck-quill segment type

Another No-Hackle in water

Duck-Quill No-Hackle

wings slope back at an approximately 45-degree angle. Some ties have wings fully upright, but this is not realistic for most mayflies.

6. Dub the thorax with fine orange dubbing, wrapping it on either side of the wings.

7. Tie in a bright yellow hackle and wrap it two turns behind and two turns in front of the wings. Clip top and bottom so the V opens on the bottom of the body.

8. Wrap a fairly large head, tie off, and cement the head.

Note that this pattern can also be tied with single wings of hair or feather fibers. These are effective, and easier and quicker to tie, but they do not look quite as natural on the water. They may be as effective as the shaped shoulder feather wings, but for those large and experienced trout in gin-clear water, we have more confidence in the shaped-wing pattern.

The most important point to remember when tying no-hackle flies is to spread the tail fibers as much as possible in a horizontal plane. This will ensure a proper position on the water and guarantee upright wings. Excellent flotation will be assured if light-wire hooks and dubbed bodies are used.

SPINNERS

Six basic spinner patterns have proven extremely effective for us. The first three are no-hackle types: the Hen Spinner, the Partridge Spinner, and the Poly Spinner. Two have their wings constructed of hackle wound either conventionally or parachute style; one pattern, especially in larger sizes, uses both feathers and hackle.

The first type—the Hen Spinner—is tied with hen-hackle tips that are wide and webby. When tied fully spent, these present a beautiful wing outline, lying flush in the water. When preparing these feathers, it is important to trim the excess fibers at the butts with scissors. If the fibers are stripped, the quill is weakened. Most tiers make the mistake of mounting the wings conventionally, i.e., with their concave sides down. *It is very important that the concave sides face up.* This ensures that the fly will land properly on the water, float better, and look more realistic.

Another critical factor is selecting the right color for the wings. Over the years, most of the commercially tied Hen Spinners we've seen have wings that are much too light in color. Many are even being tied with white feathers. On the water, light to medium gray looks more natural. It is better to err on the darker than the lighter side.

Also, remember that spinners—especially freshly fallen ones—do not always have their wings in the fully spent position. They can be partially spent, totally spent, or have one wing up and one wing down. Often the deadliest Hen Spinner has one wing flush in the film and the other angled up at 45 degrees. It is also advisable to point the wings slightly forward to compensate for the current and casting forces.

Here are a few streamside tips for fishing these spinners. Carry some felt-tip markers in various shades of gray so you can "doctor up" a fly that is too light. Remember also that spinners are the final stage of the mayfly and die

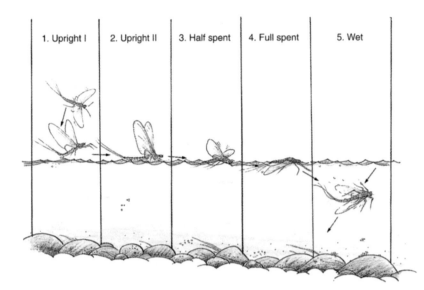

| 1. Upright I | 2. Upright II | 3. Half spent | 4. Full spent | 5. Wet |

Spinner sequence and possible patterns:

1. Flight and ovipositing

2. Upright spinner

3. Half-spent spinner

4. Full-spent spinner

5. Wet or drowned spinner

soon after laying their eggs. They cannot escape the stream and will eventually drown or go awash in a back eddy. Try fishing the Hen Spinner wet after the trout have stopped feeding on the surface.

The second type of spinner—the Partridge Spinner—uses light partridge breast feathers tied spent or half spent. They are deadly during the *Ephemerella dorothea* spinner fall. These feathers, when wet, not only become quite transparent, but their speckled appearance also simulates the venation of the naturals. The easiest method of assembly is to tie them on in a clump and figure-8 them into two equal sections. Both the Partridge and Hen Spinners must be well soaked in dry-fly flotant. Other body, breast, and shoulder feathers have also proven successful for this type of fly.

The third type—the Poly Spinner—is another no-hackle type and has become one of the most popular of the spent-wing patterns. Even though it is not as deadly for selective trout as some of the other imitations, it has the advantage of being very easy to tie. However, fly tiers must resist the temptation to use too much material for the wings. Many of the commercially tied versions have an unnatural "shaving brush" quality, and even though they float well, these patterns simply do not work on tough trout. Color is critical here as well—better too dark than too light.

Hackle Spinner

The fourth spinner type is simple to tie and is constructed of wound hackle. Spinners with their wings upright can be represented with fully wound hackle, whereas intermediate- to full-spent positions can be represented by trimming to shape. Another method of obtaining these positions is to put the dubbing on last and figure-8 the hackle fibers into position. Depending on the species being imitated, the most effective colors are light blue dun, medium blue dun, and bronze blue dun. In some cases, the addition of one or two turns of grizzly increases the effectiveness greatly.

Hen Spinner

No-Hackle Partridge Spinner

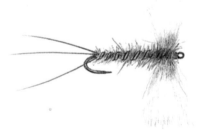

Downwing Poly Spinner

Hexagenia limbata dun

A para-tied caddis imitation showing use of the rubber band technique.

Pale Morning Dun No-Hackle Dun with duck quill segment wings

Also, a more realistic and durable wing outline can be maintained if a very fine tying thread is wound through the hackle. This procedure acts to stiffen and flare the fibers.

Parahackle Spinner

In 1990 we devised a new way to mount parachute hackle that resulted in a unique series of spinner patterns. This technique is based on wrapping one or more hackles around a tightly stretched strand of rubber and then allowing the rubber to return to its normal size. This process completely locks the hackle in place and results in an incredibly durable fly. It also permits one or more hackles to be mounted almost anywhere on a hook. Tiny size #22 to #28 flies are tied with ease.

Parachute hackle spinners float like a cork compared with conventionally hackled spinners, because more individual fibers come in contact with the water per turn of hackle. Realism is also improved, with the hackles radiating from a center position. This type of pattern has been especially deadly for imitating the tiny *Trico* and *Baetis* spinners.

Conventional Spinner

Effective imitation of the larger flies, in sizes #4 to #10, is accomplished with hen-hackle tips accompanied by sparse, undersized hackle. Both hackle and hackle tips should blend together to form the general color of the wing. On some of the larger flies, such as *Hexagenia*, double wings can be used, putting grizzly on top and blue dun on the bottom. With this combination, the grizzly represents the dark splotches in the venation, and blue dun represents the general coloration on the water. The grizzly tips can be seen through the blue dun but are toned down to a more realistic shade.

In general, light hooks and dubbed bodies should be used to provide proper flotation, and tails should be long, stiff fibered, and spread. For the larger flies, however, excellent bodies, either regular or extended, can be fashioned from materials such as deer body hair and some of the new synthetic yarns. Tails should be spread, not for mechanical reasons, as they are for the no-hackle duns, but because they add greatly to the realistic appearance of the artificial.

DOWNWINGS

The materials and techniques required for caddisfly, stonefly, and midge imitations are basically identical to those used for the upwings. The bodies of all stages—nymph, pupa, and adult, for example—are mainly constructed of fur or dubbing. Wing cases are made of ostrich herl, quill segments, fur, and shoulder feathers. Wings are fashioned from hen-hackle feathers, duck quill, partridge, hair, and hackle fibers. Probably the major difference is the use of more hackle in simulating flying or skittering adults.

1. Green rock worm—*Cheumatopsyche*
2. Wiggle larva—*Hydropsyche*
3. Simple campodeiform larva

Our caddisfly imitations are divided into five types: worms, pupae, emergers, adults at rest, and flying adults. A simple yet deadly pupa pattern for size #20 and smaller consists merely of a fur body and either a collar or beard made of partridge. The most common body colors are green, tan, and gray. For size #18 and larger, wing pads and a fuzzy, shaggy head can be added. The wing pads are best simulated with duck-shoulder feathers or quill segments. Dark gray to black are the most common colors. The pupal head is made by forming a small clump of dark gray fur just behind the eye of the hook; this fur should then be picked with a dubbing needle to create a shaggy texture.

It is important to note that caddis pupae swim *by moving their middle legs—which are fringed for that purpose—back and forth*. Therefore, when we are imitating a pupa swimming from the bottom to the top, we add two small cock hackle tips to the normal pupa. These are tied in so they stick out at a 45-degree angle from the body. They will then move back and forth when the fly is raised from the bottom.

Caddis emergers and crippled caddis are as important as, or even more so than, mayfly emergers. They are tied the same way as the mayfly emergers, except that their cases are translucent instead of opaque. Most are a light golden color, which is perfectly imitated by ginger Z-Lon. The case should be pointed like a natural's.

One of the most effective and exacting imitations of an adult caddis at rest is a fat fur body with a pair of wide, webby hen hackles tied flat. If hackle is desired, add sparse blue dun or grizzly tied palmer, clipped top and bottom. An even more realistic version can be made by winding the hackle on only the front one-third of the body. Other materials that make excellent wings for this type of fly include duck-quill segments, partridge, and hen-hackle fibers. The duck-quill-segment type looks more like a real caddisfly, if the wings are put on separately with concave sides down and tips to the outside. A more generalized but very effective pattern is one that uses groundhog hair for the wings. This type of material is recommended for unknown or strange water situations.

The most common imitation of a flying caddis is the Adams-type fly. Just vary the body and wing coloration to suit the natural. A selection of these flies with green, tan, and gray bodies tied in sizes #16 through #20 will cover most flying-caddis situations. Other types used to simulate flying or

Two caddis pupa imitations

Left: weighted pupa; right: unweighted deer hair back surface pupa

Hackle Tip Legged Caddis Emerger

Snowshoe Hare-Wing Cinnamon Sedge Emerger

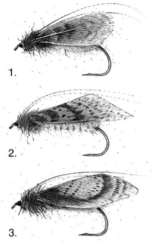

Three no-hackle adult caddisflies:

1. Hen-Wing Caddis

2. Turkey Wing Segment Caddis

3. Partridge and Tape-Wing Caddis

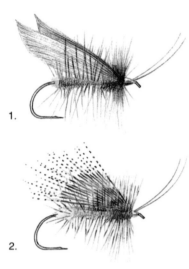

Two adult fluttering caddis:

1. Henryville Caddis

2. Partridge Caddis

skittering caddis are palmer hackle flies. One consists of only a fur body and palmer hackle; another has a pair of duck-quill wings added, before the front hackle is wound; another is the Elk-Hair Caddis, with fur body, palmer hackle, and buoyant elk hair to imitate the wings. If quality hackle and light hooks are used, these flies float high and are easy to skitter and skip over the water.

Most midge patterns are tied on the smallest of hooks, primarily #24 and #28, and we find that these minute imitations are much more effective if kept simple and uncomplicated. Either an all-fur body or a combination thread-and-fur body is all that is required for the pupal imitation. The abdomen, whether fashioned from fur or thread, should be very slim, whereas the thorax should be more robust and made of fur. Small wing pads made from quill segments or shoulder feathers can be added over the thorax if a more detailed pattern is desired. Black, olive, and brownish olive are the most common body colors, whereas wings are usually blackish or light gray.

Midge emergers are an important pattern to carry in your fishing vest. They are extremely effective on the western spring creeks and at any time you are fishing to a flush emergence of midges. They are tied like the caddis emergers.

Adult midges are best imitated with a slim fur body and wings of either hen-hackle tips or duck-quill segments tied flat over the body. Partridge may also be used effectively as a wing material.

Flying adults can be simulated with tiny hackle flies, tied regular or palmer style. Probably our most effective pattern has blue dun tails, a dark mole body, and slightly oversized hackle—dark blue dun and grizzly mixed. This fly rides high on the water and imitates the skittering adult. Since the development of our rubber-mounted hackle technique, our favorite tie is now a gray fur body with grizzly parachute hackle.

STONEFLIES

With the exception of double wing cases, stonefly nymphs are tied with materials and techniques identical to those used for mayflies. Quite often

Adult Elk-Hair Cinnamon Caddis

Caddis emergences

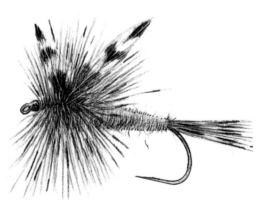

Adams Fly

Whitlock's Glass-Bead Midge Pupa

Olive Midge Pupa

Midge Emerger Pupa

Whitlock Brown Stonefly Nymph

Kaufmann's Stonefly Nymph

Adult natural *Pteronarcys*

Hair-Wing Stonefly

the fur bodies are weighted with lead to facilitate the bottom bumping that is sometimes needed for these patterns. For nymphal imitations, size #12 and larger, goose-quill fibers are more realistic than partridge for tails and legs. We prefer quill segments and ostrich clumps for the double wing cases.

Groundhog hair, because of its variegated coloration, is an excellent wing material for imitating adult stoneflies at rest. Hen-hackle tips and duck-quill segments are also good, especially on the smaller sizes, #14 and smaller. Flying stones require Adams- or palmer-type artificials, similar to those used for flying caddis. In all cases, try to match the wing and body coloration of the naturals as closely as possible.

CHAPTER 6

Streamside Procedure

THE CARDINAL RULE of streamside procedure is "get a sample." No matter how well we are acquainted with a stream and its hatches, it is imperative that we catch and examine specimens closely on every trip. As we have suggested earlier, general observation of a natural as it floats by or flies overhead is not sufficient. Specimens must be captured and held at close range so that color and size can be determined. A small and inexpensive hand magnifier should be carried at all times to help with these investigations. It is also a good idea to put some of the naturals in small containers and save them for further inspection.

When you are fishing in strange water or places where the hatch is unpredictable, there are some important preliminary steps that should be taken. The first is to fight the natural urge to get geared up and into the water as fast as possible. Those who jump out of the car, rush into the stream, and start beating the water with whatever worked well 2 weeks before, or for a friend on some other river at another time, will usually get skunked. It's far better to slow down and perform a little basic research that will give you the necessary information. The benefits will certainly outweigh the small amount of lost fishing time.

Some type of hand net or seine should be a standard item carried in the trunk of the car. An inexpensive kitchen strainer attached to a wooden handle or bamboo pole is adequate. Nymphs can easily be seined with such a device by kicking the stream bottom and holding the strainer downstream. Captured specimens can be saved for identification of the upcoming hatch and also as tying models for effective nymphal and emerging patterns. Here again, the hand magnifier is invaluable for close-up observation. Remember that seining should be performed in various places to get a good cross-sectional look at the total life in the stream. Riffles, runs, silt beds, backwaters, eddies, and weed beds should all be investigated. Items such as logs, sticks, leaves, stones, and plant life can be picked up by hand and studied closely for nymphal life. (One note of caution: Seining nymphs is illegal in some states, so be sure to check local regulations.)

Molting spinners afford a greater challenge, but they can usually be located with a little perseverance. Some species seem to prefer certain kinds of trees or bushes for their final molt, whereas others can be found on such objects as bridge abutments, cabin walls, light fixtures, and screen doors. Dead spinners from the previous day can be located in quiet backwaters on logs, snags, and weed beds, or found entangled in webs spun by spiders and insect larvae. The capture of airborne spinners from the mating flight is best accomplished with a long-handled sweep net. However, if you are quick of hand, you might be able to snare a few low-flying specimens.

Now that our initial research has been accomplished by seining for nymphs and checking for spinners, it is time to assemble the rod and do some fishing. Let's assume that there is a distinct lack of feeding or hatch activity on the stream. Probably the best bet would be to tie on a nymphal

8-foot long-handled sweep net

Long-handled seine about 5 feet in length

pattern that imitates the most predominant specimen found during the seining process or the one that appears to be ready for emergence. Nymphs that are close to hatching usually display darkened wing cases and are active. Sometimes a light line can be seen on the covert where the outer skin is starting to split. Try to match the size, shape, and color of the natural as closely as possible. Remember, it's the color and appearance of the artificial when it's *wet* that is important. Always moisten the fly in your mouth or in the stream to get the proper effect.

Try various casting, floating, and retrieving techniques with your nymph to see which is the most effective. The typical quartering upstream, dead-drift technique is not always the best. Try various combinations of casting angles. Fishing the nymph directly upstream can be very effective, but long, fine leaders and delicate casting are essential. Downstream nymphing is especially deadly on certain hatches, but it must be combined with well-executed lazy S and curve casts.

Often the long upstream cast, followed first by a slow sinking action and then by an accelerated escape-to-the-surface movement, is the most productive technique. Occasionally, a downstream cast, followed by a fast erratic retrieve, will produce strikes when all else fails. The main thing to remember when nymphing in unfamiliar waters is to *be creative*. Find out what forms of underwater life are present and then experiment with various techniques of presenting a suitable imitation.

Nymphal imitations are normally fished until emergence time; for many species it is then best to switch to an emerging pattern. This type of fly is similar to the nymph, except that wing cases are replaced with wings. These patterns are more or less a combination of nymph and dun features, and they can be fished under, in, or on the surface film. Thus, the emerging pattern is a highly versatile fly that can be used effectively during several phases of the hatch. As a result, these flies should be tied on both heavy- and light-wire hooks, and some of the light wire should be soaked in dry-fly flotant. Most nymphs split out of their cases at the surface and struggle a bit as they float along. To simulate this activity, an emerging pattern tied on a light hook should be drifted through rising trout with an occasional twitch. Some nymphs, however, uncase their wings underwater and swim to the surface in the dun form. Simulation of this habit is accomplished by sinking a heavy-wire pattern and then raising it in front of a feeding fish.

The emerging fly is most deadly right at the beginning of the hatch. This is the period when the fish are just beginning to snare a few duns on the surface, but they are still taking most of their food slightly under or in the film. They have become conscious of wings emerging into view but are reluctant to feed steadily on the surface. The sight of emergent wings seems to excite the trout into frenzied feeding activity and solid strikes. Even after most of the fish have started to feed steadily at the surface, the emerging pattern can be very effective. A light-wire version, soaked in flotant and then drifted along the surface, is sometimes more deadly than a delicate high-floating dun pattern.

As the hatch progresses, a moment is usually reached when most of the trout become partial to duns only. They know exactly what they want and

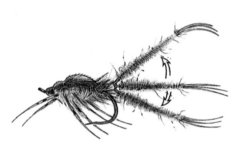

Swisher-Richards Wiggle Nymph showing how abdomen wiggles and articulates. Note hinge.

become very selective. This is the beginning of great frustration for many fishermen, when actually it should be the period when the greatest harvest is reaped. This is the time when the trout is most vulnerable *if* the angler has the *right fly* and knows how to use it. Repeated failures during these situations can drive you crazy, but there is no need for anxiety if a little common sense is applied.

First, determine what insect the trout are feeding on and then get a sample of it. Determining which fly is being taken can sometimes be a problem, so you really have to put your nose down in the water and observe closely. If necessary, wade right into the main line of drift even if it means spooking a few fish (they'll normally return to their feeding stations within a minute or two after you leave). Once you've determined what the fish are feeding on, catch a specimen, even though you're positive you know the species. (A small aquarium hand net should be carried for this purpose.) Determine the body color, wing color, and exact size of the fly. Color can be interpreted only by each individual, but size should be accurately measured, preferably with a millimeter gauge.

In fact, size cannot be overemphasized as an essential hatch-matching characteristic, especially on the smaller insects. As we mentioned earlier, an error of only 1 mm can make an enormous difference between a natural and an artificial. The average mayfly is only about 7 mm in length, which would be a size #16. If your imitation is 1 or 2 mm too long on what would be a small or average-sized fly, it will look enormous to the trout. No matter how perfect the imitation, if it has unrealistic dimensions, it will never fool a selective riser.

With the required color and size in mind, select a fly that you think will do the job. If a suitable imitation cannot be found, sometimes another fly can be trimmed or manicured. The final alternative is to use a portable fly-tying kit, which should be standard equipment in your fishing gear. It certainly is difficult to leave rising trout, but if you are stranded without the right pattern, it is better to sacrifice a little fishing time and spend a few profitable minutes at the vise. Besides simulating color and size as closely as possible, it is important to tie a fly that will land upright and present a good wing outline. The outstanding feature of the freshly emerged dun is the wing silhouette, which creates a sailboatlike appearance. This feature must be imitated in the artificial. Once the right pattern has been fashioned, it should be fished with or without movement, depending on the behavior of the drifting dun.

The fall of a spinner flight can provide fantastic fishing for the initiated and much anxiety for the neophyte. An angler who is prepared with the right pattern—and who can determine when to use it—will enjoy some of the finest fishing available. However, the uninitiated often have great difficulty figuring out what the trout are feeding on during these periods. This is mainly due to the fact that imagoes, especially the spent-wing variety, are very hard to see in the water. A hatch of duns is quite obvious because the upright wings are opaque and easy to see, but spinners, even as large as Hendricksons, are hard to detect because of the clear wings and low-floating body position. They can be seen in the air before the fall takes place, but if a fisherman is not oriented to this habit, they can easily go undetected. (Many anglers concentrate so hard on their fly that they are completely unaware of any activity around them.) Also, the spinners of some species seem to prefer certain riffles and runs and can easily fall upstream and go unnoticed.

The best procedure for detecting spinners is to stay as alert as possible. Look up frequently to see if flights are forming. On a bright sunny day, even high-flying spinners can be spotted as their wings glisten in the sun. Another excellent indicator is to watch for birds. When spinners are in the air, birds become very active and dive into the swarm to get an easy meal. Once the spinners are on the water, closer observation may be needed in order to see them properly. Always get a sample with the hand net and examine it for color and size. Patterns are simple to tie, consisting of tails, dubbed bodies, and hackle or hackle points for the wing. When hackle is used, it is left full or trimmed to various angulations, depending on the wing position of the natural. Flotation is a problem with spent-wing patterns, so extra-fine-wire hooks are essential.

The portable streamside tying kit is indispensable. It is a rare trip when we do not use ours at least once while on the river. It need not be fancy or large, but it should include a number of basic tools and materials. The ideal vise should be mounted on a pedestal so it can be used anywhere. Other standard tools would include scissors, hackle pliers, dubbing needle, razor blades, and tweezers. Because most flies can be made from just two materials, fur and hackle, keep a small box of fur or dubbing in assorted colors and several necks as staples in your kit. Besides hooks and thread, other important items include wood duck, duck shoulder, turkey, and partridge.

Keeping a diary or some other form of written notes concerning each trip is another key part of our streamside procedure. This collection of notes can be invaluable, and the more of it that is collected, the greater chance you will have successful fishing in the future. Since most hatches occur at approximately the same time every year on the same stream, the record of these details can be used year after year as an accurate guide to good fishing. Typical notes should include the stream name and section fished, the date, type of water, weather, water temperature, water condition, hatch and time of hatch, feeding activity, feeding time, flies used, and fishing success.

To anticipate the time of the hatch, here is a general rule to follow: *Mayflies will emerge at the most pleasant time of day for the season.* In the spring, this period occurs in the afternoon, usually from 1:00 p.m. to 4:00 p.m., but as the days get warmer, the flies tend to hatch both earlier and later in the day. During hot, muggy weather there will be hatches in the evening and early morning. Then, as the summer fades, afternoon hatches are again the rule. Once you learn when the individual hatches occur, you can plan your streamside arrival to coincide with the peak fishing period of the day.

Probably the most important attribute of a really successful fly fisherman is common sense. It should be obvious that if we are to simulate the main food source of the trout, we must learn all we can about aquatic insect life. In order to produce effective imitations, it would seem evident that specimens must be caught and examined closely. Also, we must study the activities and habitat of the various species in order to present our artificials in a convincing manner. These are undoubtedly sound and logical procedures. Unfortunately, not enough fishermen pursue such a course of study and action. It takes only a modest amount of effort to develop these effective streamside methods, and much is to be gained.

STREAM LOG								
Date:							No.	
Stream:		Section:			Type:			
Fast	Med	Slow	6AM	Noon	6PM	Midnight	6AM	
Time Fished: Total Hours:								

Weather Conditions:	Hot	Cool	Sunny	Cloud	Rainy	Windy	Storm	Temp

Water Conditions:	Clear	Discolor	High	Medium	Low	Temp

Hatches:	Species	Activity	Stage	Time

Fishing:	Feeding	Activity	Method	Artificial	Time

Fish Released: (Quantity and Size)	Brooks	Browns	Rainbows	Cutts	Others

A blank page from our streamside record book

The Early Season

DURING THE EARLY season, the most pleasant time of day for both the angler and the trout is the afternoon. This is the time when all the important hatches occur, so we can call this period the "season of the afternoon hatches." In late April and early May, the water temperature will often drop into the low 40s during the night, causing the trout's metabolism to be very inactive. Then, as the morning sun hits the water, the temperature will rise slowly and hit a peak in the early afternoon. When the 50-degree mark is reached, the trout's metabolism is raised to a point at which good feeding activity can take place. Occasionally fish will feed at a temperature slightly less than this figure, but increased activity results when the thermometer climbs to a higher level.

Of course, if the weather is unseasonably warm, minimum feeding conditions may occur as early as 11:00 a.m., moving up the hatch accordingly. However, in general, at the start of the early season, the major hatching activity takes place during the afternoon, with the peak coming between 2:00

and 4:00 p.m. Major spinner falls usually occur soon after this period. As the weather becomes warmer, the hatches and spinner falls get later and later, until such flies as *Ephemerella dorothea*, which began as an evening hatch, become a late-evening hatch, and the Hendrickson spinner falls are at dusk. The beginning of the hotter weather, usually around the first week in June, marks the start of the midseason.

Hendrickson No-Hackle

In Michigan there are likely to be three mayflies on the water for opening day, which is during the last week in April. These species include *Baetis tricaudatus, Paraleptophlebia adoptiva,* and *Ephemerella subvaria.* In the eastern part of the country, where the season begins slightly earlier, opening-day anglers will probably run into hatches of both *Epeorus pleuralis* and *Paraleptophlebia adoptiva.* These are all midday to early-afternoon hatches, coming when the water temperature reaches its daily peak. During this part of the season, hatch-oriented anglers need not be concerned about hitting the stream before late morning or noon. As the season progresses, such major species as *Ephemerella invaria, Leptophlebia cupida,* and *Stenonema vicarium* can emerge both earlier and later as water temperatures rise. In general, however, the flies of the early season provide pleasant daytime fishing.

As the water reaches optimum temperature, flies begin to appear, and on rich, varied rivers there are often multiple hatches in the afternoon. Sometimes two to three species of mayfly hatch at once and the fish can be very selective, not always choosing the larger—or what appears to be the most numerous—species. When you include all of the other insects—caddisflies, stoneflies and midges—it can be difficult to determine what the fish prefer. On a single river, fish in one type of habitat may be exposed to more of a certain species than fish in another type of water, and they will feed accordingly. For instance, a slow stretch may have mostly *Paraleptophlebia adoptiva,* and fish in these areas will be keyed to them. In faster areas, *Ephemerella subvaria* will be more numerous, and trout under these lines of drift will want a good Hendrickson imitation. It is important to study the emergence charts in order to be prepared for overlapping hatches and selective trout.

We have talked about smooth-flowing rich rivers, but some, such as the Rogue in Michigan, are almost embarrassingly rich. On a warm May afternoon, it can have stoneflies, two species of caddisflies, midges, two or three species of mayflies, and a couple of craneflies, all at once. This situation produces a tremendous amount of feeding activity, but also can pose quite a complicated problem. With the possibility that the trout are feeding on either nymphs, pupae, emerging duns, or spinners, the angler has the perplexing problem of choosing from among as many as fifty patterns. You have to be alert and observant—otherwise, by the time all fifty patterns have been tried, willy-nilly, hit or miss, the hatch will be over.

In order to identify and then simulate each species properly, we have listed all available data concerning the early-season flies. The same procedure will be followed in the two succeeding chapters about the midseason and the late season. This data will include the insect's scientific name, common name, emergence date, size, nymphal habitat, description of the natural in its various stages, description of the corresponding artificials, and any available information about technique and procedures. Since emergence dates vary slightly depending on your locality, the best idea is to compile your own hatching chart for the rivers you fish most often.

Blue-Winged Olive (East, Midwest, and West)

Genus and species: *Baetis* (all species) and *Plauditus* (formally *Pseudocloeon*)
Family: Baetidae
Emergence: April 1 to October 30
Size: 4 to 10 mm (#16 to #26 hook size)
Nymph habitat: Shallow gravel runs and submerged vegetation

NATURAL	ARTIFICIAL
NYMPH	
Body: Brown or olive brown	**Body:** Dark brown or medium olive and medium brown rabbit fur mixed
Wing pads: Blackish	**Wing pads:** Black ostrich clump or black crow quill segment
Tails: Three, olive brown	**Tails:** Wood duck or merganser dyed olive
Legs: Olive brown	**Legs:** Wood duck or merganser dyed olive
DUN	
Body: Olive or olive brown	**Body:** Medium olive or medium olive and medium brown rabbit fur mixed
Wings: Light or medium gray	**Wings:** Light or medium gray hen-hackle fibers, clump
Tails: Two (except *tricaudatus*), light gray or whitish, typical	**Tails:** Light gray hackle fibers
Legs: Light gray or whitish, typical	**Hackle:** None or light gray, parachute

Nymph

Dun

Spinner

SPINNER

Body: Medium or dark brown	**Body:** Medium or dark brown rabbit fur
Wings: Hyaline	**Wings:** Light gray hen-hackle tips, spent
Tails: Two (except *tricaudatus*), light gray or whitish, typical	**Tails:** Light gray hackle fibers
Legs: Light gray or whitish, typical	**Hackle:** None

The *Baetis* complex, or blue-winged olives, provides some of the most prolific hatching activity on rivers and streams across the country. They are not only widespread, but they are also on the water all season long. We have witnessed beautiful hatches of *Baetis tricaudatus* in Colorado during the month of March and of *Baetis hiemalis* on Michigan streams in mid-November. In both cases the trout were feeding heavily on the emerging duns.

The features and coloration of *Baetis* are so similar that in many cases identification at the species level can only be determined by an entomologist. For the fly fisherman, it will be much more practical to cover the numerous blue-winged olives as one group. In general they can be divided into two fairly distinct color types. This holds true not only for the duns but also for the nymphs and spinners.

Most duns fall into either the light gray wing/olive body or medium gray wing/olive-brown body classification. Nymphs are generally brown or olive brown, whereas spinners are medium or dark brown. For the angler who wants to keep his *Baetis* patterns to a minimum, the best approach would be to carry duns with olive-brown bodies and medium gray wings, nymphs with olive-brown bodies, and spinners with bodies spun from a combination of medium and dark brown fur. This follows the theory that the trout pick out the color they want to see. This theory may or may not be valid, but we've found it to be generally effective for numerous hatches. If this approach is followed, use two parts of medium olive fur to one part of medium brown for the dun body. This keeps the pattern light enough for some species, yet provides enough brown to work for the darker species such as *tricaudatus* and *cingulatus*. Also use medium gray wing material. A wing that is too dark normally works much better than one that is too light.

Most *Baetis* nymphs are either olive, brown, or olive brown. For a single pattern, it is best to mix one part medium olive fur to one part medium brown fur. The same applies to the spinner: Mix medium and dark brown fur, one to one.

The nymphs of *Baetis* are streamlined and very vigorous swimmers, so patterns should be slender and fished with lots of action. Nymphal and emerging imitations are quite effective just before and during the hatch. For the smaller species, sizes #20 and #24, excellent wing cases for the nymph can be fashioned by spinning on a clump of blackish, fine-textured fur, such as mole. More realism is added by picking the fur slightly. For the emerging pattern, use tiny dark gray hackle tips to replace the wing-pad material.

Baetis duns can be found on the water at any time of the season and day, especially from 11:00 a.m. until dusk. A few species are comparatively large in size, #14 and #16, but most are in the 4- to 6-mm category, or #20 to #24. Too often, because of their size, they are completely ignored by the angler. In early May, for example, *Baetis tricaudatus* is found on the water simultaneously with the slightly larger *Paraleptophlebia adoptiva* and the much larger Hendricksons. If they appear in significantly greater numbers, the fish will feed on them heartily. Many times the fisherman will think the large species is what the trout are taking, when they are actually feeding on the small *Baetis*. A parallel situation exists when the *cingulatus* hatch is on during late May and early June. The duns of this species emerge along with the larger and better-known *Ephemerella dorothea*, although on many occasions the trout seem to prefer the smaller fly. These duns are minute, size #20 and #22, and can be extremely difficult to see, especially when they are mixed with the #16 sulphurs.

The hen-hackle fibers used for the wings of the subimago pattern are easier to tie and also form a more definite outline if they are clipped to shape after mounting. Equally effective wing materials include turkey breast, duck shoulders, and quill segments.

Spinners of the eastern and midwestern species normally return to the water during the late afternoon and evening, whereas western species prefer either early-morning or evening flights. Some females have the peculiar habit of crawling or diving underwater to lay their eggs, making both wet and dry patterns important. The wet imago is tied on a slightly heavier hook with the wings slanted more to the rear.

The most important species in Montana are *Baetis tricaudatus* and *Plauditus punctiventris* (the latter used to be known as *Pseudocloeon edmundsi*). Both have a peak emergence from May through June, and September through October. The size of *Baetis tricaudatus* varies from #16 to #24, the larger ones arriving in the spring. *Plauditus punctiventris* come in sizes #20 to #26.

Quill Gordon (East)

Genus and species:	*Epeorus pleuralis*
Family:	Heptageniidae
Other common names:	Gordon Quill, Dark Gordon Quill
Emergence:	April 20 to May 20
Size:	9 mm to 11 mm (#12 to #14 hook size)
Nymph habitat:	Swift gravel to rocky riffles

NATURAL	*ARTIFICIAL*

NYMPH

Body: Dark grayish brown	**Body:** Gray and brown rabbit fur mixed
Wing pads: Brownish black	**Wing pads:** Black ostrich clump
Tails: Two, tannish with dark flecks	**Tails:** Wood duck
Legs: Tannish with brown mottling	**Legs:** Wood duck

DUN

Body: Yellowish with dark brown markings	**Body:** Pale yellow and dark brown rabbit fur mixed
Wings: Dark gray	**Wings:** Dark gray duck-quill segments
Tails: Two, tannish	**Tails:** Ginger, widely spread
Legs: Tannish	**Hackle:** Sparse bronze blue dun or none

SPINNER

Body: Yellowish with dark brown markings	**Body:** Pale yellow and dark brown rabbit fur mixed
Wings: Hyaline	**Wings:** Light blue dun hen-hackle tips, spent
Tails: Two, dark brown	**Tails:** Dark brown hackle fibers
Legs: Tannish with dark brown markings	**Hackle:** None

Emergence of the Quill Gordon usually marks the beginning of good dry-fly fishing for eastern anglers. This hatch provides excellent early-season activity even though the weather may be cold, snowy, and blustery. Our last encounter with *Epeorus pleuralis* occurred at Henryville, with 4 inches of snow on the ground and a maximum water temperature of slightly less than 50 degrees. Numb fingers combined with pounding hearts produced some of the finest fishing of the season. A blanket of floating duns, unable to warm their muscles enough to escape the lines of drift, caused frenzied feeding for almost 2 hours. After a long winter of anticipating the first good hatch, this was like a dream come true.

Such episodes are typical of the Quill Gordon hatch. The weather is often cold and uncomfortable, causing many anglers to pass up excellent streamside action in favor of fireside activities. Most fishermen find it difficult to believe that good fly hatches can exist during such miserable weather. By taking advantage of these situations, one soon learns to look forward to the so-called miserable weather rather than dreading it.

The nymphs of *Epeorus pleuralis* are generally found where fast-water situations prevail. They have large distinct gills that are used as suction cups for clinging to rocks and stones, even in the swiftest of currents. When emergence time approaches, the nymphs migrate to the downstream side of underwater objects, where the nymphal skin is cast off. The newly hatched dun ascends, pierces the surface film, and then floats along to dry its bedraggled wings.

This peculiar type of underwater hatching makes an emerging pattern very effective, at least during the initial stages of the hatch. The emerging artificial is tied similarly to the No-Hackle Dun except that a heavy-wire hook is used and the duck-quill wings are shorter and slanted more to the rear. It is best fished by casting upstream, allowing it to sink, and then twitching it up through the currents in front of feeding fish. The emerging pattern should also be tied on light-wire hooks for use when the trout become more conscious of surface feeding. Sometimes it works well through the rest of the hatch. A time usually comes, however, when only a high-riding, upright-wing dun will work. The duck-quill segment pattern listed is excellent, but other wing materials, such as duck shoulder and turkey breast, are equally effective. The turkey-wing version is best tied in a clump with a few turns of parachute hackle.

The imagoes return during the middle of the day and on occasion can be quite important, especially on warmer days. An alternative spinner pattern can be tied using bronze blue dun hackle or light blue dun hackle, clipped top and bottom.

Slate-Wing Mahogany Dun (East, Midwest, West)

Genus and species:	*Paraleptophlebia adoptiva* (East, Midwest); *Paraleptophlebia bicornuta, Paraleptophlebia debilis* (West)
Family:	Leptophlebiidae
Emergence:	April 20 to June 15 (East, Midwest); August 20 to end of September (West)
Size:	**7** to 9 mm (#16 to #18 hook size)
Nymph habitat:	Shallow gravel-bottomed areas

NATURAL	*ARTIFICIAL*

NYMPH

Body: Medium to dark brown	**Body:** Dark and medium brown rabbit fur mixed
Wing pads: Black	**Wing pads:** Black crow quill segment
Tails: Three, tannish olive	**Tails:** Wood duck
Legs: Tannish olive	**Legs:** Wood duck

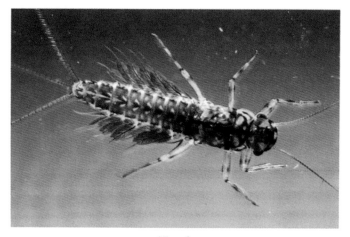

Nymph

Dun

DUN

Body: Medium to dark brown
Wings: Slate gray
Tails: Three, brown
Legs: Brown

Body: Dark and medium brown rabbit fur mixed
Wings: Dark gray duck shoulder
Tails: Brown hackle fibers
Hackle: Dark bronze blue dun hackle or none

SPINNER

Body: Dark reddish brown
Wings: Hyaline

Tails: Three, grayish brown
Legs: Brownish

Body: Dark reddish brown fur
Wings: Bronze blue dun hackle, clipped top
and bottom
Tails: Bronze blue dun-hackle fibers
Hackle: None

These little mahogany-bodied duns make up one of the earliest hatches of the season in both the East and Midwest. They often appear on the water with other larger species, such as *Ephemerella subvaria*, and close observance is required to discover which is being taken. Many times the angler will assume that the fish are feeding on the larger fly, when they are actually preferring the *adoptiva* duns.

Emergence takes place at the surface, making the use of an emerging pattern very effective when fished over rising trout. This fly is fashioned by substituting dark gray hackle points for the wing pads of the nymphal dressing. A light-wire hook should be used to provide proper flotation.

The hatching activity usually begins around 11:00 a.m., and it continues sporadically all afternoon. In very cold weather the duns will ride the water a long distance because of cold wing muscles that must be warmed sufficiently before flight can occur. The spinners return around midday and can be important when they are most numerous on the water. In the West these insects emerge in late summer and fall. The hatch usually starts about 10:00 a.m. and lasts until early afternoon. The western trout seem to prefer a nymph imitation but will hit duns and emergers. The spinners, however, are not very important.

Hendrickson (East, Midwest)

Genus and species: *Ephemerella subvaria*
Family: Ephemerellidae
Other common names: Beaverkill, borchers
Emergence: April 25 to June 15
Size: 9 to 12 mm (#12 to #14 hook size)
Nymph habitat: Swift gravel riffles of any size stream

NATURAL	*ARTIFICIAL*

Nymph

NYMPH

Body: Dark chestnut brown
Wing pads: Brownish black
Tails: Three, amber with dark bands
Legs: Amber with dark bands

Body: Dark reddish brown rabbit fur
Wing pads: Black ostrich clump
Tails: Wood duck
Legs: Wood duck

DUN

Body: Various combinations of olive, tan, and yellow
Wings: Medium to dark gray
Tails: Three, light olive with dark flecks

Legs: Light olive with dark flecks

Body: Tan, olive, and yellow rabbit fur mixed

Wings: Dark gray mallard shoulder
Tails: Bronze blue dun hackle fibers, widely spread
Hackle: Sparse dark blue dun V-hackle or none

SPINNER

Body: Dark chestnut brown
Wings: Hyaline
Tails: Three, light olive with dark flecks
Legs: Olive brown

Body: Chestnut brown rabbit or buffalo fur
Wings: Light gray hen-hackle tips, spent
Tails: Bronze blue dun hackle fibers
Hackle: None

Dun

Spinner

Peak emergence in Michigan is from May 5 to May 15, slightly earlier in the East, and later in the colder streams.

The nymphs become active around noon. Imitations should be fished deep and dead-drifted with an occasional twitching motion. Emergence begins around 2:00 p.m., so it's wise to put on an emerging pattern just before this point. It should be fished shallow or in the film, also using a gentle twitching action. Even when the duns start popping up, the emerging pattern can be used effectively well into the hatch, although as the fish become more selective it will cease to produce, and the dun imitation is required. The most essential requirement of the dun is a wing that closely simulates the size, color, and silhouette of the natural. It is essential that the artificial land on the water with its wings in an upright position. This is one of the most significant features of the floating dun.

Depending on weather conditions, the hatch may last 30 minutes to 3 hours, but about 2 hours is normal. Often during an early May afternoon, we get caddisflies, *Baetis vagans,* and *Paraleptophlebia adoptiva,* along with *Ephemerella subvaria.* You must be alert to discover which species the fish are rising to. Individual fish in different areas sometimes display different tastes. This is due to the abundance of one species over others in a particular location. The smaller flies are less discernible to the fisherman, although there may be more of them present.

On warm afternoons in early May the spinners fall in the water about 4:00 to 5:00 p.m., lying flush in the film, and they become almost invisible. If the fish resume feeding after the hatch is over, they are probably feeding on the spinners. The rise form is now much less hurried and more regular and deliberate than the splashing and noisy feeding to the duns. As the days get warmer, the spinner fall gets later and later, until eventually it comes at dusk. The spinner fall is more concentrated than the emergence and lasts only about 30 minutes, but a good imitation produces some of the best fishing.

A heavy Hendrickson spinner fall is something to remember. Every trout in the stream seems to take part in the feeding activity. As compared with the difficulty encountered with some other species, this is relatively easy fishing. Imitations of the imago are simple to fashion, but it's important to carry patterns displaying two or three wing silhouettes. Some of the naturals floating down will have upright wings, some spent wings, and some half-spent wings. Full hackle will imitate the upright version, and the others require trimming. If you prefer tying only one pattern, tie the full-hackle variety and carry scissors in your vest. We like the hen-wing spinner best when the naturals are full spent. Light hooks and top-quality hackles are an absolute necessity for the proper flotation of the full-spent and half-spent artificials.

Coloration of the Hendrickson dun can vary tremendously from stream to stream—even from different areas on the same stream. The suggested pattern for the subimago has a body constructed of yellow, tan, and olive fur, which is normally effective but should actually be matched to the naturals being imitated. For the wings, the proper shade of gray should be selected from the mallard shoulder area. The feathers chosen can be used either natural or trimmed to shape. Turkey-breast feathers, dyed and cut, also make durable and highly effective wings. If hackle is not used on the pattern, then the tail fibers must be spread widely to act as outriggers. This feature ensures that the fly will land on the water in an upright position.

Black Quill (East, Midwest)

Genus and species:	*Leptophlebia cupida*
Family:	Leptophlebiidae
Other common names:	Whirling dun, early brown spinner
Emergence:	April 25 to August 15
Size:	10 to 12 mm (#12 to #14 hook size)
Nymph habitat:	Slow current and backwaters, in leaf drift or silt- and trash-covered areas

Nymph

NATURAL / *ARTIFICIAL*

NYMPH

NATURAL	ARTIFICIAL
Body: Dark brown	**Body:** Dark brown rabbit fur
Wing pads: Blackish	**Wing pads:** Black crow quill segment
Tails: Three, brown	**Tails:** Dark brown mallard breast
Legs: Brown	**Legs:** Dark brown mallard breast

DUN

NATURAL	ARTIFICIAL
Body: Dark brown	**Body:** Dark brown rabbit fur
Wings: Slate gray washed with brown	**Wings:** Dark elk hair, clump
Tails: Three, light olive brown	**Tails:** Dark bronze blue dun
Legs: Olive brown	**Hackle:** Dark bronze blue dun, parachute

SPINNER

NATURAL	ARTIFICIAL
Body: Dark reddish brown	**Body:** Dark reddish brown seal or buffalo fur
Wings: Hyaline	**Wings:** Bronze blue dun hen tips, spent
Tails: Three, grayish brown	**Tails:** Dark bronze blue dun
Legs: Medium brown	**Hackle:** None

Peak emergence of this species occurs during mid-May, but sparse, sporadic hatches may be found throughout the greater portion of the season. The nymphs are easy to recognize by their large, double, platelike gills. They do not burrow, but instead clamber about on the stream bottom using their camouflage for protection. At hatch time they either crawl out on a log or stone or, in quiet backwaters, shed their skin at the surface. In general, the nymphal pattern has not been too deadly for us, but on occasion a slightly weighted version used with a sinking line has been effective.

The duns emerge rather sporadically, starting at midday and continuing through the afternoon hours. The spinners form their flights during mid- to late afternoon and may be found on the water until dusk. These flies are seldom present in great numbers, but because of their size, they offer an enticing meal for a trout.

Gray Fox, American March Brown (East, Midwest)

Genus and species: *Stenonema vicarium, Stenonema ithaca*
Family: Heptageniidae
Other common names: Ginger quill
Emergence: May 10 to July 15
Size: 10 to 16 mm (#10, #12, and #14 hook size)
Nymph habitat: Moderate to rapid current, clinging to the underside of stones, in leaf drift or gravel riffles

NATURAL	ARTIFICIAL

NYMPH

Body: Medium brown to dark brown on top, amber underneath	**Body:** Dark brown and light brown rabbit fur mixed
Wing pads: Dark brown	**Wing pads:** Dark brown mottled turkey quill segment
Tails: Three, brownish	**Tails:** Brown mallard breast fibers
Legs: Amber banded with brown	**Legs:** Brown mallard breast fibers

DUN

Dun

Body: Various, including tannish mottled with brown, typical	**Body:** Cream German fitch and brown rabbit fur mixed
Wings: Tannish olive mottled with dark brown	**Wings:** Mallard breast feathers dyed tannish olive, clump
Tails: Two, amber mottled with brown	**Tails:** Brown hackle fibers
Legs: Amber banded brown	**Hackle:** Honey, parachute

SPINNER

Spinner

Body: Various, including tannish mottled with brown, typical	**Body:** Cream German fitch and brown rabbit fur, mixed
Wings: Hyaline, light brown mottlings	**Wings:** Bronze blue dun hackle and sparse grizzly, clipped top and bottom
Tails: Two, mottled brown	**Tails:** Brown hackle fibers
Legs: Amber banded with brown	**Hackle:** None

These large mayflies are important in the East and of local importance in the Midwest. When present in good numbers, they normally bring out some of the better fish and cause heavy feeding activity. Duns can hatch in the afternoon, especially on dark cloudy days, although emergence is more often at dusk. Nymphs and emerging patterns are highly effective, as it sometimes takes half a minute or more for the dun to escape the nymphal shuck. Struggling slightly under or in the surface film, they provide a very tempting treat for the trout.

For the emerging fly, use a clump of wood duck or brown mallard breast to imitate the sprouting wings. They should be tied short, about two-thirds body length, and laid back at a 45-degree angle. Fish this pattern near but under the surface film with a twitching motion, which will simulate the struggle of the natural.

After complete emergence has been accomplished, the duns will float for a long period before taking to the air. A commotion is created as they flutter their wings in an effort to leave the water. This disturbance, coupled with their lengthy ride on the water, makes these elegant creatures a favorite of large trout.

Western March Brown (West)

Genus and species:	*Rhithrogena morrisoni*
Family:	Heptageniidae
Emergence:	May 20 to June 15
Size:	8 to 11 mm (#14 to #16 hook size)
Nymph habitat:	Gravel-bottom streams of any size

NATURAL	*ARTIFICIAL*

NYMPH

Body:	Head and thorax very dark olive brown, paler underneath	**Body:**	Dark olive dubbing
Wing pads:	Black	**Wing pads:**	Black crow quill
Tails:	Three, cream	**Tails:**	Cream boar
Legs:	Olive with brown bands	**Legs:**	Brown partridge, dyed olive

DUN

Body:	Olive	**Body:**	Olive dubbing
Wings:	Light gray with strong dark speckles	**Wings:**	Mallard flank feathers dyed gray and shaped with a wing burner
Tails:	Three, brown	**Tails:**	Brown Chinese boar
Legs:	Brown	**Hackle:**	Brown, clipped top and bottom

SPINNER

Body:	Reddish brown above, yellowish brown underneath	**Body:**	Yellowish brown dubbing
Wings:	Hyaline	**Wings:**	Light gray hen-hackle tips
Tails:	Nearly white	**Tails:**	Cream cock hackle fibers
Legs:	Pale amber	**Hackle:**	None

Nymph

This species is the first large mayfly to emerge on western rivers, hatching about 10:00 a.m. and lasting 1 to 2 hours. The spinner falls come at the same time, and fish feed on both stages. On Henry's Fork, the emergence is from the last week in May to mid-June. The Yellowstone, Madison, and Gallatin Rivers have later emergences that start in July and can last until early September.

Two other species of *Rhithrogena*—*R. futilis* and *R. uindulata*—are also present in the West. These produce fishable spinner falls, but the duns do not seem to be important. The same spinner imitation will work for all three species.

Sulphurs, Pale Afternoon Duns (East, Midwest)

Genus and species:	*Ephemerella invaria* and *rotunda*
Family:	Ephemerellidae
Other common names:	Light Hendrickson, PAD
Emergence:	May 3 to July 20
Size:	8 to 10 mm (#16 hook size)
Nymph habitat:	Gravel-bottom streams of any size

NATURAL	*ARTIFICIAL*

NYMPH

Body: Head and thorax very dark brown, paler underneath	**Body:** Dark and medium brown fur mixed
Wing pads: Three, amber with brown bands	**Wing pads:** Black crow quill
Legs: Amber with brown bands	**Legs:** Brown partridge

DUN

Body: Yellowish orange	**Body:** Yellow dubbing with a little orange mixed in
Thorax: Orange	**Thorax:** Orange dubbing
Wings: Blue dun	**Wings:** Mallard feathers from the base of the wings, shaped with a wing burner
Tails: Three, brown	**Tails:** Brown Chinese boar
Legs: Light brown	**Hackle:** Yellow, clipped top and bottom

SPINNER

Body: Reddish brown above, yellowish brown underneath	**Body:** Yellowish brown dubbing
Wings: Hyaline	**Wings:** Light gray hen-hackle tips
Tails: Nearly white	**Tails:** Cream cock hackle fibers
Legs: Pale amber	**Hackle:** None

Nymph

Dun

Spinner

Ephemerella invaria and *Ephemerella rotunda* are the most widely distributed species of the genus in the East and Midwest. The eastern equivalent of the pale morning duns of the West, they produce some of the finest fishing and come in the afternoon when the weather is at its best. The species are so close in appearance that a single pattern can be used for both. The spinners fall in the evening and produce some frantic feeding for about 45 minutes. Since all ephemerids take a long time to unfold their wings, an emerger pattern is especially effective during the hatch. The emergence follows the end of the little black caddis on the Au Sable in Michigan.

The color of these species can vary significantly. In some areas the insects have some olive in the bodies. The hatch usually lasts for about 2 weeks, but recently we found a tailwater river in Tennessee where the hatch started in late April and was still going in November. We have no idea why this condition exists on this river, but we certainly enjoyed it. The water from the dam comes from the bottom of the lake, so the temperature is a constant 47 degrees. Perhaps this has something to do with the long emergence, but there are many other rivers in the area with the same conditions where the emergence period is normal.

Pale Evening Dun (East, Midwest)

Genus and species: *Ephemerella dorothea*
Family: Ephemerellidae
Other common names: Sulphur dun, pale watery dun
Size: 6 to 9 mm (#18 to #20 hook size)
Emergence: May 25 to July 5
Nymph habitat: Swift gravel runs and riffles

NATURAL	*ARTIFICIAL*

NYMPH

Body: Brown with orangish or yellowish cast, heavily freckled or mottled	**Body:** Brown mixed with yellow or orange rabbit fur
Wing pads: Dark brown, freckled with light brown and yellow	**Wing pads:** Dark brown turkey-quill segment
Tails: Three, amber with brown bands	**Tails:** Wood duck
Legs: Amber with brown bands	**Legs:** Wood duck

DUN

Body: Yellow, orangish yellow, or olive yellow	**Body:** Yellow, or yellow mixed with either orange or olive rabbit fur
Wings: Light gray	**Wings:** Light gray hen-hackle fibers, clump
Tails: Three, yellowish	**Tails:** Honey-hackle fibers
Legs: Yellowish	**Hackle:** Honey, parachute

SPINNER

Body: Yellowish brown	**Body:** Brown and yellow rabbit fur mixed
Wings: Hyaline	**Wings:** Light gray hackle
Tails: Three, yellowish	**Tails:** Honey-hackle feathers
Legs: Yellowish	**Hackle:** None

Nymph

Dun

Spinner

This insect is an evening emerger, coming at the same time as the little yellow stonefly. The stones begin their egg-laying flight about 1 hour before dusk and provide some fine dry-fly fishing. Just as the light begins to fade, the fish will stop hitting the imitations of the stonefly but will keep on feeding. It is now too dark to see insects on the water, but if the angler shines a light on the water he will see it is covered with emerging duns of *Ephemerella dorothea*. Switch to a #20 Pale Evening Dun Emerger and you will again be into fish.

The nymphs become very active at hatch time, and the fish feed heavily, picking the naturals off the bottom before they can swim to the surface. Heavy-wire patterns or sinking lines are a must during these periods. Artificials should be twitched right on the bottom for best results. An emerging pattern can be fashioned by replacing the wing cases on the nymph with medium gray hackle tips. This fly is sometimes very effective during the entire hatch period. We would suggest that when you fish the nymphal or emerging pattern you work downstream and use a dead-drift float. This technique is especially effective on the sulphur hatch, probably because of the orientation of the natural in the surface film. Very few hatches provide as many problems of imitation as this one, and the best way to cope is to carry a wide variety of imitations and try to be creative.

The spinners return at or slightly after dusk and are well imitated with a fur body and wound hackle wings. Full-hackle and trimmed-hackle wing patterns should both be available for the spinner fall. The full hackle provides superior flotation, but the spent and half-spent versions are often necessary for proper simulation. Two other patterns are extremely effective during the dusk and after-dark spinner falls. One uses light gray hen-hackle points, tied one-half or fully spent, with no hackle. The other has wings made from a clump of light gray partridge, which is split and figure-eighted into the spent or semispent position. A few turns of undersized bronze blue dun hackle completes the dressing.

Gray Drake (East, Midwest)

Genus and species:	*Siphlonurus rapidus, Siphlonurus alternatus, Siphlonurus quebecensis*
Family:	Baetidae (now Siphlonuridae)
Size:	*Siphlonurus rapidus,* 9 to 12 mm (#14 hook size)
	Siphlonurus alternatus, 14 to 17 mm (#12 hook size)
	Siphlonurus quebecensis, 14 to 16 mm (#12 hook size)
Emergence:	*Siphlonurus rapidus,* May 26 to June 19
	Siphlonurus alternatus, June 17 to July 26
	Siphlonurus quebecensis, May 22 to June 26
Nymph habitat:	Still water

NATURAL	*ARTIFICIAL*

NYMPH

Body:	Mottled light and dark brown with olive overtones (*Siphlonurus quebecensis* lighter)	**Body:**	Spun fur mixture of light brown, dark brown, olive
Wing pads:	Black	**Wing pads:**	Black crow
Tails:	Ginger with brown bands	**Tails:**	Wood duck
Legs:	Ginger with brown bands	**Legs:**	Wood duck

DUN

Body:	Purplish gray with olive reflections	**Body:**	Dun imitation not needed
Wings:	Dark smoky olive		
Tails:	Olive gray		

SPINNER

Body:	Females pale olive abdomen because of underlying eggs; males gray semihyaline abdominal segments above, reddish brown or purplish brown, thorax dark reddish brown	**Body:**	Pale olive gray spun fur
Wings:	Hyaline with dark veins, stigmatic area lightly washed with gray	**Wings:**	Gray hen-hackle tips
Tails:	Brown rapidly fading to smoky white	**Tails:**	None

Spinner

The three species of *Siphlonurus* are all so similar in color that only one imitation in two sizes is needed. The nymphs migrate to still water before emergence, often far back into swampy areas, where they crawl out on shore to hatch. As a result, the duns are of no importance to anglers. The spinner falls are another matter entirely, and they provide excellent evening fishing. The spinners fall at dark in swift water and are large enough to tempt the bigger trout to feed.

Anglers are often mystified by the gray drake because they see the spinners in the air but they don't see them fall on the water. The reason is that on some occasions they are seeing traveling females. During a mating flight of mayflies, the males swarm over the water and the females fly through the swarm. The males catch the females and fertilize the eggs. The females then fly upstream to drop their eggs, and some species fly as far as 3 miles. The angler is probably seeking a flight of females traveling to a suitable rapids. On a large river such as the Muskegon, the riffles may be a mile apart. As a result, one angler may not get a fall while another fishing the next riffle upstream may have very good fishing.

Yellow Cahill (East, Midwest)

Genus and species:	*Stenacron canadense*
Family:	Heptageniidae
Other common names:	Cream mays, yellow mays
Emergence:	May 15 to August 15
Size:	8 to 11 mm (#12 and #14 hook size)
Nymph habitat:	Moderate to rapid current in shallow riffles, under stones and detritus

NATURAL	ARTIFICIAL

NYMPH

NATURAL	ARTIFICIAL
Body: Dark brown on top, pale brownish olive underneath	**Body:** Medium brown and light olive rabbit fur mixed
Wing pads: Dark brown	**Wing pads:** Mottled dark brown turkey quill segment
Tails: Three, medium brown	**Tails:** Mallard flank feather, dyed brown
Legs: Banded light and dark brown	**Legs:** Mallard flank feather, dyed brown

DUN

NATURAL	ARTIFICIAL
Body: Various, from yellowish olive to yellow, often with orange	**Body:** Blended dubbing to match naturals in area, yellowish to yellow orange
Wings: Mottled; creamy, tannish, whitish, or yellowish	**Wings:** Yellow mallard flank feathers typical
Tails: Two, tan or cream	**Tails:** Honey-hackle fibers
Legs: Pale amber to white banded with brown	**Hackle:** Honey, parachute

Nymph

Dun

Spinner

SPINNER

Body: Tannish with an amber cast is typical, but can vary from whitish to orangish yellow

Wings: Hyaline, slight dark mottlings

Tails: Two, tan or cream

Legs: Tannish banded with brown

Body: Blended fur to match naturals in area, cream or pale yellowish rabbit fur typical

Wings: Bronze blue dun hackle and sparse grizzly, clipped top and bottom

Tails: Ginger hackle fibers

Hackle: None

The duns of this closely related group hatch over a large portion of the season, reaching their peak in the East from mid-June to mid-July, and in the Midwest during late July and early August. They are similar in appearance, both in size and in coloration. Most of the subimagoes are some shade of yellow.

The heaviest hatching periods occur just before dark, but sporadic activity can take place during midday and afternoon. If the fish feed on them at all, it is usually right at dusk. Unfortunately, these flies are rarely on the water in great enough numbers to cause heavy surface feeding. They normally emerge when other more important species are hatching in greater numbers. Occasionally, however, when they are the predominant insect on the water, excellent dry-fly fishing is available. The fish do not seem to be very selective at these times, probably because of the sparseness of the hatch. The spinners return at dusk and ride the water for a considerable distance before depositing their eggs. This means that the angler must decide which stage the fish are feeding on and carry both dun and spinner patterns.

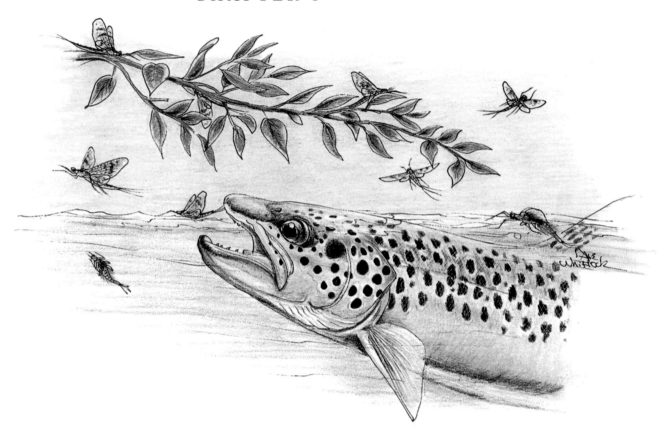

CHAPTER 8

The Midseason

HATCHES OF THE midseason represent a transition from afternoon activity to evening and night emergence (except in the West, where now it is really spring). As the days become warm, early-morning activity also begins to develop. In fact, we could call this the season of the dusk and dawn hatches. The same general rule concerning the hatch periods that applied to the early season also applies to the midseason. Decide what time of day is the most pleasant for you, and that is often the best time for the emergence to take place. In the heat of summer, the most pleasant time for us is the cool of early morning or late evening.

This is the season of giant mayflies, such as the green drake *(Ephemera guttulata)*, the brown drake *(Ephemera simulans)*, and the enormous Michigan mayfly *(Hexagenia limbata)*. These large ephemerids bring out the "old lunkers" that rarely feed on the surface. Fish of more than 5 pounds are not uncommon. They are called "washers" in the Jordan River area of Michigan, because when they rise to a *Hexagenia limbata,* it sounds like a hog falling in the water, with the waves washing up on both banks. Explosive hatches of huge duns and tremendous spinner falls, with females writhing on the surface to expel egg sacs, make old cannibal trout lose all their caution and feed almost between the angler's feet.

Not to be ignored are the smaller species in the #18 and #24 size range, which come in the early morning from sunup to about 10:00 a.m. The "washers" will not be on the prowl at this time, but great numbers of 10- to 18-inch fish will be rising freely to the smaller flies. This light-tackle fishing is just as much, or more, fun than the night fishing, and during this season you can enjoy both.

Green Drake, Coffinfly (East)

Genus and species: *Ephemera guttulata*
Family: Ephemeridae
Emergence: May 20 to June 15
Size: 18 to 22 mm (#8 and #10 hook size)
Nymph habitat: Nymphs burrow in mud banks and silted areas

NATURAL	ARTIFICIAL

NYMPH

Body: Amber with distinct olive cast	**Body:** Creamy tan German fitch and light olive rabbit fur mixed
Wing pads: Dark brown	**Wing pads:** Dark brown ostrich clump
Tails: Three, light olive	**Tails:** Light partridge dyed olive, short
Legs: Tannish olive	**Legs:** Light partridge dyed olive

DUN

Body: Creamy yellow with brownish markings	**Body:** Light deer or elk body hair, tinted yellow, extended, brown thread ribbing
Wings: Light gray with distinct olive cast and brown mottlings	**Wings:** Clump of deer or elk body hair tinted olive
Tails: Three, dark brownish olive	**Tails:** Moose mane or pheasant tail fibers
Legs: Creamish with brownish markings	**Hackle:** Dark ginger and grizzly, parachute

SPINNER

Body: Light cream, brown markings on thorax	**Body:** Light cream deer body hair, extended, white thread ribbing
Wings: Hyaline, heavily mottled with dark brown markings	**Wings:** Clump of dark brown elk hair, sparse
Tails: Three, brown	**Tails:** Moose mane or pheasant tail fibers
Legs: Yellowish, forelegs brown	**Hackle:** Bronze blue dun, parachute

Dun

For many eastern anglers, the *Ephemera guttulata* hatch is the peak of excitement for the entire season. Just the sight of one green drake struggling on the surface of a placid pool is enough to quicken the heartbeat and bring about a feeling of great anticipation. This is the period when many of the old lunkers come out of their hiding places and feed freely on the surface. At no other time of the season are such large trout so susceptible to the dry fly.

The nymphs of *guttulata* belong to the family Ephemeridae and are characterized by legs flanged for burrowing, mandibles bearing long tusks, and fringed, feathery gills. They are usually found among the silt and debris that collect around rocks and large boulders and also in the mud banks of quiet backwaters. At hatch time, they crawl out of their burrows and swim rapidly to the surface, where the dun emerges almost instantly. During this period, a nymphal pattern fished in such a manner is very deadly. You can simulate this phenomenon by sinking a heavy-wire imitation to the bottom and then using a high-rod technique to swing it quickly to the surface. Further realism can be added by using a quick, but subtle, wrist action to impart an undulating movement to the artificial.

The emerging pattern for *guttulata* should be tied on lighter-wire hooks and fished in the film. To construct this imitation, use the nymphal dressing, except for the wing pads, which instead should be a clump of four dark gray hackle points tied short. A twitching action should be used to simulate the struggle of shedding the nymphal shuck.

The heaviest emergence of these olive-tinged duns comes in the evening, but sporadic activity can occur throughout the afternoon. They encounter great difficulty in getting off the water, creating quite a commotion as they struggle along and make numerous unsuccessful attempts to fly. This characteristic, combined with their extremely large size, makes *Ephemera guttulata* an almost irresistible morsel for even the most wary old fish. When on the water in great abundance, as they often are, the green drake duns can cause big trout to throw caution to the wind and to feed voraciously. Most anglers make a great effort to produce drag-free, dead-drift floats when using the dry fly, but the green drake is one of many hatches during which a well-executed twitch is not only permissible but very deadly.

The spinners of *guttulata,* more commonly known as coffinflies, normally return at dusk 3 days after emergence. It is quite a spectacular sight to watch them swarm high over the stream and gradually dip lower and lower toward the water's surface. When the egg-laying process commences, trout of all sizes are excited into a frenzied feeding activity. Once a good riser is located, he should be stalked and tested without hesitation. Time and effort must be put to maximum use as these periods are often short lived, and because of the relatively large size of the naturals, much less feeding is required to satisfy even the largest appetites.

Slate Drake (East, Midwest)

Genus and species:	*Isonychia bicolor*
Family:	Baetidae (now Isomyehiidae)
Other common names:	Leadwing coachman, dun variant, slate drake, white-gloved howdy
Emergence:	May 20 to September 20
Size:	13 to 16 mm (#10 and #12 hook size)
Nymph habitat:	Moderate to swift currents

Nymph

Dun

NATURAL   *ARTIFICIAL*

NYMPH

Body: Dark brown   **Body:** Dark brown rabbit
Wing pads: Blackish   **Wing pads:** Black ostrich clump
Tails: Three, medium olive   **Tails:** Medium brown mallard breast
Legs: Light olive, brown bands   **Legs:** Wood duck

DUN

Body: Dark reddish brown   **Body:** Reddish brown rabbit fur
Wings: Dark slate   **Wings:** Dark gray elk hair, clump
Tails: Two, tan   **Tails:** Light brown hackle fibers
Legs: Forelegs brown, middle and hindlegs cream   **Hackle:** Bronze blue dun, parachute

Spinner

SPINNER

Body: Reddish brown   **Body:** Reddish brown rabbit fur
Wings: Hyaline   **Wings:** Light gray hen-hackle tips
Tails: Two, cream   **Tails:** Ginger hackle fibers
Legs: Forelegs brownish, feet white on female,   **Hackle:** None
middle and hindlegs cream

This large mayfly is found both in the East and Midwest, but it seems more important to eastern anglers. We've encountered sporadic hatches on the Au Sable system. However, we have seen nothing to compare with those on Art Flick's Schoharie. Degradation of the green drake hatch in recent years has made the slate wing one of the most important large trout hatches of the season.

The emergence period is very long, from late May to late September, but usually peaks during mid-June in the East and mid-July in Michigan.

Nymphs of *Isonychia* are long and streamlined, and are vigorous swimmers. When emergence time approaches, they move into shallow, quieter water, usually along the banks, and crawl out on stones to hatch. The trout are aware of this migration and follow along for an easy meal. Nymphal imitations fished in a like manner can be very productive during this period.

Owing to this method of emergence, the duns are relatively less available to the trout than for most other hatches. A fair number, however, do manage to fall or get blown into the water. Coupled with their large size and tendency to struggle on the surface, this makes the emergence of the large mahogany duns a special treat for the trout. The hatch comes in the evening during sunny and seasonable weather, but it may also occur during sunlight hours on cloudy days. The imagoes return in the evening, causing a situation in which both duns and spinners are on the water at the same time. Anglers must pay close attention to know which form the trout are feeding on.

Duns drifting relatively motionless in the current are best imitated with the elk-wing parachute form. Deer body hair dyed dark gray is a good substitute for the elk. When the duns are active, or being blown by the wind, a high-riding hackle fly is deadly. It can be skittered and skated. For this pattern, use dark blue dun hackle wound conventionally with no wings. High-quality dry-fly tackle must be used for both tails and hackle.

Brown Drake (East, Midwest, West)

Genus and species:	*Ephemera simulans*
Family:	Ephemeridae
Emergence:	May 25 to July 15
Size:	10 to 14 mm (#10 and #12 hook size)
Nymph habitat:	Stream bottoms with a mixture of sand and gravel

NATURAL	*ARTIFICIAL*
NYMPH	
Body: Amber with medium brown markings	**Body:** Creamy tan German fitch and medium brown rabbit fur mixed
Wing pads: Dark brownish black	**Wing pads:** Dark brown ostrich clump
Tails: Three, amber	**Tails:** Light tan partridge, short
Legs: Amber	**Legs:** Light tan partridge
DUN	
Body: Grayish yellow with dark brown markings	**Body:** Yellow, light gray, and brown rabbit fur mixed
Wings: Gray, heavily spotted with dark brown	**Wings:** Dark deer body hair, clump
Tails: Three, amber	**Tails:** Ginger hackle fibers
Legs: Amber	**Hackle:** Brown and grizzly, parachute

Dun

NATURAL	*ARTIFICIAL*

SPINNER

Body: Dark brown, yellowish underneath	**Body:** Yellow and light brown rabbit fur mixed
Wings: Hyaline, heavily spotted with dark brownish black	**Wings:** Brown and grizzly hackle, full or clipped top and bottom
Tails: Three, pale yellowish brown	**Tails:** Ginger hackle fibers
Legs: Pale yellowish brown	**Hackle:** None

The nymphal pattern is effective just before the hatch and should be fished with a fairly active retrieve. When tied on a light-wire hook and fished in the film, it is also deadly during the initial phase of the emergence. However, the fish soon become partial to the freshly hatched subimagoes and, at that point, a dun pattern must be used. The deer body hair tied in a clump makes an excellent wing outline and provides a perfect base for securing the parachute hackle. An alternative body material for both dun and spinner is deer hair dyed to the proper shade.

In Michigan, the brown drake is the first large fly of the year that provides good dusk and after-dark fishing. Because of their size and time of emergence, big fish are induced to feed on the surface. The hatch is normally at its peak sometime between June 5 and June 15, a week or so before the even larger *Hexagenia limbata*. Duns and spinners are both on the water from sundown until well after dark, making it difficult to discover which stage the fish are feeding on.

The brown drake immediately follows the famous green drake (*Ephemerella grandis*) hatch in the West. Except for a slight size variation, both species look similar on the water. The trout can tell the difference, so the angler must be able to recognize the change and act accordingly. Several times we've been fooled by this situation, thinking the fish were taking green drakes when they had actually switched to the brown variety. The importance of collecting specimens and examining them in your hand cannot be overstated.

Slate-Maroon Drake (West)

Genus and species:	*Ironodes nitidus*
Family:	Heptageniidae
Emergence:	June 1 to July 15
Size:	11 to 14 mm (#12 to #14 hook size)
Nymph habitat:	Fast water, rocks, and gravel

NATURAL	*ARTIFICIAL*
NYMPH	
Body: Dark brownish gray with darker mottling on back	**Body:** Brown and gray rabbit fur mixed
Wing cases: Dark brown	**Wing cases:** Very dark brown quill segment
Tails: Two, mottled brown	**Tails:** Brown partridge
Legs: Mottled brown	**Legs:** Brown partridge
DUN	
Body: Maroon underneath, mottled brown on top	**Body:** Maroon rabbit fur
Wings: Dark gray	**Wings:** Dark gray quill segments
Tails: Two, gray	**Tails:** Gray hackle fibers
Legs: Gray with brown markings	**Hackle:** None
SPINNER	
Body: Yellowish brown, segments 2 through 7 semitransparent	**Body:** Yellow and brown rabbit fur mixed
Wings: Hyaline with distinct reddish brown veins	**Wings:** Light gray hen-hackle tips, spent
Tails: Two, pale yellowish brown	**Tails:** Honey-hackle fibers
Legs: Amber shading to brown	**Hackle:** None

This rather spectacular ephemerid produces a mid- to late-morning hatch that is normally short in duration but great in number. Fish are attracted to this fat, juicy mayfly, which usually creates heavy feeding activity. A weighted nymph fished in the deep runs just before and during the hatch is often deadly. This is a common species found widely over the western states on both sides of the Continental Divide.

Slate-Wing Olive (East)

Genus and species: *Ephemerella* (now *Drunella*) *attenuata*
Family: Ephemerellidae
Emergence: June 5 to July 15
Size: 6 to 9 mm (#16 and #18 hook size)
Nymph habitat: Gravel riffles and slow currents in streams of all sizes

NATURAL	ARTIFICIAL

NYMPH

Body: Tannish brown	**Body:** Tan and brown rabbit fur mixed
Wing pads: Dark brown	**Wing pads:** Dark brown ostrich clump
Tails: Three, tannish and short	**Tails:** Tan partridge
Legs: Tannish mottled with brown	**Legs:** Brown partridge

DUN

Body: Medium olive	**Body:** Medium olive rabbit fur
Wings: Dark gray, almost black	**Wings:** Dark gray turkey breast, clump
Tails: Three, olive	**Tails:** Olive hackle fibers
Legs: Light olive	**Hackle:** Light olive, parachute

SPINNER

Body: Thorax dark brown, abdomen medium brown	**Body:** Dark brown and medium brown rabbit fur mixed
Wings: Hyaline	**Wings:** Light gray hen-hackle tips
Tails: Three, light olive	**Tails:** Light olive hackle fibers
Legs: Light olive	**Hackle:** None

Drunella attenuata is found only in the East, but it is closely related to the midwestern species *Ephemerella lata* (page 92). To the angler, they can be considered identical, except for one minor difference: coloration of the nymphs. The *attenuata* nymphs are much lighter, having a distinct tannish cast, as opposed to the much darker *lata*. The duns normally hatch around midday, but can appear sporadically from early morning to late afternoon, depending on the weather conditions. The marked contrast of blackish wings over bright olive bodies simplifies identification. The spinners return to the water for mating and egg laying at dusk the following day.

Western Green Drake (West)

Genus and species: *Ephemerella* (now *Drunella*) *grandis*
Family: Ephemerellidae
Emergence: June 15 to July 15
Size: 14 to 16 mm (#10 and #12 hook size)
Nymph habitat: Medium to fast rock and gravel runs

	NATURAL	*ARTIFICIAL*

NYMPH

Body: Dark reddish brown	**Body:** Dark blackish brown mole fur
Wing pads: Black	**Wing pads:** Black quill segment
Tails: Three, dark brown	**Tails:** Dark brown partridge
Legs: Dark brownish black	**Legs:** Dark brown partridge

DUN

Body: Green with dark brown rings; dark brown markings only on dorsal in freshly hatched duns	**Body:** Medium green deer hair, extended body ribbed with dark brown thread
Wings: Dark slate gray	**Wings:** Dark elk hair, clump
Tails: Three, green and brown	**Tails:** Olive hackle fibers
Legs: Light yellowish olive shading to brownish green	**Hackle:** Olive, parachute, sparse and short

SPINNER

Body: Dark brown with wide pale margins so as to appear ringed	**Body:** Reddish brown rabbit fur ribbed with light gray muskrat fur
Wings: Hyaline	**Wings:** Pale gray hen-hackle tips
Tails: Three, dark brown	**Tails:** Bronze blue dun hackle fibers
Legs: Pale tan	**Hackle:** None

Nymph

Dun

Drunella grandis is one of the largest mayflies found in the West, and on many rivers it is the most important hatch of the season. Because of its large size, giant trout can be found feeding on the surface during this hatch. We have landed rainbows as large as 5 pounds at western green drake time and have heard of 10-pounders being taken. Many fish as large as 18 or 20 inches are common during a good day. These nymphs are large, fat, and evidently very desirable.

The hatch seems to start with a few flies coming off in the morning for 4 or 5 days. Suddenly the hatch will start in the morning and last until about 5:00 in the afternoon, with duns literally covering the water, perhaps one dun for every square foot. After 2 or 3 days of peak hatching, it will taper off and there will be just a few flies in the morning for about a week On cold, cloudy days, we have seen this hatch hold off until 4:00 in the afternoon and emerge heavily until dark. We have never seen a spinner fall, and knowledgeable guides who fish many rivers in the West, all of them with good green drake hatches, have also told us that they have never seen a spinner fall. It probably comes after dark, or early in the morning.

It's worth noting that there is really more than one species of western green drake. The other important species are *Drunella doddsi, Drunella coloradensis,* and *Timpanoga hecuba.* In Montana, all four species are present on the Gallatin. The Lamar, Soda Butte, Yellowstone, and Slough Creek all have green drake hatches. Fall hatches occur on the Lamar, Slough Creek, and Soda Butte.

Any of our dun patterns work well: the Paradun, the No-Hackle, and especially the extended-body types. An exceptional one is the V-Hackle Partridge Drake. The wings are partridge feathers dyed dark gray and tied much the same way as a fan wing, with the hackle tied on normally and clipped on the top and bottom so that the only fibers are coming out the sides. An extremely productive imitation for this hatch is the Green Drake Emerger. This has a trailing shuck of opaque dark brown yarn, a body of olive dubbing with a yellow rib, and a hackle of grizzly dyed yellow olive.

Local anglers use a conglomeration of large flies such as Goofus Bugs, Grizzly Wulffs, Gray Wulffs, and Irresistibles, all of which seem to work fairly well. However, you do get refusals with these flies. Even after the hatch has tapered off, the fish seem to be on the lookout for these large mayflies in the mornings between 10:00 a.m. and 1:00 p.m., and large fish can be found rising, cruising, and feeding on the occasional dun. The date for this hatch around the area of West Yellowstone is June 22 to July 4, varying according to altitude and unseasonable weather.

One note on the color of the duns: The freshly hatched female has a bright green body with slight brown markings on the back. However, the same dun 1 hour later is much darker, mostly dark reddish brown with light olive rings. The fish see the bright green, not the later darker fly. Most species of dun become darker on aging, but in this species the problem was so pronounced we had to transport camera equipment to the riverbank to get a better look.

Slate-Brown Dun (West)

Genus and species: *Epeorus longimanus*
Family: Heptageniidae
Emergence: June 15 to July 15
Size: 10 to 11 mm (#14 hook size)
Nymph habitat: Small to medium-sized streams above 5,000 feet elevation, on large rocks

NATURAL	*ARTIFICIAL*

NYMPH

Body: Dark grayish brown, light brown underneath	**Body:** Brownish gray muskrat fur
Wing pads: Dark brownish black	**Wing pads:** Dark brown or black quill segments
Tails: Two, tan with dark brown markings	**Tails:** Brown partridge fibers
Legs: Tan with dark markings	**Legs:** Brown partridge fibers

DUN

Body: Light gray with dark markings on back	**Body:** Light gray muskrat fur
Wings: Dark gray	**Wings:** Dark gray duck-shoulder feathers
Tails: Two, gray with brown markings	**Tails:** Medium gray hackle fibers
Legs: Tan shading to brown	**Hackle:** None

SPINNER

Body: Pale reddish brown, although may vary to reddish brown according to locality	**Body:** Tan beaver or rabbit fur
Wings: Hyaline	**Wings:** Light gray hen-hackle tips, spent
Tails: Two, tan mottled	**Tails:** Tan hackle fibers
Legs: Tan	**Hackle:** None

Nymph

Epeorus species are common in the East and West and rare in the Midwest, with the sizes of the various species ranging from 7 to 11 mm. Nymphs are two tailed and flat bodied with a large head. *Epeorus longimanus* is found in small and medium-sized streams above 5,000 feet elevation in fast water. They are replaced by *Epeorus albertae* on lower, warmer stretches of the same river. Hatching time is about 11:00 a.m., and the spinner fall is in the early afternoon. Hatches are usually short but heavy. A nymph fished in fast runs before and during the hatch is effective.

Speckled Spinner (West)

Nymph

Genus and species:	*Callibaetis coloradensis, Callibaetis nigritus* (both now *Callibaetis ferrugineus*)
Family:	Baetidae
Emergence:	June 15 to September 30
Size:	8 to 10 mm (#14 and #16 hook size)
Nymph habitat:	Slower rivers with aquatic vegetation

NATURAL	*ARTIFICIAL*

NYMPH

Body:	Grayish brown	**Body:**	Light muskrat fur
Wing pads:	Dark mottled brown	**Wing pads:**	Dark brown turkey-quill segment
Tails:	Three, light brown	**Tails:**	Light brown mallard
Legs:	Light brown	**Legs:**	Light brown mallard

DUN

Dun

Body:	Brownish with an olive tint	**Body:**	Medium brown and medium olive rabbit fur mixed
Wings:	Dark gray, paths of veins and cross-veins white	**Wings:**	Slate gray hen-hackle fibers, clump
Tails:	Two, tannish with brown at joinings	**Tails:**	Cream hackle fibers
Legs:	Tannish cream	**Hackle:**	Cream, parachute

SPINNER

Spinner

Body:	Light grayish tan with tiny dark brown speckles	**Body:**	Light gray muskrat fur
Wings:	Hyaline, dark brown splotches on leading edge	**Wings:**	Dark brown partridge or merganser flank fibers, spent
Tails:	Two, whitish with brown at joinings	**Tails:**	Cream hackle fibers
Legs:	Tannish cream	**Hackle:**	None

These mayflies are primarily lake dwellers, preferring to live among vegetation. The genus is found over virtually all trout states from New York to California. In most areas they are only locally abundant on trout streams. Most species of *Callabaetis* are adapted to slow, warm-water situations. However, *Callabaetis ferrugineus* has adapted to a colder-water environment and is found in canyons, mountains, and mountain valleys at elevations usually above 4,500 feet. In lakes, ponds, and slow-flowing rivers, nymphs are found in silted bottoms or among submerged vegetation.

The western rivers in which they are particularly important are the spring creeks. One important feature of these rivers is that they maintain a fairly constant level. There is no great runoff during the spring to scour the bottom. Vegetation, such as filamentous algae, and smooth, slow-flowing currents provide the perfect habitat for the nymphs of *Callibaetis*. Henry's Fork of the Snake is a wide, spring-creek river, but little over knee deep. It emerges full blown from an underground source and is fishable when the Madison and Yellowstone are in flood stage. Its gravel bottom is carpeted with bright green vegetation.

The duns of *Callibaetis ferrugineus* hatch at dusk, after dark, and at mid-day. They are a brownish olive insect and have dark gray wings, with the paths of the veins and cross-veins being white. Adult bodies are thickly speckled with minute brown dots, set in small depressions. The forewings of the female spinners are darkly pigmented on the leading edges. Nymphs are streamlined and fitted for swimming and darting in slow water. The spinner falls come in the morning from 9:30 to 11:00 and in the evening from 7:00 to 9:00. The imagoes sometimes fall with the smaller but more numerous *Ephemerellas,* but the fish often prefer the larger *Callibaetis.* Rainbows from 15 inches to 26 inches are not uncommon during this hatch and spinner fall.

Tiny Blue-Winged Olive (Midwest, West)

Genus and species:	*Pseudocloeon anoka* and *Pseudocloeon edmundsi* (both now *Plauditus punctiventris*)
Family:	Baetidae
Emergence:	June 20 to September 30
Size:	4.5 to 5 mm (#24 hook size)
Nymph habitat:	Shallow gravel runs and submerged beds of vegetation

NATURAL	*ARTIFICIAL*
NYMPH	
Body: Greenish olive, streamlined	**Body:** Greenish olive rabbit fur
Wing pads: Brownish olive	**Wing pads:** Dark brown ostrich clump
Tails: Two, light olive	**Tails:** Light olive hackle fibers
Legs: Light olive	**Legs:** Light olive hackle fibers
DUN	
Body: Greenish olive	**Body:** Greenish olive rabbit fur
Wings: Light gray, one pair only	**Wings:** Light gray hen-hackle fibers, clump
Tails: Two, light gray	**Tails:** Light gray hackle fibers
Legs: Light gray	**Hackle:** None, or light gray parachute, two turns only

Dun

Spinner

SPINNER

Body: Light olive brown with orangish cast

Wings: Hyaline
Tails: Two, white
Legs: White

Body: Blend of olive, light brown, and orange rabbit fur
Wings: Light gray hen-hackle tips, spent
Tails: Light gray hackle fibers
Hackle: None

Even though these mayflies are very small in size, they are extremely important to anglers in all sections of the country. They occur in great numbers, causing the fish to move out into midstream and feed freely. *Plauditus* is multibrooded, so emergence can take place almost anytime after mid-June. However, there are two peak periods, the first occurring from late June to mid-July, and the second during late September. On dark cool days these little flies begin emerging about 11:00 a.m., continuing sporadically until dark. On warm sunny days they hatch in fantastic numbers, beginning about an hour before sundown and ending shortly after dark.

When emergence time approaches, most of the mature nymphs are found crawling on submerged vegetation. Nymph patterns fished in these areas, or slightly downstream from weed beds, can be very successful. As the hatch progresses, more and more fish switch to the floating duns. At this stage, a delicate #24 no-hackle dry fly is most effective. If the tails are properly split and good wing outline is maintained, these minute imitations will float upright and closely resemble the naturals on the water. The spinners normally return at dusk and are taken quietly and subtly by the trout. Once again, you will have to observe closely to see which stage the fish are actually feeding on.

Giant Michigan Mayfly (East, Midwest, West)

Genus and species:	*Hexagenia limbata*
Family:	Ephemeridae
Other common names:	Michigan caddis
Emergence:	June 20 to July 30
Size:	18 to 33 mm (#2, #4, and #6 hook size)
Nymph habitat:	Silt beds and mud banks, usually in shallow water along the stream's edge

NATURAL   *ARTIFICIAL*

NYMPH

Body: Amber with medium brown markings   **Body:** Creamy tan German fitch and brown rabbit fur mixed

Wing pads: Brownish black   **Wing pads:** Dark brown ostrich clump
Tails: Three, amber   **Tails:** Light tan partridge, short
Legs: Amber   **Legs:** Light tan partridge

DUN

Body: Varies from yellow to grayish brown, with purplish brown back markings   **Body:** Natural deer body hair tied parallel to shank, ribbed with yellow tying thread
Wings: Smoky gray with olive reflections   **Wings:** Dark elk or deer body hair, clump
Tails: Two, yellowish brown   **Tails:** Two pheasant tail fibers
Legs: Yellowish brown   **Hackle:** Brown and grizzly, parachute

SPINNER

Body: Yellowish with purplish brown back markings   **Body:** Yellow deer body hair tied parallel to shank, ribbed with brown tying thread, regular or extended body

Wings: Hyaline   **Wings:** Double hen-hackle tips, grizzly over light gray, spent

Tails: Two, yellowish brown   **Tails:** Two long pheasant tail fibers
Legs: Yellowish brown   **Hackle:** None

Nymph

Dun

Spinner

This is the famous Michigan "caddis" hatch. It is not actually a caddisfly, but years ago someone called it that and confusion has reigned ever since. For many anglers, these gigantic flies mark the peak of the season, especially on the larger streams such as the Pere Marquette, Au Sable, and Jordan. *Hexagenia limbata* is the midwestern equivalent of the eastern green drake hatch.

These largest of trout-stream mayflies, with their fat, meaty bodies, entice large fish to feed on the surface. They hatch in tremendous numbers on warm muggy nights, beginning in the second or third week of June. Peak emergence almost always comes around the Fourth of July.

Final molting to the spinner stage occurs in 24 to 72 hours, depending on the weather. The imagoes normally fall from dusk to 11:00 p.m., with the females releasing their eggs in a death struggle after hitting the water. The rise form is a spectacular, deep, loud slurp.

In streams, the life cycle requires 2 years. As our stomach analysis showed, the fish feed regularly on the nymphs during the fall and winter months. The opportunity arises when nymphs leave their burrows and swim around to molt, which occurs about thirty times as they grow. The nymphs make U-shaped holes as they burrow in the mud banks along the edge of the stream.

Before emergence, the nymph is sometimes effective if fished just under the surface, near the silt beds where the naturals emerge. Occasionally, it will also fool a wise old feeder when every dry fly in the box has failed. Try this technique dead-drift and, if the offering is rejected, add a slight twitch as the nymph comes into the trout's window. The addition of hackle tips to simulate partially sprouted wings is sometimes also very effective.

Emergence of the duns and the return of the spinners usually take place at dusk or well after dark, and on some nights occur after midnight. Occasionally the subimagoes will hatch sporadically throughout the day and the imagoes will fall an hour or two before dark. This happens frequently on Michigan's Manistee River and results in some fantastic big-fly fishing during daylight hours. The fish become highly selective under these conditions, and realistic patterns are a necessity. These experiences indicate that parachute hackle and clump wings are most effective when simulating the large flies.

The double hen-wing spinner imitation is the most deadly and realistic pattern we've developed, and it has the added advantages of floating well and being very durable. The grizzly tips simulate the dark wing markings; while the light gray tips tone down the grizzly and provide the general coloration and appearance of spent wings in the film. Another effective yet simple-to-tie pattern consists of a yellow and brown fur body with gray and grizzly hackle, clipped top and bottom, for wings. The only drawback is poor flotation, which results from the weight of a large hook and too little hackle. Lightweight, short-shank hooks and extended quill bodies improve buoyancy only slightly, and they have the added disadvantage of being brittle.

One fly that deserves mention for use on the *Hexagenia* hatch is the extended-body, impala-wing fly. This one is especially effective after dark, toward the end of the spinner fall. It is hackleless, floats low in the water, and will produce equally well with or without movement. This pattern has an extended body of natural deer body hair coming off a lightweight short-shank hook. Two pheasant-tail fibers protrude beyond the body to form the tails. Light gray impala is used for the spent wings, and tan mohlon (a synthetic yarn) is wrapped around the wings to form an enlarged thorax. The mohlon thorax not only creates a realistic silhouette but also adds greatly to the flotation of the fly.

It should also be mentioned here that in the Midwest the wiggle nymph imitation has become a top fly for steelhead. Anglers are using it with great success in the fall, winter, and spring.

Flavs or Slate-Winged Olive (West)

Genus and species:	*Ephemerella flavilinea* (now *Drunella flavilinea*)
Family:	Ephemerellidae
Emergence:	June 25 to August 20
Size:	8 to 10 mm (#14 and #16 hook size)
Nymph habitat:	Gravel runs, medium to fast water

NATURAL	*ARTIFICIAL*

NYMPH

Body: Dark brown	**Body:** Dark blackish brown mole fur
Wing pads: Black	**Wing pads:** Black quill segment
Tails: Three, dark brown with black bands	**Tails:** Dark brown partridge
Legs: Dark brown	**Legs:** Dark brown partridge

Spinner

NATURAL	ARTIFICIAL

DUN

Body: Medium greenish olive	**Body:** Medium greenish olive rabbit fur
Wings: Dark slate	**Wings:** Dark gray elk hair, clump
Tails: Three, dark olive gray	**Tails:** Dark olive hackle fibers
Legs: Light olive shading to brown	**Hackle:** Olive, parachute

SPINNER

Body: Light translucent reddish brown	**Body:** Reddish brown buffalo fur
Wings: Hyaline	**Wings:** Light gray hen-hackle tips, spent
Tails: Three, brown with dark joinings	**Tails:** Brown hackle fibers
Legs: Brown shading to dark brown	**Hackle:** None

The western slate olive dun is a fly very closely resembling the green drake, and it immediately follows the green drake hatch. The dun is almost indistinguishable in appearance from *Drunella grandis* except that it is smaller. Even so, it is still a good-sized, juicy mayfly, and fine fish are attracted to it. The hatch lasts a long time—almost 2 months—so it is extremely important. The duns usually emerge from about 5:00 to 6:30 p.m. until dark, but on dark cloudy days we have seen them hatching all day, beginning at 11:00 a.m. The spinner fall is usually in the morning from about 9:00 a.m. until 1:00 p.m. However, some spinners also fall in the evening.

Drunella flavilinea and *Drunella grandis* belong to the same subspecies, along with *Drunella lata* of the Midwest, and these nymphs are all similar in color and shape. For this reason, a weighted nymph fished in the deep runs is often successful before the hatch. Emergence from the nymphal shuck takes place on the surface. We have noticed, in fact, that these flies often have trouble getting one wing out of the shuck, and they flail around on the water while emerging. Thus the artificial, if given a little action, will get fish from their feeding lanes to take a fly acting in this manner.

These insects start hatching just about the time that the *Drunella grandis,* or western green drake, is about finished. Once again, the hatch starts when most western streams are high with spring runoff water. Anglers who prefer to fish to rising trout at the beginning of the hatch tend to seek out water such as the large and small spring creeks and high meadow streams that do not get these floods. Therefore we run into these flies, which fishermen on the large runoff rivers, such as the Madison and the Big Hole, do not encounter. These hatches are present on the "freestone streams," but these bodies of water are usually too dark to allow the trout to feed on the surface until later, at the tail end of the hatch.

A brown-bodied Hen Spinner is a killer in the morning after a hatch the previous evening. All of our dun patterns are effective during an emergence, and it is a good idea to be prepared with two or three different types. Then if you miss a strike, a slightly different style can be substituted. Often the change of flies will result in a fine fish.

CHAPTER 9

The Late Season

As WE HAVE seen, the midseason is characterized by two radically different types of angling: evening fishing with very large flies, and early-morning fishing with relatively small flies. During this time there are normally two pleasant periods each day. The first is when the water is warmed by the morning sun, and the second occurs after the heat of midday, when the water cools in the evening. However, as the late season begins around the middle of July, the night hatches fade, whereas the morning hatches increase their intensity and length.

By this time the heat of summer is at its peak, causing high evening water temperatures. Here again, the "pleasant time of day" rule seems to apply, as the hatches occur in the early morning when the water is at a comfortable temperature. This period shifts to midday in September, and then moves to the afternoon as the weather gets slowly colder during late fall. As the season ends, the cycle is complete, with hatches coming at the same time as they did when the season opened.

This late season, to us, is the most interesting time of all, and also the most challenging. The naturals are very small, mostly in the 3.5- to 5-mm range, making light and delicate equipment the order of the day. We use #4 rods and lines, combined with size #22 to #28 flies and 6X to 7X leaders. Hatches of these tiny flies are very dependable, much more so than the larger species. Good fish feed with extreme regularity and must rise more often to get a full meal. They seem to lose much of their natural caution. In fact, it is sometimes difficult to put them down, especially at the peak of the hatch, when they are gorging heavily.

The fish, however, are very selective, and correct imitations are a must if you are to be at all successful. Contrary to popular opinion, just any small fly will not suffice. A 5-mm imitation of a *Tricorythodes* dun, when the natural is only 3.5 mm long, is useless. The difference between a #22 and #28 does not appear great, but relatively speaking it is more than 40 percent, and the fish can easily recognize the difference. When fishing to these small flies, you should carry a millimeter gauge and try to measure the naturals.

The major difficulty with small standard imitations is that too much hackle is used and it is usually too long. Hackle on these flies only obscures, or completely obliterates, the delicate outline of the insect and gives the impression of a fuzzy dandelion seed.

For years we incorrectly blamed the small hooks for not holding well. Only one or two fish out of ten might be landed. However, we found that when we follow two rules, #28s are just as efficient as #14s. First, the fly must be the right size, color, and silhouette. Second, the fly must float and behave in the same manner as the natural. In general, for freshly hatched duns and newly fallen spinners, imitations must float high in the film and not be waterlogged. To accomplish this task, you must saturate the fly with a waterproofing agent. Then, after drying completely, either add a more viscous flotant, such as silicone, or rub in a paste dressing. The first step prevents waterlogging, and the latter provides the film necessary for proper flotation.

When we started following these rules we landed many more fish and, in fact, had trouble unhooking them. We now use barbless hooks, which hold just as well as regular hooks and permit release without injury. This ease of unhooking not only protects the trout but also preserves delicate dry flies. An even further advantage is that more valuable fishing time is gained. The time that would normally be spent unhooking barbed flies and changing crushed, slimy dressings can always be spent more profitably during the all-too-short hatch period.

Yellow May, Yellow Drake (East)

Genus and species:	*Ephemera varia*
Family:	Ephemeridae
Emergence:	June 25 to July 25
Size:	13 to 16 mm (#10 and #12 hook size)
Nymph habitat:	Mixture of sand and gravel, also in silt and mud banks

Nymph

Dun

Spinner

NATURAL   *ARTIFICIAL*

NYMPH

Body: Amber with dark brown markings

Wing pads: Dark brown
Tails: Three, amber
Legs: Amber

Body: Creamy tan German fitch and brown rabbit fur mixed
Wing pads: Dark brown ostrich, clump
Tails: Light tan partridge, short
Legs: Light tan partridge

DUN

Body: Pale yellow, brown markings on back

Wings: Light yellowish gray, spotted with brown

Tails: Three, yellow mottled with brown
Legs: Yellow, brown markings on forelegs

Body: Deer body hair tinted yellow, yellow thread ribbing
Wings: Clump of light deer body hair, tinted yellow
Tails: Light ginger hackle fibers
Hackle: Light ginger and grizzly, parachute

SPINNER

Body: Pale yellowish olive with brown markings on back
Wings: Hyaline spotted with dark brownish black
Tails: Three, yellow mottled with brown
Legs: Yellow, brownish markings on forelegs

Body: Pale yellow and light olive rabbit fur mixed
Wings: Grizzly hen-hackle tips, spent
Tails: Light ginger hackle fibers
Hackle: Bronze blue dun, sparse and undersized

The nymphs of *Ephemera varia* possess many of the same characteristics as those of *Ephemera guttulata,* such as flanged legs, tusks, feathery gills, and rapid emergence. However, they can be differentiated from the green drake nymphs by their smaller size, darker coloration, and distinctive markings, both dorsally and ventrally. The underside of the abdomen displays blackish longitudinal markings, and the back of the entire body exhibits a unique pattern. This aesthetic dorsal design is a deep chocolate brown in coloration and is discernible in both the subimago and imago stages.

Emergence normally occurs at twilight, but when the weather is cloudy and cool the duns can be seen sporadically all day. Their beautiful color and large size make a very impressive sight, especially when either duns or spinners appear in any great quantity. Adults usually return to the stream the day after emergence and begin their mating flight at dusk.

Slate-Winged Olive (Midwest)

Genus and species:	*Ephemerella* (now *Drunella*) *lata*
Family:	Ephemerellidae
Emergence:	July 1 to August 10
Size:	6 to 10 mm (#16 or #18 hook size)
Nymph habitat:	Gravel riffles in streams of all sizes

NATURAL	*ARTIFICIAL*

NYMPH

Body: Brownish black, robust	**Body:** Dark Belgian mole fur
Wing pads: Brownish black	**Wing pads:** Black crow quill segment
Tails: Three, brown	**Tails:** Brown partridge
Legs: Brownish black	**Legs:** Dark brown partridge

DUN

Body: Olive	**Body:** Olive rabbit fur
Wings: Dark gray, almost black	**Wings:** Dark gray turkey breast, clump
Tails: Three, olive	**Tails:** Olive hackle fibers
Legs: Olive	**Hackle:** Olive, parachute

SPINNER

Body: Males brown, females light olive	**Body:** Medium brown or light olive rabbit fur
Wings: Hyaline	**Wings:** Light gray hen-hackle tips, spent
Tails: Three, light olive	**Tails:** Light olive hackle fibers
Legs: Light olive	**Hackle:** None

Drunella lata is one of the first good early-morning hatches of the season. Emergence can begin as early as 6:30 a.m. and continue until noon, with the peak period occurring from 7:00 to 9:00 a.m. The duns appear sporadically over an extended period, rarely hatching in large numbers at one time. Often they are on the water with other more numerous species—such

Dun

as *Plauditus punctiventris (Pseudocloeon anoka)* and *Tricorythodes stygiatus*—causing the fish to ignore them completely. However, there is a period in mid-July when *Plauditus* is fading and *Tricorythodes* is barely existent that provides excellent early-morning activity.

The nymphal imitation is sometimes effective before any surface activity is noticed. It should be fished along the bottom of gravel riffles with an occasional twitch. As the hatch commences, an emerging pattern is very productive when floating in the film dead-drift. The emerging pattern is the same as the nymphal imitation, except that dark grayish black points are used in place of wing pads. These emergent wings should be three-quarters the body length and tied back at a 45-degree angle. The suggested pattern for the subimago can be tied without hackle as long as the tails are split properly.

The spinners of *Drunella lata* return just before sundown and fall for almost an hour after dark, providing tremendous evening fishing. In the Midwest, this is the last hatch of good-sized flies of the season, and the fish seem to know it. After these juicy morsels leave the water, most of the good hatches are size #20 or smaller. The spinners are far more important than the duns for two reasons. First, the duns hatch sporadically over a 4- or 5-hour period in the morning, resulting in a low-intensity emergence and slow feeding activity. (The following evening, the same number of flies return as spinners and fall en masse in about 90 minutes, causing frenzied activity.) Second, the duns must compete with other more numerous species in the morning, whereas the spinners have little or no competition in the evening.

Pale Morning Dun #1 (West)

Genus and species:	*Ephemerella inermis*
Family:	Ephemerellidae
Other common names:	Olive quill
Emergence:	May to July 15
Size:	5.5 to 7 mm (#16 to #20 hook size)
Nymph habitat:	Gravel and aquatic vegetation, all speeds of water

NATURAL	*ARTIFICIAL*

NYMPH

Body: Dark brownish olive	**Body:** Dark brown and medium olive rabbit fur mixed
Wing pads: Dark olive brown	**Wing pads:** Olive brown duck-quill segment
Tails: Three, brown with black bands	**Tails:** Dark brown partridge or merganser flank fibers
Legs: Brownish olive	**Legs:** Dark brown partridge or merganser flank fibers

DUN

Body: Bright, light olive yellow	**Body:** Light olive and light yellow rabbit fur mixed
Wings: Light gray	**Wings:** Light gray hen-hackle fibers, clump
Tails: Three, tan with dark brown at joinings	**Tails:** Bronze blue dun hackle fibers
Legs: Light olive	**Hackle:** Light olive, parachute

SPINNER

Body: Male yellowish brown, female yellowish olive	**Body:** Mix either dark brown or light olive with yellow rabbit fur
Wings: Hyaline	**Wings:** Medium gray hackle, clipped on bottom
Tails: Three, light tan with brown joinings	**Tails:** Bronze blue dun hackle fibers
Legs: Olive tan	**Hackle:** None

Ephemerella inermis is the most widespread and numerous of the western *Ephemerellas* and is characterized by a beautiful but elusive olive yellow cast. The fish become extremely selective during this hatch and an artificial, either too large or off color, is usually ignored. The fly resembles the eastern *Ephemerella invaria* (page 62) but is a trifle smaller and more olive. The spinner fall is at 9:30 a.m. on Henry's Fork of the Snake, and they literally carpet the water for about 2 hours. The duns start emerging around 11:00 a.m. and continue all afternoon. At about 6:00 p.m. the spinner fall starts

Nymph

Dun

Spinner

again and lasts until dusk. Trout rise all day to this hatch, and rainbows as large as 8 pounds can be taken on #20 dry flies. Often there are so many naturals on the water that you must cast your artificial to fit in with the feeding rhythm of the fish. Otherwise it will drift along untouched with hundreds of the naturals.

Before we fished Henry's Fork, we would never have believed so many mayflies could hatch in such great numbers so steadily for many hours and over 2 months. Even more amazing is the fact that great hatches of *Tricory-thodes, Plauditus (Pseudocloeon), Callibaetis, Baetis,* and two other species of *Ephemerellas* are hatching simultaneously. This very large spring creek is the most prolific insect factory we have ever seen.

The dun is best imitated by a #16 or #20 hen-hackle fiber wing, chartreuse fur body, and sparse parachute hackle. Other patterns equally as effective are the duck-shoulder and duck-quill segment type with no hackle. A killer pattern for the spinner is an olive yellow fur body tied with full medium gray hackle and then clipped only on the bottom. A small dark brown nymph is also deadly just before and during the early part of the hatch.

These insects exhibit a wide range in size, becoming smaller as the season progresses. The other pale morning dun is *Ephemerella infrequens*, which is very similar in appearance but larger (7 to 9 mm). On rivers that have both species, they are separated by elevation.

The nymphs apparently have two color phases, one being olive and the other very dark, almost black. Trout key on one or the other, based on our experiments. When we were fishing Nelson's Spring Creek one summer, we could see the trout nymphing. They would not take flies that afternoon, nor would they take our normal olive nymphs. We picked up some rocks and found mature nymphs of both colors. As soon as we tied on a black imitation, we were immediately into fish.

There is another insect on the spring creeks of Montana that closely resembles the pale morning dun. It hatches in July and August and is of the family Baetidae, genus *Centroptilum*. No special imitation is needed for them as they are so close to the pale morning dun, except that they have only two tails and emerge in the late afternoon and evening.

Tiny White-Winged Black (East, Midwest, West)

Genus and species:	*Tricorythodes* (various species)
Family:	Leptohyphidae
Emergence:	July 1 to September 30
Size:	3 to 6 mm (#20 to #28 hook size)
Nymph habitat:	Quiet water where silt and debris collect

NATURAL	*ARTIFICIAL*
NYMPH	
Body: Dark brown with rings in abdomen, or black	**Body:** Dark brown or black rabbit fur, thick at thorax
Wing pads: Blackish brown	**Wing pads:** Dark Belgian mole clump
Tails: Three, tannish	**Tails:** Tan hen-hackle fibers
Legs: Tannish	**Legs:** Tan hen-hackle fibers
DUN	
Body: Brownish black, robust thorax	**Body:** Brownish black mole fur, heavy at thorax
Wings: Whitish	**Wings:** Light gray hen-hackle fibers, clump
Tails: Three, whitish	**Tails:** Light gray hackle fibers
Legs: Whitish	**Hackle:** None

Dun

Spinner

NATURAL	ARTIFICIAL

SPINNER

Body: Brownish black, robust thorax
Wings: Hyaline, whitish
Tails: Three, whitish, four times body length
Legs: Reddish brown fading to white

Body: Brownish black mole fur, heavy at thorax
Wings: Light gray hen-hackle tips, spent
Tails: Long light gray hackle fibers
Hackle: None

Few anglers are familiar with these extremely small but important mayflies. This is probably because they come after the larger, well-known hatches are over, and also because of the time of their hatching activity. Emergence takes place somewhat later on western streams, with mating flights forming almost immediately. Subimaginal skins, whitish in appearance, are a welcome sight to the angler. Their presence is a good indication that the spinners will be on the water shortly.

The nymphs of *Tricorythodes* are easily recognized by the enlarged triangular gill plates of the second abdominal segment and by the long slender hairs that cover the body, legs, and tails. The hair collects trash and debris, which can be seen clinging to the various parts of the body. Nymphal patterns are sometimes effective at the beginning of the hatch, and they should be fished in the film dead-drift. The fish, however, seem to prefer the winged stages, especially the spinners. This preference is undoubtedly due to the fact that the imagoes return to the water in such fantastic numbers.

When the emergence is well under way, imitations of the freshly hatched duns should be used, at least until the first spinners begin to fall. A clump of light gray hen-hackle fibers makes an excellent wing outline and is very durable. Turkey-breast and duck-shoulder feathers, in the proper color, can also be used effectively.

Soon after the first spinners begin to fall, a point is reached at which some fish are still feeding on the duns, whereas others have switched over to the spent variety. Sometimes they all seem to switch at once, but at other times some individuals show distinct preferences. These situations require close observation so that you can judge which pattern should be used. Eventually, however, the imagoes dominate completely, and the spinner pattern becomes essential. By this time, fish of all sizes have moved into their feeding positions, and they are rising eagerly. During this period, the fish also become extremely selective, creating a situation in which it is imperative to have the *right fly*.

The suggested spinner pattern, using hen-hackle points for the wings, is normally very deadly, but there are times when a hackled fly is preferable. Substitute light gray or bronze blue dun hackle for the hen points. Keep the wing outline sparse and delicate by using no more than two or three turns of hackle. Because some species have a lighter abdomen, you might try either whitish or olive—a feature that can be incorporated to give more realism. Probably the most important requirement for these small flies is to maintain realistic dimensions. *Tricorythodes stygiatus* requires a #28 or #24 hook size (#28 is best). A #22 will be completely ignored, except in the West, where the insects are much larger. As a double check on size, put the natural and artificial side by side for comparison.

The western species is *Tricorythodes minutus* and is considerably larger (#18 to #24) than the most common eastern species, *Tricorythodes stygiatus* (#26 to #28). In the West, the females are olive and the males are black. The dun stage on western rivers is much more important than in the East, where most of the fishing is to the spinner fall. The males emerge in the evening and the females emerge in the morning. This morning fishing to the duns can be very good, but make sure your imitation has an olive body. For the angler equipped with the right pattern in the right size, this hatch in all parts of the country provides the ultimate in small-fly, fine-tackle fishing.

Pink Lady (West)

Genus and species:	*Epeorus albertae*
Family:	Heptageniidae
Size:	9 to 11 mm (#14 hook size)
Emergence:	July 5 to August 15
Nymph habitat:	Medium to fast gravel runs

NATURAL	*ARTIFICIAL*

NYMPH

Body:	Gray with brown markings	**Body:**	Brownish gray muskrat fur
Wing pads:	Dark gray	**Wing pads:**	Dark gray quill segment
Tails:	Two, gray with brown markings	**Tails:**	Light partridge
Legs:	Gray with brown markings	**Legs:**	Light partridge

DUN

Body:	Females pink with brown markings on back, males pale olive	**Body:**	Light brown and pink rabbit fur mixed
Wings:	Medium gray	**Wings:**	Medium gray duck-shoulder feathers
Tails:	Two, ginger	**Tails:**	Ginger hackle fibers
Legs:	Cream with tan markings	**Hackle:**	None or medium gray V-hackle

SPINNER

Body:	Females pink with light grayish tan, males pale olive	**Body:**	Pink with tan beaver or rabbit fur or synthetic
Wings:	Hyaline	**Wings:**	Light gray hen-hackle tips, spent
Tails:	Two, brown	**Tails:**	Brown hackle fibers
Legs:	Brown	**Hackle:**	None

This pink mayfly is widely distributed over the West. It occurs in the lower, warmer stretches of streams and gradually replaces *Epeorus longimanus*, which is found in the upper, colder stretches. The spinner fall is in early morning and late evening. Nymphs are found in fast water, and the adult duns emerge underwater, making a small wet fly a killing pattern during the hatch.

Two other species of *Epeorus*—*Epeorus grandis* and *Epeorus deceptivus*—are less common but are present in the West. *Epeorus grandis* is a large species found in small fast streams at about 5,000 feet with a daytime temperature of 45 degrees or lower. It hatches in early June, July, and early August. *Epeorus deceptivus* is similar to *Epeorus longimanus*, also about 8 to 9 mm long, and the spinner is light brown.

Pale Morning Dun #2 (West)

Genus and species: *Ephemerella infrequens*
Family: Ephermerellidae
Emergence: July 15 to October 10
Size: 7 to 9 mm (#16 to #18 hook size)
Nymph habitat: Under rocks and gravel in moderate to slow currents

NATURAL	ARTIFICIAL

NYMPH

Body: Medium brown	**Body:** Medium brown fur
Wing pads: Dark brown	**Wing pads:** Dark brown ostrich clump
Tails: Three, tan, mottled with dark brown	**Tails:** Dark brown partridge
Legs: Tan, mottled with dark brown	**Legs:** Dark brown partridge

DUN

Body: Yellowish with distinct olive cast	**Body:** Pale yellow and light olive rabbit fur mixed
Wings: Light yellowish gray	**Wings:** Light gray duck shoulder, tinted yellow
Tails: Three, light olive	**Tails:** Light olive hackle fibers
Legs: Light olive	**Hackle:** None or sparse light olive V-hackle

SPINNER

Body: Chocolate brown with yellowish cast	**Body:** Reddish brown and yellow fur
Wings: Hyaline	**Wings:** Bronze blue dun hackle
Tails: Three, light tan	**Tails:** Bronze blue dun hackle fibers
Legs: Tan, forelegs brown	**Hackle:** None

Ephemerella infrequens is undoubtedly one of the most important and prolific hatches in the West. It is a medium-sized fly and emerges in fantastic numbers, two factors that combine to provide an enormous food supply for the trout. It also hatches over a long period of time, staying on the water for a major portion of the later season. With all of these available meals floating by their noses, the trout automatically become highly selective.

Another factor that contributes greatly to this selectivity is the elusive coloration of the duns. To the naked eye, the body color appears to be a cream or pale yellow shade. In fact, most of the local fly shops have row after row of cream- and yellow-bodied flies—most of which are ineffective when floated over selective trout.

After experiencing the same frustrations as everyone else, we discovered through our close-up photographs that the subimaginal body has shades of both yellow and olive, and the wing is light gray tinted with yellow. This information, incorporated into a no-hackle fly, resulted in some very effective patterns. The one outlined here has wings fashioned from light gray duck-shoulder feathers that have been tinted with yellow. Great pains should be taken to select feathers with plenty of body—ones that will hold their shape when wet. Even the highest-quality feathers will slim down in water, so it is a good idea to begin with a broader outline than displayed by the natural.

Two other wing variations that have also proven effective on finicky rivers should also be mentioned here. One is a matched pair of duck-quill segments dyed to the proper yellowish gray shade. These actually appear to be most realistic, but they are not as durable. We recommend that these be used without hackle, although sparse light olive V-hackle can be added if preferred. The other variation is a clump of yellowish gray turkey-breast fibers with a few turns of light olive hackle, parachute style. The body used with all wing variations is the same: a mixture of pale yellow and light olive fur.

As hatch time approaches, the nymphs of *infrequens* get very active on the stream bottom. This situation provides excellent action if sinking lines and weighted artificials are used. Imitations must be twitched right on the bottom to be effective. Even after the hatch is in full progress, many fish can be observed snatching up nymphs before they can make their rapid dash to the surface. Nymphing in this manner, although certainly effective, is not very enjoyable.

As the hatch progresses, most of the fish become surface oriented and start feeding on flies that are drifting close to the water's surface. This activity suggests at least three patterns that could be used to imitate the various stages in the hatching process. The first would be an emerging pattern, devised to simulate the nymph as its wings unfold from the wing case. This stage takes place as the natural swims within a few inches of the water's surface. The required pattern is the same as suggested for the nymph, except that the wing pads are replaced with medium gray hackle points tied short.

After their nymphal cases have been shed, it is common for many of the duns to drift along slightly awash, trying to dry their bedraggled wings. This condition creates the need for a second emerging-type pattern similar to the suggested dun imitation. However, the duck-shoulder feathers should be tied short and the pattern pulled into the film to form a low silhouette. The third pattern, of course, is an imitation of the fully emerged dun that is floating on the surface with upright wings.

We have yet to experience a heavy spinner fall of this species. On several occasions, however, sporadic mating flights have been observed until twilight, causing light feeding activity.

Slate-Gray Dun (West)

Genus and species: *Heptagenia elegantula*
Family: Heptageniidae
Emergence: August 5 to September 25
Size: 9 to 10 mm (#14 or #16 hook size)
Nymph habitat: Warmer silted streams below 6,000 feet

	NATURAL	ARTIFICIAL

NYMPH

	NATURAL	ARTIFICIAL
Body:	Grayish brown	**Body:** Grayish brown muskrat or rabbit fur
Wing pads:	Dark gray	**Wing pads:** Dark gray quill segment
Tails:	Three, gray, banded	**Tails:** Dark partridge fibers
Legs:	Gray with dark markings	**Legs:** Dark partridge fibers

DUN

	NATURAL	ARTIFICIAL
Body:	Grayish olive with brown bands	**Body:** Light gray and olive rabbit fur mixed, ribbed with brown thread
Wings:	Dark gray	**Wings:** Dark gray duck-shoulder feathers
Tails:	Two, gray	**Tails:** Gray hackle fibers
Legs:	Tannish shading to brown	**Hackle:** None

SPINNER

	NATURAL	ARTIFICIAL
Body:	Brownish yellow	**Body:** Medium brown and yellow rabbit fur mixed
Wings:	Hyaline	**Wings:** Light gray hen-hackle tips, spent
Tails:	Two, dark gray	**Tails:** Dark gray hackle fibers
Legs:	Dark gray	**Hackle:** None

Dun

Gray Drake (West)

Genus and species:	*Siphlonurus occidentalis*
Family:	Baetidae (now Siphlonuridae)
Emergence:	August 10 to October 10
Size:	12 to 15 mm (#10 and #12 hook size)
Nymph habitat:	Quiet water, especially around the edges of trout streams and in backwaters

NATURAL	*ARTIFICIAL*

NYMPH

Body: Brownish gray with dark brown markings	**Body:** Gray muskrat fur
Wing pads: Dark brownish gray	**Wing pads:** Dark brown quill section
Tails: Three, tan marked with brown	**Tails:** Brown partridge
Legs: Tan marked with brown	**Legs:** Brown partridge

DUN

Body: Olive gray with dark brown markings	**Body:** Gray deer hair, elongated body, ribbed with dark brown thread
Wings: Dark slate	**Wings:** Two partridge breast feathers dyed dark gray
Tails: Two, dark gray	**Tails:** Dark gray hackle fibers
Legs: Gray shading to dark gray brown	**Hackle:** One short hackle tied in normally with fibers clipped top and bottom (V-hackle type)

SPINNER

Body: Dark grayish brown with light rings	**Body:** Dark grayish brown muskrat fur
Wings: Hyaline	**Wings:** Light gray hen-hackle tips, spent
Tails: Two, dark grayish brown	**Tails:** Dark brown hackle fibers
Legs: Dark grayish brown	**Hackle:** None

Spinner

This large mayfly is quite common on most western trout streams. It is found all over the Rockies from Colorado to California. The nymph is a free-swimming type with a flattened body and large head, and according to Edmunds is omnivorous, feeding on plant and insect life in slow-moving water on the stream bottom. Gray drakes are found in streams at elevations of 3,000 to 5,000 feet, usually with a daytime temperature of 45 to 65 degrees. The spinner fall is in the midmorning and in the evening, although on a cloudy day it will be found at midday. The emergence occurs sporadically from about 11:00 a.m. until 1:00 p.m. There are usually few duns on the water, but the fly is so large and enticing that fish seem to be on the lookout for it. The nymph imitation is good when fished with a darting motion along the edges of the stream. You will find that the gray drake is quite common on the Snake, Yellowstone, and Madison Rivers.

White Fly (East, Midwest, West)

Genus and species: *Ephoron album, Ephoron leukon*
Family: Polymitarcidae
Emergence: July, August, and September in the evening; spinner fall is after dark
Size: 8 to 12 mm (#16 hook size)
Nymph habitat: Gravel-bottomed streams of any size

NATURAL	*ARTIFICIAL*
NYMPH	
Body: Cream with tan thorax, looks almost exactly like a *Hexagenia* nymph, only smaller	**Body:** Cream fur
Wing pads: Black	**Wing pads:** Black crow quill
Tails: Three, amber with brown bands	**Tails:** Wood duck
Legs: Amber	**Legs:** Brown partridge
DUN	
Body: Cream with tan thorax	**Body:** Cream and tan spun fur
Wings: Light gray	**Wings:** Light gray hen-hackle tips
Tails: Three, cream	**Tails:** Cream cock hackle
Legs: Cream	**Legs:** Cream cock hackle
SPINNER	
Body: White with tan thorax	**Body:** Cream spun fur, tan for thorax
Wings: Gray	**Wings:** Light gray hen-hackle tips
Tails: Nearly white	**Tails:** Cream cock hackle
Legs: White	**Hackle:** White

These burrowers are usually found in warmer trout streams and smallmouth bass streams of medium to large size, mainly in the East and Midwest, but there are hatches on some western streams. The white fly produces some of the finest fishing in late summer. The emergence comes in the evening and the spinners fall after dark. They produce some frantic feeding for about 1 hour or more. These flies mate the same night they hatch; they do not live overnight. The females never molt, whereas the male does.

If everyone knew how enjoyable the late season was, it might lose one of its sweetest charms—solitude. Gone are the hordes of opening week, gone are the multitudes who line every hole, reserving them for the night hatches of *Hexagenia limbata* (page 84) or *Ephemera simulans* (page 74). The majority of anglers hang up their rods after the large flies are done for the season, and consequently we find beautiful runs deserted, with day-hatching mayflies abounding, along with pleasant weather and free-rising trout. To us, a 15-inch brown on #28 and 7X is far more thrilling than a 24-incher on heavier tackle. If we had to pick only one season, this would be the one.

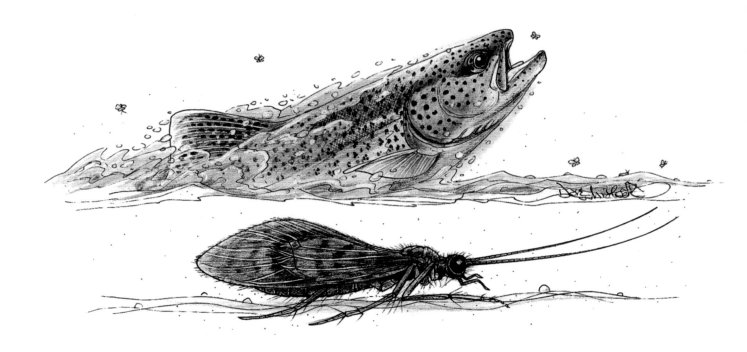

CHAPTER 10

Caddisflies: The Tentwings

CADDISFLIES ARE NOTORIOUSLY more difficult to fish to than are mayflies. Because they are usually considered second in importance to the more glamorous mayfly, many anglers do not afford them equal study. However, on many streams—including some of the best fly-fishing rivers in the country—caddisflies become the *most* important insect. This is especially true on the very rich tailwater rivers. It may be that caddisflies are relegated to second place because the complexity of their emergence and ovipositing gives anglers more trouble.

There are dozens of different caddis patterns. That there are so many patterns tells the story: No single fly was really consistent during caddis activity. One day a pattern may work very well, and the next day it fails miserably. The fault lies not so much with the patterns themselves as with the type of pattern the angler chooses during caddis activity and how he fishes it. If you thoroughly understand the habits, biology, and vulnerable stages of caddisflies, you will be able to choose and fish the correct pattern at precisely the right moment.

Caddisflies undergo a complete metamorphosis, which consists of egg, larval, pupal, and adult stages. This is different from mayflies, which undergo an incomplete metamorphosis: egg, nymph, and adult. Caddis hatches are much more difficult to master than mayfly hatches for a number of reasons. The main problem is that a large number of species oviposit by diving or crawling underwater to lay their eggs on the bottom. The angler cannot tell the difference between these females swimming back to the surface and flying off and the newly emerged caddis that came from a pupa swimming to the surface. But the outlines of the emerging pupa and the adult female swimming to the surface are radically different, and the angler must be able to figure out which stage the trout are feeding on. Otherwise he will be unable to choose the correct pattern or fish it in a natural manner.

Mayflies undergo a dramatic physical change from the dun stage to the spinner stage, making it easy to tell whether emergence or ovipositing is taking place. Caddisflies do not undergo this change and look very much alike from the time they emerge to the time they are ovipositing. In addition, caddisflies live much longer than mayflies as adults, and so they are often seen over the water when they are doing nothing more than flying around.

How, then, can one differentiate between an emergence and ovipositing? Often you can't, and to make things even more difficult, both often occur at the same time. How do you discover whether the trout are feeding on emerging pupae, egg-laying females returning to the surface, or adults that have just emerged? This is why anglers have more trouble with caddis than with mayflies or stoneflies, which by comparison are easy to recognize. We will offer some solutions to these annoying problems in this chapter.

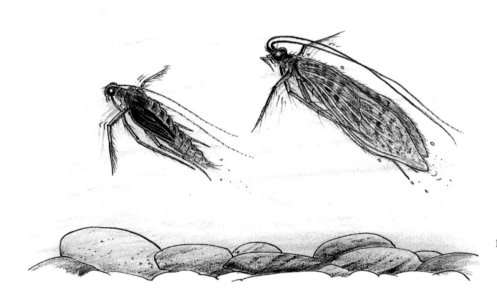

Pupal and adult caddis

LARVAE

Caddis larvae hatch from eggs on the bottom of the river or lake and live as larvae for about 30 weeks. Some species build a case in which they live until they mature. Some are free living, crawling on the bottom without a case. Other species are net builders, constructing various types of devices that filter food from the current while also spinning a silken retreat close by. These species include the common net builders, Hydropsychidae, which are the most important group of caddisflies to fly fishermen.

Two or three weeks before emergence, the free-living caddis larvae and the net builders build a case, and all the larvae begin pupation. When the pupa is mature, it chews its way out of the pupal case and swims to the surface, where it sheds its pupal skin and emerges as a winged adult. The important thing to know about the free-living larval forms is that they are taken by trout both on the bottom and as they swim up and sink down during "behavioral drift." This drift occurs just before dawn and just after sunset.

The larvae swim up in the current by wiggling their bodies, thus sweeping their anal parts with their brush of hairs (apical bristles) back and forth. The worm swims with its head down and its tail up. These characteristics would dictate a larval imitation that can wiggle and be dead-drifted on the bottom, then be manipulated to swim up in the current, then allowed to drift back down to the bottom. The imitation we will explain does fulfill these requirements. We also need an imitation that need not wiggle but can be fished dead-drift on the bottom.

Trout consume free-living caddis worms in large numbers. These food items come in various colors, but green, olive gray, and tan are the most prevalent. The heads, legs, and thorax are usually tan or brown. We include the common net builders in this group because they do not build a case until just after pupation. Caddis larvae are usually considerably longer than the pupae they turn into. A 9-mm pupa may come from a 14-mm worm.

Trout also eat cased caddis in large numbers, especially in the fall, winter, and spring. At these times there is little other insect activity, and the cased larvae crawl around exposed on the bottom of the stream when most of the

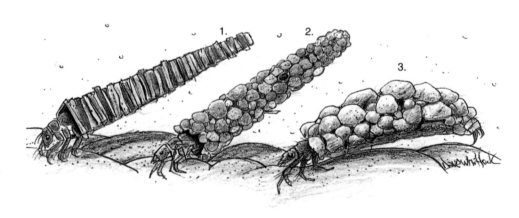

1. *Microsema* cased larva

2. *Oecetis inconspicua* cased larva

3. Glossosomatidae saddle-cased larva

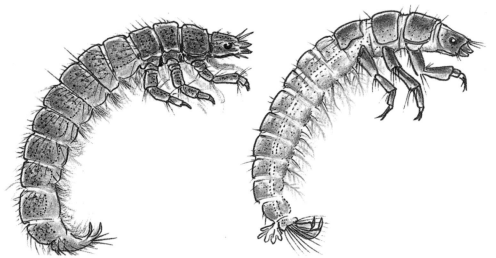

Two caddis larvae: *Rhyacophilia* and *Cheumatopsyche*

summertime vegetation has disappeared. (Most trout streams, of course, are closed at these times.) During the lush summer months, plenty of soft prey is available, and trout probably prefer these to the cased larvae. Some of these cased larvae are very large, so imitations of them make good searching patterns when used at the right time.

When the pupae are mature, they chew their way out of their cases, swim to the surface, and emerge into the adult insect. Once out of the pupal shuck they quickly fly to the stream bank. Usually the pupae swim from the bottom of the stream directly to the surface and shed their pupal skin, which can take a while. This is the stage of the emergence when they are the most vulnerable. Once free of their pupal shuck they get off the water very quickly.

Little black caddis pupa

Some genera, such as *Hydropsyche, Cheumatopsyche,* and *Ceratopsyche* (by far the three most important genera to anglers), drift near the bottom as pupae for a long stretch before swimming to the surface. They can also drift just under the surface for quite a distance before successfully emerging. Often the pupae fail to penetrate the surface film on the first attempt. They may drift just under the surface or sink to the bottom, where they rest while gathering strength for another attempt at breaking through the film. Quite a few get stuck in the shuck and drift along in the film until they eventually die. These crippled caddis are extremely vulnerable.

The key information to remember when constructing and fishing caddis pupae is that they often drift on the bottom before swimming to the surface, sometimes for a considerable distance. Caddis pupae drift in a tucked position, then swim to the surface using their middle legs for propulsion. This is completely different from mayfly nymphs, which swim by undulating their abdomens and sweeping their tails up and down. Caddis pupae have fringes of hair on their middle legs, an adaptation for swimming. They can often drift just subsurface before emerging. While drifting, they are also in this tucked position.

This indicates that we need a weighted pupal imitation that will sink to the bottom and appear to sweep its legs back and forth while swimming to the surface. We need another weighted imitation that can be drifted on the bottom in the tucked position and an unweighted pattern that can be dead-drifted just under the surface.

EMERGERS AND CRIPPLED CADDIS

Once they are out of the shuck, adult caddisflies usually get off the water very quickly. Imitating the stage just preceding the fully winged adult gives us a better chance of a surface take, because the fish seem to realize the insect is more vulnerable at this time. Quite a few adults also become trapped (crippled) in the pupal skin and never escape. Fortunately, one pattern imitates both emergers and cripples. The artificial should appear partly out of its shuck, which is teardrop shaped, light golden in color, translucent, and trails behind the body. The pattern should float and be fished dead-drift. This is the most valuable pattern during an emergence.

ADULTS

Caddis adult imitations are most effective after the hatch, during the egg-laying flights, although we do fish them on the emergence. Some species carry an egg-ball mass and deposit their eggs much like mayflies, bouncing on the surface, dipping their abdomens in the water, and occasionally going slightly under the water. This action requires a dry adult imitation. Some species dive or crawl underwater to deposit their eggs, so a wet fly is also sometimes a necessity. The same pattern fished wet or dry is effective depending on which stage the fish are feeding upon.

Emergence and egg laying occur simultaneously much of the time. This really creates a problem when dealing with a species that lays its eggs un-

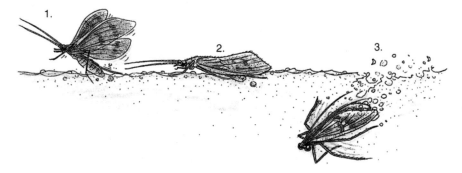

Three types of ovipositing adults:

1. Over surface
2. On surface
3. Below surface

derwater, because the adults flying off on the emergence and the adults coming out of the water after laying their eggs look alike in the air. Determining if trout are taking emerging pupae or adult females is important, because underwater the silhouettes of the pupa and the adult are much different. The solution is to be aware of which families of caddisflies dive underwater for egg laying and which act more like mayfly spinners.

When we do not know if we are fishing to a species that oviposit beneath the surface, we can use a dropper and fish the pupa, emerger, and adult. If we are catching many more fish on one or the other fly, we can be pretty certain the fish are feeding on that stage. Of course, if we can identify the caddisflies we are fishing to, we don't have to guess. Appendix B, "Keys to Families and Genera of Caddisflies," provides an easy means to identify caddisflies to the family level. The following is the information you need to fish each hatch.

Families That Oviposit Like Mayflies

1. Brachycentridae (humpless case makers): Little black caddis, American grannom, little grannom
2. Glossosomatidae (saddle case makers): Small black caddis
3. Helicopsychidae (snail case makers): Speckled Peter
4. Lepidostomatidae (lepidostomatid case makers): Little brown-green sedge
5. Leptoceridae (long-horned case makers): White miller, gray- and tan-wing long-horned sedges
6. Molannidae (hood case makers): Gray checkered sedge
7. Odontoceridae (strong case makers): Dark blue sedge
8. Phryganeidae (giant case makers): Large rush sedge

Two-caddis rig with pupa as dropper

Families That Oviposit in the Water

1. Hydroptilidae (microcaddis) and Philopotamidae (finger-net spinning caddis): Small black caddis
2. Polycentropidae (trumpet-net and tube-making caddis): Little red twilight sedge, dinky light summer sedge, brown checkered summer sedge
3. Rhyacophilidae (free-living caddis): Green sedge
4. Psychomyiidae (net-tube spinning caddis): Dark eastern woodland sedge, dinky purple-breasted sedge

Families That Oviposit by Both Methods

1. Brachycentridae (humpless case makers): Little black caddis, American grannom, little grannom
2. Hydropsychidae (common net spinners): Cinnamon sedge, spotted sedge, little olive sedge, zebra caddis

A NONCONFORMIST FAMILY

1. Limnephilidae (northern case makers): These are extremely varied forms. Approximately half of the species in this family usually deposit eggs above water on plants or stones, where rains wash them into the stream. These species belong to the subfamily Limnephilinae. The other half of the family dive or crawl underwater to deposit their eggs.

Some caddis species are very easy to distinguish merely by looking at them. Some of the smaller ones appear very similar but act very different. Once a family is identified, the angler can go to the descriptions of the families, genera, and species and usually be able to name the hatch. In those few important cases in which there can be some confusion as to the genus, we have also provided an easy key to the important genera. Although these keys are very simple to use, they do require the use of some magnification. As we mentioned earlier, a simple 10X slide magnifier can be obtained from a camera shop and a 30X hand lens is usually available at a biological supply company.

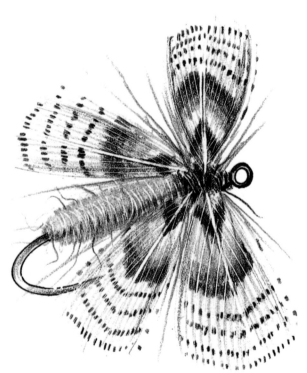

Quad-Wing Spent Caddis with partridge wings and green Antron body

Spent caddis

SPENT CADDIS

After the adult caddis has deposited the eggs, whether by crawling under the water or by dipping on its surface, some adults fall to the water and drift motionless in the current. At this point they will look like normal adults, with wings held in a V back over their bodies, and we use the same adult pattern used during egg laying. Later, as their muscles relax, the four wings fan out. A spent caddis resembles a moth with its wings out flat.

The Quad Wing Caddis imitation is deadly at times, especially at dusk, when the egg-laying flight is over. The pattern is also useful in the late afternoon during the early season, after the little black caddis emergence and egg-laying flight is over. The Quad Wing is also a very good pattern to fish wet when females are diving underwater, laying their eggs, and returning to the surface. Another good time to fish the Quad Wing is early in the morning, after an evening or nighttime egg-laying flight, when fish are on the lookout for spent caddis left over from the night before. Spent caddis are fished dead-drift on the surface, except when imitating underwater egg layers.

CADDIS TACTICS

We will begin this section with dry-fly and emerger strategies, because dry-fly fishing is often more fun than wet-fly fishing, at least for us, and we believe for most other people, too. All of these techniques are for trout feeding selectively on caddisflies during the emergence and egg-laying flights. We know from stomach analysis that more pupae than adults are usually taken during the emergence. Nevertheless, trout take many emergers and some adults during the hatch, and we usually start fishing with them even though we know we might hook more fish on a pupa. It is possible to combine a dry fly and a pupa, or an emerger and a pupa, in the same cast, thus enjoying the best of both worlds.

DRY-FLY STRATEGY

Caddisflies face upstream while escaping the pupal shuck and just afterward. To take advantage of this habit, we try to approach a fish feeding on the surface as closely as possible, slightly up and across stream or directly upstream. Using an adult dry imitation or an emerger, we cast upstream from the fish, the distance depending on the depth of water and where the trout is holding. The deeper the lie, the farther upstream we will cast.

The distance also depends on how selective the fish may be. For instance, the Muskegon River in Michigan is stocked with approximately one million 8- to 12-inch rainbows and browns in the spring. The river is so rich in aquatic insects (mostly caddisflies) that the fish grow more than an inch each month. Since most fly fishermen practice catch-and-release, by the fall these fish are much larger, have been caught many times, and are highly selective. In the spring and early summer they are fairly easy to take. By fall they rise from the bottom to examine the artificial, then turn and follow it for as much as 10 feet before either taking or refusing the offering.

If everything is not absolutely natural, you will get a refusal. Because the trout follow the fly for such a long distance, if you make a presentation 5 feet above the rise you will be at least 5 feet short of the trout's holding position and he will never see it. Less sophisticated fish, and fish in extremely fast water, will not follow a fly nearly as far. You may have to experiment a little to discover the best spot to present the fly.

When a fish closely examines a fly over such a long distance, a long and drag-free float is essential. Either a curve cast or a reach cast—the latter being much easier to learn—will allow the fly to face upstream and produce these kinds of floats. (For further details on types of casts, consider reading our book *Fly Fishing Strategy*.) These are the same techniques we use for trout feeding on mayfly duns and spinners.

The method for fishing emergers is the same as for fishing adult dries. After all, it is still dry-fly fishing, even though the shuck should be slightly *subsurface* and the body should be *on* the surface. Fishing emergers is usually more effective than fishing adults when caddisflies are actually hatching, because emergers imitate a stage when the insect cannot immediately escape. Emergers now serve a dual role, because the pattern also mimics a crippled insect that can't get away from the trout.

One technique for fishing these patterns is different from the method described earlier. Placing yourself directly upstream from the riser, make the cast straight downstream, feeding line from the rod tip to prevent drag. When the fly is a foot or so above the riser, twitch it just a little, but not enough to introduce drag (or at least very little drag). This imitates the commotion of an insect struggling to leave the pupal shuck. The struggle is visible on smooth water and even on fairly fast-moving water. Simulating this action seems to trigger more strikes than a dead drift.

Standing directly upstream allows us easily to place the fly so it faces upstream. If you do not get a strike on the first cast, slide the rod tip sideways to move the fly and leader away from the fish's lie. Then when you pick up the fly it does not disturb the trout. Lift the fly gently from the water and cast again. If you cannot get directly upstream, at least try to cast the fly so that it faces upstream by using a curve or reach cast.

Fish feeding on an emergence may be taking pupae just under the surface, emergers in the film, or both. A good tactic is to use an imitation of a pupa as a dropper and a floating emerger as a strike indicator. The approach could be up and across or directly downstream. Using a pupa and a dry emerger at the beginning of the hatch will tell you which stage the fish

Dolophilodes distinctus

are feeding on, although you will catch fish on both imitations. The dry imitation can be slowly skittered or twitched; this imparts a corresponding action to the wet pupal imitation that is almost irresistible to trout feeding on emerging pupae.

In the spring, some species of small, dark caddis *(Dolophilodes distinctus)* swim to the surface, then skip over to shore as pupae. To fish this emergence, position yourself up and across the stream, cast a little up and beyond the trout, then skate the pupal imitation across the stream toward shore as slowly as possible. This is similar to the way a Neversink Skater is fished—only more slowly.

The last technique for fishing surface flies is used when trout are feeding on spent females. This is basically the same as the first technique (upstream dead-drift), so normal adult or spent patterns are used (Quad Wing and Delta Wing Caddis). If an emergence and a spinner fall are occurring at the same time, a pupa or an emerger can be tied on as a tail dropper and a dry adult as the second fly. You will soon discover which form the fish are feeding on.

SUBSURFACE STRATEGY

The first subsurface technique is used for the pupal drift, which starts before the emergence (sometimes long before, as in the case of Hydropsychidae). Position yourself up and across from a suspected lie. Then the fly is similarly cast up and across from the lie and allowed to sink. At this point you must dead-drift the fly past the trout. You can use a weighted imitation or place a split shot about 1½ feet above the fly. A strike indicator makes it easier to fish these bottom-drifting pupae. If you don't get a strike when you think the fly is drifting by a fish, cast again and swim the imitation to the surface in front of the fish.

The second technique is used for pupae drifting just under the surface. This is the same method described in the previous section, in which a pupal imitation is used as a tail fly and a floating emerger as the dropper. The emerger serves both as a strike indicator and as a way to discover which stage the fish prefer.

The third technique is used when fish are feeding on egg-laying females, either crawling underwater or swimming up after laying eggs. A normal adult dry, such as a Delta Wing or a Quad Wing fished wet, is a good choice at these times. Cast across and a little upstream so the fly can sink. When it is across from you, put tension on the line and allow the fly to drag across the stream, either imparting no action or twitching the fly as it swings across the stream. Both approaches should be tried, as one is sometimes more effective than the other. Often the strike comes just at the end of the swing. Remember that these flies can be weighted to get down quickly. A pupa can be added as a dropper if an emergence is taking place at the same time and if you are in doubt about the trout's preference.

When trout are feeding on pupae rising from the bottom to the top, a weighted imitation is essential. The fly is cast above a likely feeding spot, allowed to sink to the bottom, and then twitched up to the surface when you believe the fly is in front of the fish. Swimming pupae look different from drifting pupae, so the fly should be tied to imitate the swimming legs, which stick out from the sides.

Anglers who like to fish after dark or before dawn have an opportunity to fish the behavioral drift, on which the trout feed as they do on a major hatch, except that all of the activity is subsurface. The larvae raise themselves up and down in the current while drifting downstream. To imitate this movement, use a wiggle larva, cast it upstream, allow it to sink, then swim the imitation up in the current and allow it to sink again.

The last tactic is used when searching the water with a larval imitation. Fish feed on caddis worms and cased caddis at times when no hatch is occurring. In fact, on especially rich tailwater streams, there may be thousands of them per square foot. This technique is exactly the same as the first method outlined in this section (dead-drift on the bottom), except that a larval imitation is used instead of a pupa. A strike indicator once again makes this strategy more productive.

CHAPTER 11

Tying the New Caddis Patterns

WHEN YOU ARE fishing to the various stages of caddisflies, you'll find that these patterns are good examples of effective materials and techniques. Each tie is for a specific genera or species but can also be used for all species of caddisflies. In other words, if you prefer one method of tying an adult, such as the Tape Wing with game-bird body feathers, you can use this technique for all species of adult caddisflies simply by varying the size, shape, and color. If you fish mostly fast water and prefer deer-hair wings, you can also use this method for all species.

The Tape Wing pattern is especially effective, as it has sheen and is translucent, as are the wings of the natural caddisflies. If you need to tie hair wings, you can make them more effective by tying in a little gray Z-Lon under the wing to add some sheen. The Teardrop Emerger is a great pattern because its shuck is translucent, and it has the teardrop shape of the natural.

Little green sedge

Green caddis

CAMPODEIFORM LARVAE

Campodeiform larvae are larvae that do not build cases, except just before pupation. They are also the free-living types, tunnelers, net spinners, and roamers. They include the very important common net spinners (Hydropsychidae), and the true free-living worms *(Rhyacophilia)*.

Simple Larval Imitations

Little Olive Caddis Larva *(Cheumatopsyche)*

Materials

HOOK: Tiemco TMC #2487, 2XS, #14 to #16
BODY: Green spun fur or synthetic dubbing
HEAD: Black beadhead
RIB: 6X mono
TAIL: Cream soft hackle

Tying Procedure

1. Wrap the hook with tying thread.
2. Secure the beadhead.
3. Take the thread to the rear of the hook, and tie in the very short tail and mono ribbing.
4. Dub the body and bring the ribbing to the beadhead.
5. Tie off behind beadhead.
6. Pick out the dubbing on the bottom of the hook to imitate legs and gills.

Cinnamon Caddis Larva #1 *(Hydropsyche)*

Materials

HOOK:	Tiemco TMC #2487, #12 to #14
BODY:	Tan spun fur or synthetic dubbing
LEGS:	Soft hackle
HEAD AND THORAX:	Black thread and brown fur
RIB:	Gold wire
TAIL:	Cream soft hackle

Tying Procedure

1. Wrap the head at the bend of a curved-shank hook.
2. Dub a thorax.
3. Tie in a soft hackle feather for legs.
4. Tie in a wire rib.
5. Dub this half of the body to the hook eye and wrap the rib.
6. Whip finish and cement.
7. Cut off the bend of the hook near the head.
8. Lash a piece of mono to project off the back of the second curved-shank hook, loop it through the front section, and lash it back to the hook. Make sure the loop is open to free movement. Superglue the wrapping or it will slip.
9. Tie in the wire for the rib.
10. Dub the back half of the body.
11. Tie in the short tail fibers.
12. Wrap the rib and tie off. Pick out fur on bottom.

Exact Imitations

These are meant to be fished dead-drift when no hatch is in progress. Stomach analysis proves that trout eat these larvae all year long.

Cinnamon Caddis Larva #2 *(Hydropsyche)*

Materials

HOOK:	Tiemco TMC #3761, 1XL, 2X heavy, #14 to #16
BODY:	Gray or green spun fur or synthetic dubbing
LEGS:	Tan turkey tail fibers
HEAD AND THORAX:	Liquid latex and acrylic paint mixed
RIB:	Clear mono thread
TAIL:	Cream soft hackle

Tying Procedure

1. Tie in two pieces of lead wire just behind the eye, on the sides of the hook, to extend to the end of the thorax area.

2. Take the thread back to a little beyond the bend in the hook; tie in the short tail section and the ribbing.
3. Dub the abdomen to the thorax area; wrap the ribbing and tie off.
4. Paint the thorax and head sections with light tan acrylic paint mixed with liquid latex mix.
5. Paint in the dorsal plates with dark brown acrylic paint and liquid latex mix.
6. Attach the short legs by dipping the butts of the feathers' fibers in liquid latex and placing them in position.
7. Pick out the fur on the bottom of the abdomen to imitate the gills.

Green Rock Worm *(Rhyacophilia)*

Materials

HOOK:	Tiemco TMC #3761, 1XL, 2X heavy, #6 to #12
BODY:	Bright green Antron yarn
LEGS:	Tan turkey tail or pheasant tail fibers
HEAD AND THORAX:	Liquid latex and acrylic paint mixed
WEIGHT:	Lead wire
TAIL:	Cream soft hackle
THREAD:	Tan

Tying Procedure

1. Tie in the lead wire so that the middle of the body is fatter than the ends.
2. Take the thread back to a little beyond the bend of the hook and tie in the yarn.

Green Rock Worm *(Rhyacophilia)*

3. Twist the yarn tightly and wrap it to the thorax area. To imitate the worm's deeply segmented abdomen, wrap yarn so the turns do not (or just barely) touch.
4. Shape the thorax and head with thread and tie off.
5. Paint the thorax and head sections with light tan acrylic paint mixed with liquid latex.
6. Attach the short legs by dipping the butts of the feather fibers in liquid latex and placing them in position.
7. Paint in the dorsal plates with light brown acrylic paint and liquid latex mix.

(Should a leg from one of these two imitations come off when fishing, it can simply be replaced by repeating step 6.)

PUPAE

These patterns are meant to be fished dead-drift on the bottom, swimming up to the surface, and dead-drift just under the surface before and during an emergence.

Cinnamon Caddis Pupa *(Hydropsyche, Ceratopsyche)*

Materials

HOOK:	Tiemco #100, #14 to #18, light wire
BODY:	Cinnamon spun fur or synthetic dubbing; add pheasant tail fibers for naturals with darker backs
LEGS:	Brown soft hackle
HEAD:	Brown thread with mono eyes (optional)
WING CASE:	Black Z-Lon
RIB:	Gold wire
ANTENNAE:	Wood duck flank

Tying Procedure

1. Tie in a strand of black Z-Lon on the bottom of the hook perpendicular to the shank, at a point one-third forward from the bend.
2. Tie in the wire rib on the bottom of the hook.
3. Tie in pheasant tail fibers for those flies with darker backs.
4. Dub the body past the Z-Lon to cover three-quarters of the shank.
5. Fold the pheasant tail fibers (if used) forward and tie off.
6. Wrap the rib forward and tie off.
7. Pull the Z-Lon forward and tie off on the bottom of the hook.
8. Tie in beard style six fibers of brown soft hackle for legs.
9. Tie in mono eyes or burn your own by centering an appropriate length of mono using hackle pliers.
10. Dub a head by figure-eighting around the eyes with dubbing.

11. Tie in antennae.
12. Whip finish and cement.

If you want the fly to sink, it should be weighted. And if you are imitating the swimming pupa, add a pair of small, fringed hackle tips for the middle legs. The thorax wing cases and head can be formed with liquid latex and black or dark brown acrylic paint. A very realistic head, thorax, and wing case can be produced by building these up in layers.

EMERGERS/STILLBORNS

Imitations of emerging caddis far outproduce all other dry-fly imitations during a hatch. These are our most reliable patterns at emergence time. We believe that a teardrop-shaped shuck is the key because it looks just like the naturals.

Bob's Teardrop Emerger: Little Olive Caddis *(Cheumatopsyche)*

Materials

HOOK:	Tiemco TMC #2487, #18 to #20
SHUCK:	Ginger Z-Lon
BODY:	Green spun fur or synthetic dubbing
LEGS:	Tan hackle
HEAD:	Black thread
WING:	Snowshoe rabbit

Tying Procedure

1. Dub a quarter of the body, starting from the bend.
2. Tie in Z-Lon so that it surrounds the hook and projects past the body by at least ⅟₁₆ inch more than the body length.
3. Tie an overhand knot around the Z-Lon with a scrap of tying thread approximately three-quarters of the body length from the rear of the fly.
4. Cut the Z-Lon ⅟₁₆ inch from the knot and melt it with a lighter or hot-tip cauterizing tool; superglue the tip.
5. Tie in a wing of deer hair, snowshoe rabbit hair, or poly yarn extending rearward.
6. Dub the body forward, leaving room for hackle legs and head.
7. Tie in and wrap two turns of hackle.
8. Fold the wing forward and tie down. Trim off any excess.
9. Dub a small head, whip finish, and cement.

Simple Teardrop Emerger

Simple Teardrop Emerger: Cinnamon Sedge *(Hydropsyche, Ceratopsyche)*

Materials

HOOK: Tiemco TMC #2487, #16
SHUCK: Ginger Z-Lon
BODY: Cinnamon dubbing
HEAD: Black thread
WING: Snowshoe rabbit or synthetic yarn

Tying Procedure

1. Tie in a small bunch of ginger Z-Lon and trim it so it is two-thirds as long as the body and in a teardrop shape.
2. Dub the body.
3. Tie in a short section of snowshoe rabbit hair or synthetic yarn so it slopes back over the body and is two-thirds as long as the body.
4. Tie in a head and whip finish.

ADULTS

Cinnamon Sedge Adult *(Hydropsyche, Ceratopsyche):* **Tape Wing Caddis**

Materials

HOOK: Tiemco #200, #16 to #18
BODY: Cinnamon spun fur or synthetic dubbing
WING: Game-bird body feathers on Scotch tape (coastal deer hair can be substituted for simplicity)
LEGS: Brown hackle
HEAD: Black thread
ANTENNAE: Brown mallard side feathers

Cinnamon Sedge Adult

Tying Procedure

1. Prepare the wings:
   a. Place a body feather of a bobwhite, dark partridge, or ruffed grouse on a piece of frosted Scotch tape.
   b. Brush Seal-All cement over the feather. (The glue on the Scotch tape is not waterproof.)
   c. When the glue is dry, fold the taped feather in half at the stem and clip to shape.
2. Tie in the hackle-stem antennae.
3. Dub a fat body.
4. Tie in the hackle and clip on the top. You can clip on the bottom while on the stream, if necessary.
5. Tie in the prepared wing, and superglue the wing at the point of attachment. This keeps the wing from twisting when casting.
6. Tie in the head and whip finish.

Note that when viewed from the bottom, the wing needs to form an angle of 15 degrees from the outside edges. This is narrower than many patterns would indicate.

SPENT CADDIS

Female caddisflies die after ovipositing. Once their muscles have relaxed, they offer a distinct and large silhouette and an easy meal for the trout.

Quad Wing Spent Caddis/Little Olive Caddis

Quad Wing Spent Caddis: Little Olive Caddis *(Cheumatopsyche)*

Materials

HOOK: Tiemco #100, #18 to #20
BODY: Green spun fur or synthetic dubbing
WINGS: Partridge body feathers
LEGS: Tan hackle
HEAD: Black thread

Tying Procedure

1. Dub the body two-thirds of the way up the hook shank.
2. Tie in two partridge feathers pointing back, so that the nearest edge of the feather is close to, if not touching, the body.
3. Tie in slightly larger wings, and figure-8 around them to make these wings perpendicular to the hook shank.
4. Wrap three turns of dry-fly hackle between the front and rear wings.
5. Wrap the head, tie off, and cement.

Note that Larry Soloman's Delta Wing Caddis is the same, except only two wings are tied in, and they are usually cock hackle.

CHAPTER 12

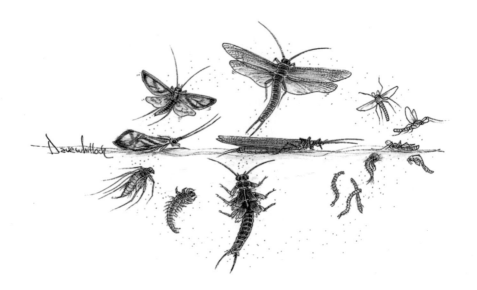

The Downwings:
Stoneflies, Midges, Craneflies,
Damselflies, Dragonflies,
and Aquatic Moths

STONEFLIES (PLECOPTERA)

STONEFLIES ARE USUALLY considered the third most important trout-stream insects. However, on certain streams with an abundance of Plecoptera, such as the fast, rocky, freestone rivers of the eastern and western mountains, they provide more food than the other insect orders. Quieter rivers usually have two or three species that can be important, but they are not present in the same numbers on faster rivers. We need only consider six major types, although there are more than 460 species of stoneflies. We call these "fisherman's classifications."

Winter Stoneflies

Tiny winter blacks (6 mm, blackish)
Early browns and blacks (12 mm, brown and black)

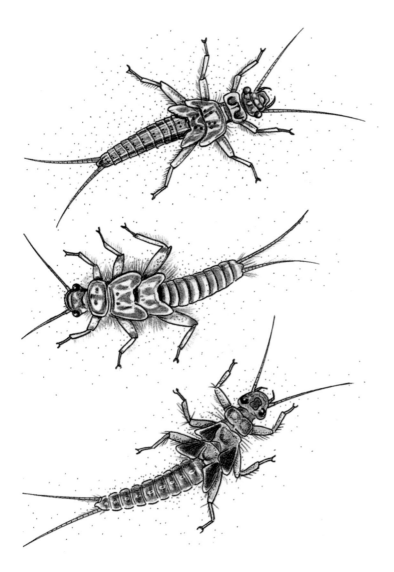

Stonefly nymphs

Whitlock Brown Stonefly Nymph

Spring Stoneflies

Salmonflies (40 mm, brownish black with orange thorax)

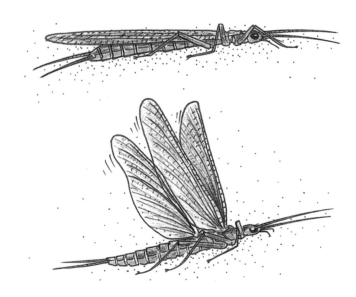

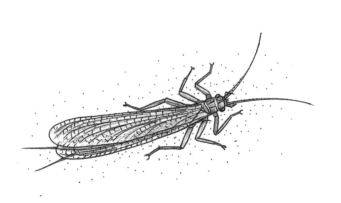

Three salmonfly adults at rest and flying

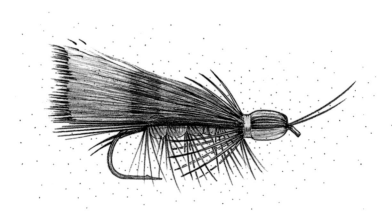

Henry's Fork Salmonfly

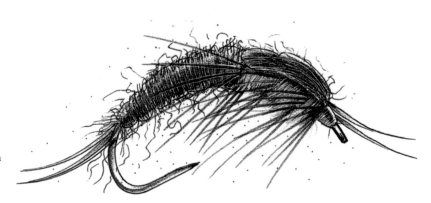

Henry's Fork Stonefly Nymph

Summer Stoneflies

Big goldens (25 mm, brownish yellow)
Medium browns (14 to 23 mm, medium brown)
Little yellows and greens (10 mm, pale yellow or olive green)

This is a fisherman's simplified list. For example, the little yellows and greens, collectively referred to as Chloroperlidae, include the genera *Alloperla, Paraperla, Hastaperla, Chloroperla,* and a few others. However, two color types in two sizes imitate them all, and we can imitate ten genera and fifty-seven species with a very few patterns. The same holds true for the other five main types of stoneflies, which means that you will only need a few patterns to imitate this entire order of trout-stream insects.

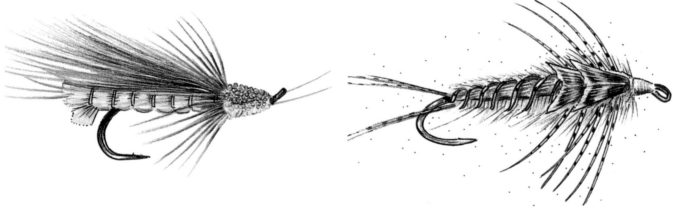

Adult female golden stonefly imitation

Pheasant-Tail Golden Stone

Kaufmann's Stonefly Nymph

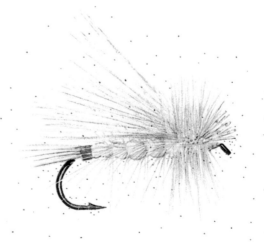

Little yellow stonefly adult imitation

Fishing to stoneflies is much easier than fishing to mayflies and infinitely easier than caddisflies. This is due to the insect's method of emergence and egg laying. All stonefly nymphs crawl to shore and out onto the bank to emerge, so a deep nymph is the angler's only choice at hatch time. Because the adults oviposit on the water's surface, only two types of patterns are needed for this stage: a flying version and a spent version. This is about as easy as it gets for fly fishing!

Stoneflies, like mayflies, undergo an incomplete metamorphosis: egg, nymph, and adult. They do not molt into a spinner as do mayflies.

Nymphs

The most important thing to remember about stonefly nymphs is that they do not swim like mayflies and caddisflies. Primarily crawlers, they swim clumsily. When dislodged from the bottom of the stream, they work their legs back and forth, which provides only a little forward motion in still water. During the emergence, and during those times when the nymphs become dislodged in a freshet, we need an artificial that can be crawled on the bottom or fished dead-drift near the bottom. Stoneflies also exhibit behavioral drift, and the same situation can be fished just before dawn and just after dark.

Adults

After dipping their eggs into the water, some adults become spent and fall into the river, where they are eaten by the trout. Other species dive to the water's surface, release some eggs, then run across the surface to shore, fly up, and repeat the whole process. In order to fish to egg layers, we need a pattern that looks like a flying stonefly and one that can be skittered over the surface. We need another pattern that looks like a spent stonefly to be fished dead-drift. And of course we need a nymph. Thus, three realistic patterns will take care of all situations for a particular species. Multiply that by the six types of stoneflies (seven including the two colors of the little yellows and little greens) and you can successfully fish every stonefly hatch in the country with twenty-one imitations.

MIDGES (DIPTERA)

Midges are usually considered the fourth most important trout-stream insects, but on certain types of water they, too, can be very important. Clear lakes, spring creeks, and clear and slow-moving rivers produce dense hatches of midges. They are especially numerous on tailwaters. Where midges are prevalent, very large fish feed on these small flies.

Like caddisflies, midges undergo a complete metamorphosis: egg, larva, pupa, and adult. Adults vary considerably in size, from as large as a size #14 and as small as size #28 or even smaller. The larger sizes are more common in lakes and ponds, and they can produce spectacular brook trout fishing

Midge larvae:
1. Cream
2. Light olive
3. Red

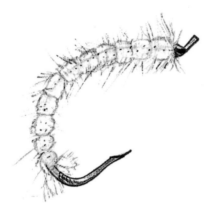

Cream Midge Larva imitations

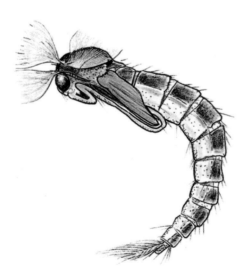

Midge natural—olive pupa

Adult midge natural

in some areas. Midges come in almost every color. The most common ones are olive, yellowish cream, black, and even red.

When fish are feeding on midges they are extremely selective, both to size and color, and to the exact stage they are feeding on. Just any old fly will not work; you need as close an imitation as possible. Although trout do eat the larvae at times, this is not a very productive stage to imitate. We will therefore concentrate on the pupal and adult stages.

The larvae live in cocoons or burrow in the bottom, where they eventually turn into pupae. When they are mature, the pupae swim to the top of the water by undulating their bodies. They usually surface in the fall season.

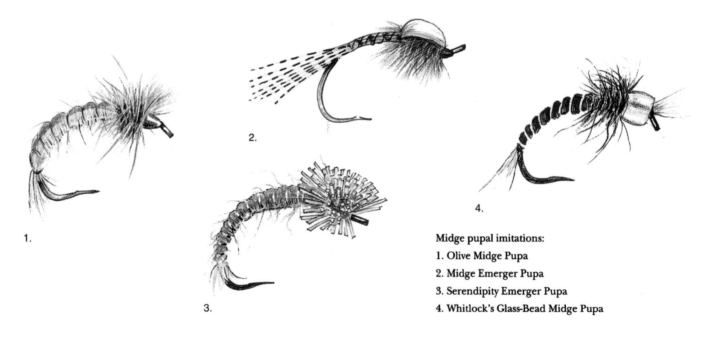

Midge pupal imitations:
1. Olive Midge Pupa
2. Midge Emerger Pupa
3. Serendipity Emerger Pupa
4. Whitlock's Glass-Bead Midge Pupa

There are more than a hundred genera and two thousand species of midges in North America, with new species being discovered almost daily. No one knows all of the important species for fly fishermen. You will have to discover what sizes and colors are prevalent on the waters you frequently fish. Local fly shops are usually helpful if you are heading off to a new river.

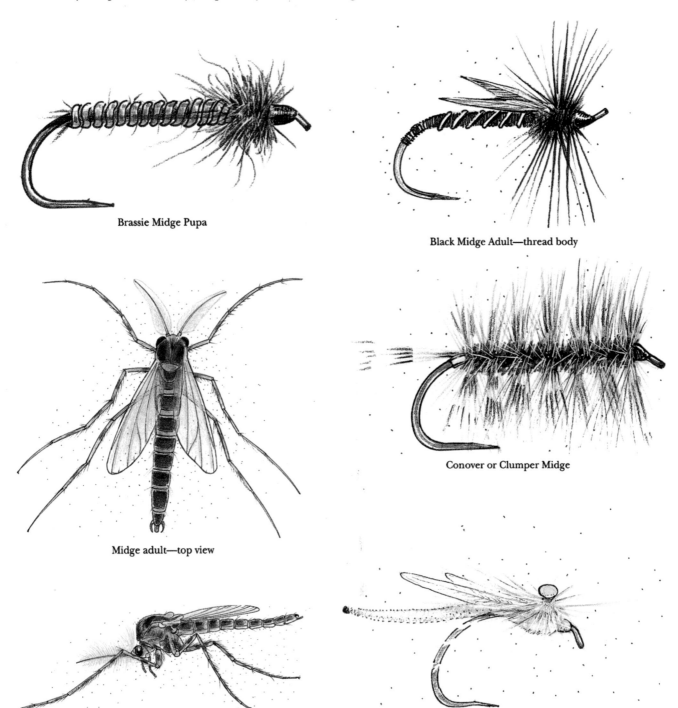

Brassie Midge Pupa

Black Midge Adult—thread body

Midge adult—top view

Conover or Clumper Midge

Midge adult—side view

Parachute Midge Adult—cream with bright orange post spot

Pupa

These are fished dead-drift just under the surface, or on the surface, like a caddis pupa.

HOOK: #18 to #28
BODY: Tying thread of the appropriate color (body should be thin)
THORAX: Darker dubbing (thorax should be thicker)

Emerger

These are fished dead-drift on the surface. This pattern is the deadliest imitation you can use during the hatch.

HOOK: #18 to #28
TRAILING SHUCK: A few fibers of muskrat fur. This material is more effective than any other fur or hair, although we are still uncertain about the reason.
BODY: Tying thread (body should be thin)
THORAX: Dubbing
WINGS: Short fibers of poly yarn

Adult

These are fished on the surface, either dead-drift or lightly twitched.

HOOK: #18 to #28
BODY: Tying thread
THORAX: Very fine dubbing
WINGS: Cream cock hackle tips spent and sloping back in a V
HACKLE: One or two turns of stiff cream cock hackle

CRANEFLIES (DIPTERA)

Craneflies belong to the same order as midges and look a lot like them, except they are larger. They also have a complete metamorphosis. Cranefly larvae range from dirty tan to dirty olive and are often quite large, from 20 to 50 mm, so they provide a juicy meal. Larval imitations should be crawled

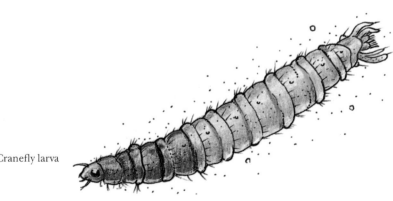

Cranefly larva

along the bottom of slow streams and lakes. In fast water they should be fished dead-drift.

The larvae crawl out of the water and pupate on shore, so the pupal stage is of no interest to anglers. Adults return to the water to lay their eggs, and at this point the trout will eagerly take them—often jumping out of the water after the flying insects. Imitations should be twitched on the surface or fished dead-drift. The most common colors are olive, cream, and yellow.

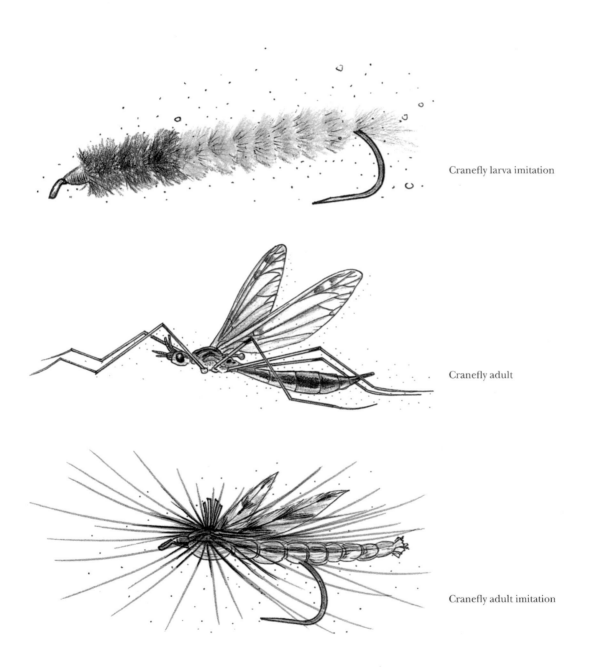

Cranefly larva imitation

Cranefly adult

Cranefly adult imitation

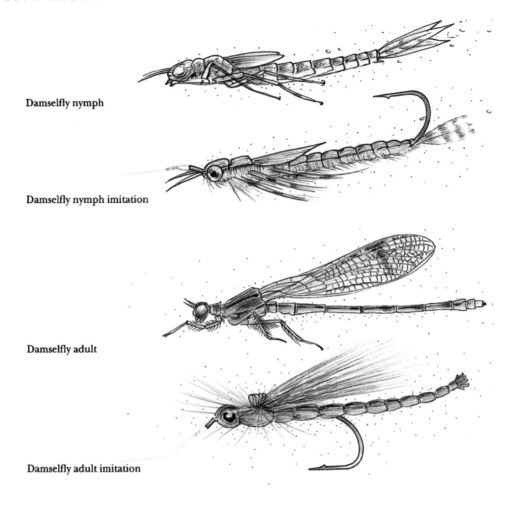

Damselfly nymph

Damselfly nymph imitation

Damselfly adult

Damselfly adult imitation

DAMSELFLIES (ODONATA)

Damselflies are abundant in streams and lakes, in both warm- and cold-water environments. Like mayflies, they undergo an incomplete metamorphosis: egg, nymph, and adult. Trout often take damselflies. We have seen large rainbows on Idaho's Silver Creek jump out of the water for damsels on the insect's mating flights.

Nymphs

Damselfly nymphs crawl or swim to plants or other structures protruding from the water, crawl up, and emerge into the adult. Trout feed on the nymphs as they migrate to shore, and imitations should be fished toward likely spots for emergence. Imitations can be weighted or unweighted, depending on the speed of the water you are fishing.

Adults

Damselfly adults are hesitant fliers at first, often falling into the water on their first flight attempts. Naturally, fish take advantage of this shortcoming, snatching the egg-laying adults and even mating pairs flying over the water.

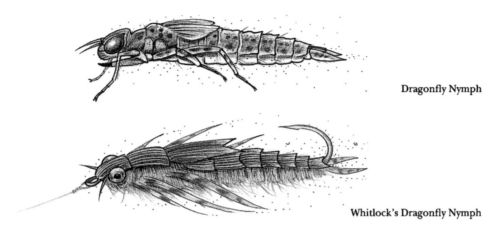

Dragonfly Nymph

Whitlock's Dragonfly Nymph

DRAGONFLIES (ODONATA)

Like mayflies, dragonflies have an incomplete metamorphosis: egg, nymph, and adult. Trout and other gamefish eat a lot of dragonfly nymphs where they are numerous, and not just as they crawl out of the water to emerge and are thus more visible. The nymphs are actively foraged all spring and summer. We have seen steelhead in the Midwest filled with them.

Nymphs

These are large insects that provide a real meal for gamefish, ranging from 12 to 50 mm in length. The nymphs are flat, with common colors of dirty olive and olive brown, both in lakes and rivers. Imitations should be fished on the bottom, either with a dead drift or with a slow or quick and jerky retrieve.

Adults

The adults are even larger than the nymphs, ranging from 12 to 75 mm in length. When they first emerge they are clumsy fliers, and fish find them relatively easy prey. As they mature they become strong, able fliers, and trout have little chance of catching them. Adult imitations should be fished close to areas where the nymphs have been crawling out and should also be given a little action to simulate an insect that has fallen into the water or failed on a first flight. Smallmouth bass seem to take dragonflies especially well. We saw a 23-inch smallmouth jump 2 feet for one on the Flat River in Michigan.

TYING REALISTIC CRANEFLIES, DAMSELFLIES, DRAGONFLIES, AND NYMPHS

Extended-body flies are the most realistic imitations for larger naturals we have even seen. They look so realistic that most people think they are extremely difficult to tie, but they are actually very easy. You will also find that they float like corks. Tie in a cock hackle in the middle of the hook. Then tie in at the eye and bend of the hook a piece of closed-cell foam

(Rainy's Fly Foam) roughly cut to the shape of the body. Paint with liquid latex obtained from your local craft shop (we use Rub-R-Mold). The wings—hackle tips or any suitable feather—are attached to the fly by dipping the tips of the feathers in a little liquid latex and placing them in position. When the latex is dry, we paint the bodies and feather attachment points with more liquid latex to strengthen them. The bodies can be colored with marking pens or a mixture of three-quarters liquid latex and one-quarter artist's acrylic paint. If a wing gets ripped off, the feather can be replaced by dipping another one in liquid latex and placing it in position.

This technique can also be used for imitating any other large aquatic insects, such as stoneflies. The tier can place either individual tails and/or legs on the imitations by dipping the butts of feathers in liquid latex and placing them under pressure. To make them more secure we now superglue them onto the bare closed-cell form and then paint the form with liquid latex. Do not dip the finished fly into liquid flotant; some brands contain a solvent that dissolves dried latex. You can use paste flotant, but it really isn't necessary, as the closed-cell foam will float the fly without any dressing.

A modification of the method described above can also be used to imitate larger nymphs. Obtain a drawing of the nymph you wish to tie (available in many fishing books), copy it, and then enlarge or reduce the size as needed. Mount it on a piece of cardboard and place a piece of Scotch tape over the picture so the latex will not stick to it. Extrude some liquid latex, loaded into a disposable syringe, onto the picture and allow it to dry. Tie in some lead on both sides of a hook, and paint it over with liquid latex. Peel the dried body from the picture and place it on the hook. When the latex is dry, paint more liquid latex over and under the body and hook. Place the tails, legs, and gills in position by dipping the butts in latex and holding in position. Two or more additional layers of latex can be painted on the body to build up a realistic shape. The body can be colored with marking pens and/or more liquid latex with a little acrylic paint. Both materials are water based so they mix well together.

AQUATIC MOTHS (LEPIDOPTERA)

Aquatic moths are closely related to caddisflies and undergo the same complete metamorphosis: egg, larva, pupa, and adult. The larvae develop hibernacula (protective retreats), and pupation takes place in these silken cocoons that are attached to submerged rocks or plants. Trout have little chance to feed on these stages, so they are not important for us to imitate. The pupa changes into an adult in the cocoon, and different species swim, float, or crawl to the surface. Emergence takes place mostly at night in the spring, summer, and fall, and trout certainly feed on these emerging adults. Most females dive underwater to lay their eggs, and some lay them on the underside of floating leaves.

The subfamily Nymphulinae of the family Pryalidae is primarily aquatic. The tubelike mouthpart (siphon) is usually long and coiled up. This is a

Aquatic moth adult

good way to differentiate between caddisflies (which lack this feature) and aquatic moths.

Adults

The adult moths are the only stage of this insect that trout get a good chance to feed on. This presents a special opportunity for anglers because the adults are present in large numbers during emergence and egg laying. Few fishermen are aware of these hatches, usually confusing them with caddisflies. Aquatic moths are generally a little larger than the average caddis (size #10 to #14; caddis range from size #14 to #20). Aquatic moths are usually mottled tan, buff, or cream in color, and the middle and hind legs often possess swimming hairs. The forewings are usually shorter than 15 mm, and the hindwings are finely patterned.

When collecting caddisflies along the banks of various rivers, we have been amazed at the many species of aquatic moths and the great number of individuals of each species that we found. Because almost all of the action is at dusk and later, anglers don't realize how prolific these insects really are. Those who enjoy fishing at night can take good advantage of aquatic moths. Try fishing adult dry caddis patterns wet in the appropriate size and color. This imitates both the winged adult emerging from its pupal shuck on the bottom and the adult females as they swim to the bottom to lay eggs.

CHAPTER 13

Terrestrials

THE FLIES THAT we have designated as the upwings, tentwings, and downwings comprise the major portion of the trout's diet during the greater part of the season. On most streams, mayflies provide the greatest volume of food, followed by caddisflies, stoneflies, and midges, usually in that order. At certain times and under certain conditions, however, various land-born insects, called terrestrials, can represent a significant segment of the trout's food supply.

By midsummer, on some rivers, most of the larger mayflies and stoneflies have emerged, and the quantity of nymphal life is greatly reduced. The remaining hatches are made up mainly of minute species, such as *Baetis* and *Tricorythodes,* and the immature nymphs from the earlier hatches are microscopic in size. This decreasing underwater food supply, coupled with the increasing availability of terrestrials, sets the stage for some very exciting fishing.

Many anglers retire about this time of the year, feeling that the season is over. Others become discouraged at low-water conditions and high temperatures, while some claim the streams are all fished out. The truth of the matter is that trout turn at this period to various terrestrials that supplement their basic diet of small aquatic insects. Land-born insects, such as grasshoppers, crickets, beetles, leafhoppers, and ants, become increasingly more important as the summer progresses. These creatures are not aquatic but they become available to the trout when they jump, fall, or get blown into the water. Except on rare occasions, insects such as grasshoppers, beetles, and crickets are not accessible to the fish in great numbers. However, they provide a juicy morsel for the trout at a time when their food supply is declining. As a result, very few floating specimens are required to trigger frenzied feeding activity. It is sometimes amazing how far a fish will move from its normal feeding position to take some of the larger terrestrials.

On the other hand, smaller terrestrials cause gentle, unhurried rises that more closely resemble the feeding activity associated with hatches of small mayflies and midges. These include ants, flying ants, leafhoppers, treehoppers, and small beetles. Of this group, the flying ants appear in greater numbers and cause more surface activity than any of the others.

Most of our study has been focused on aquatic insects, but we feel that attention should be given to some of the more important terrestrials. The following section includes some basic descriptive information and one or more suggested patterns.

GRASSHOPPERS

Grasshoppers belong to the order Orthoptera and have an incomplete life cycle. The adults vary greatly in size, have relatively long antennae, and most are greenish or yellowish gray in coloration. Four wings lie flat over the body. The hind pair folds fanlike under the front pair, which are straight and exhibit a leathery texture; the rear legs are longer than the others and are characterized by large, muscular femurs. These strong levers, or kickers, provide grasshoppers with the ability to propel themselves into the air with great force. This makes them difficult to catch for observation purposes but, fortunately for the fisherman, contributes to their presence in the stream.

Once the trout have become oriented to these low-floating silhouettes and have sampled a few nourishing mouthfuls, some fantastic fishing is

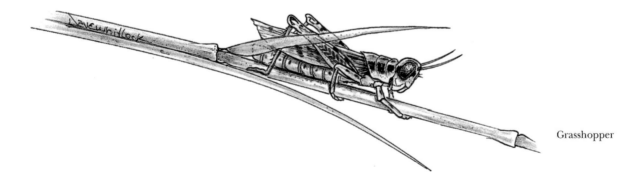

Grasshopper

possible. This period can begin in mid-July and usually peaks in August, lasting for the balance of the season. During these peak periods, large trout can be found at midday lying in some very peculiar places. They just seem to be waiting for the hoppers to come floating down. Feeding lanes normally quite narrow become very wide. In fact, a fly thrown within the trout's range of detection is simply not safe! At other times, when the fish are not quite so cooperative or anxious, various techniques may be required. Generally, a dead drift is adequate, but a well-timed twitch can be extremely effective on occasion. Frequently, bouncing the artificial off a rock or a grassy bank produces the most action, whereas at other times the splash produced by a vigorous hard-driving cast can be the key to success. Imitations should float low in the water to properly simulate the profile and position of the natural.

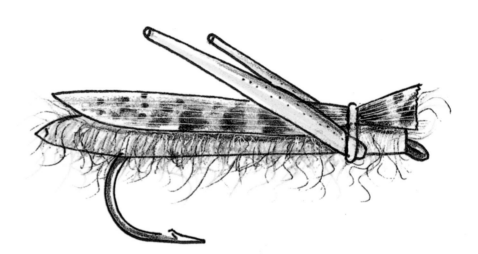

Quill Body and Legged Hopper

DP Hopper

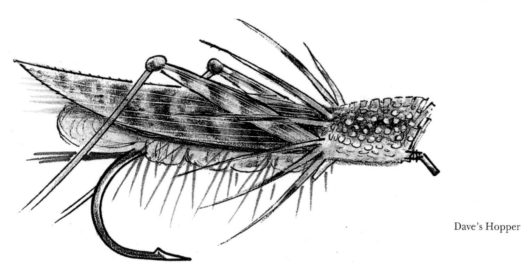

Dave's Hopper

Of the many patterns that have been developed to imitate grasshoppers, most are very effective when used at the proper time. Rather than listing all of the specific patterns here, some general tying information will be offered, along with a couple of favorite patterns. The outstanding features of the hopper include body, legs, and wings, in that order. Bodies are robust and can be imitated effectively with dubbing, synthetic yarns, and clipped deer hair dyed to the desired color. Legs, especially the hind pair, are quite significant in the outline and best simulated with quills, herl, and strands of pheasant-tail fibers. Hair—such as deer body and woodchuck—and mottled turkey all make excellent wings.

Our favorite hopper imitation is the DP, or Double Parachute Hopper. Here are the instructions.

DP Hopper

HOOK:	Mustad #94831, #2 to #12
THREAD:	6/0 to match the dubbing, usually tan, yellow, or olive
BODY:	Golden tan to light olive dubbing to match naturals
RIB:	Rust thread (optional)
WING:	Lacquered turkey quill
LEGS:	10 to 15 pheasant-tail fibers, knotted
FRONT POST:	White calf tail
REAR POST:	.035 to .045 round rubber
REAR HACKLE:	Undersized grizzly

Back in the summer of 1982, when we originated the Madam X, we didn't design it as a grasshopper imitation. However, it has since become one of the best hopper imitations in our fly box.

Madam X

Madam X

HOOK:	Mustad #94840, #6, #8, #14
THREAD:	Yellow mono cord, size 6/0 for small sizes
TAIL AND BODY:	Single clump of elk hair ribbed to hook shank
WING:	Clump of deer or elk hair tied in a bullet head
LEGS STYLE:	Two pieces of white round rubber, from .015 to .035 diameter, depending on size of fly

CRICKETS

The cricket, another member of the order Orthoptera, also represents a food source for the trout at certain times of the season. They vary widely in shape and structure, but most are of black coloration. Like grasshoppers, the crickets have an incomplete life cycle and have chewing mouthparts. They overwinter underground in the egg stage or survive in protected areas in the nymphal stage. Crickets have four wings folded over their back that are seldom, if ever, used for flying. They also have long antennae and strong "kickers," similar to the hoppers. Finding crickets in a stream is not nearly as common as finding grasshoppers, but when present they are considered a special treat by the trout. Techniques used when fishing cricket imitations parallel quite closely those used for hoppers.

Deer Hair Cricket—Impressionistic

BODY:	Black fur
WINGS:	Crow-quill segments
HEAD HACKLE:	Black deer hair, tips flared for hackle, butts clipped to form head

Deer Hair Cricket—Realistic

BODY:	Black deer hair, segmented underbody with overlay
TAILS:	Two black goose-quill segments, half of body length
HEAD:	Formed from clipping butts from body material
LEGS:	Front and middle pair out of medium black goose-quill segments, rear kickers out of heavy black goose-quill segments
ANTENNAE:	Two black polar bear hairs

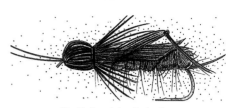

Realistic cricket imitation

LEAFHOPPERS AND TREEHOPPERS

These little creatures, called jassids, are members of the order Homoptera, which is closely related to the order Hemiptera, or true bugs. They display great variation in size and color and are equipped with mouthparts that can be used for piercing and sucking. Winged species have two pairs of wings, with the front pair longer and narrower than the hind pair. The wings are folded rooflike over the back, suggesting an opaque and leathery appearance.

Jassids feed on a wide variety of plant life and can be present in great numbers. The nymphs, however, are difficult to locate because they are very active. When a plant on which they are feeding is disturbed, they scurry to the opposite side of the leaf. The nymphs also have the strange habit of moving sideways rather than forward. Being small and light, the adults are easily blown into the stream, where they provide food for the trout and a challenge to the fisherman. Imitations must be tied on small hooks, usually size #22 to #28, but fortunately they are simple to construct.

Jassid

BODY:	Tying thread matched to body color of natural
HACKLE:	Small dry-fly quality, palmered, matched to natural; brown, black, ginger, and grizzly are all good, trimmed top and bottom
WINGS:	Two jungle-cock nails or quail-breast feathers tied flat over body

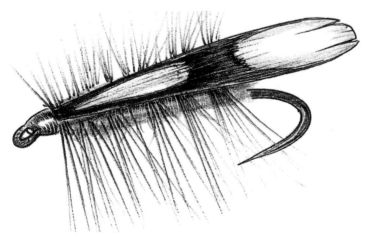

Jassid Fly

BEETLES

One of the largest orders of insects are the Coleoptera, or "sheath wings." This group of insects have complete life cycles, chewing mouthparts, and four wings. The front wings are leathery and fit over the hind part of the body like a case, meeting in a straight line along the center of the back. The hindwings are clear and fold under the front wings when the insect is at rest. Real beetles, such as ladybird beetles, potato beetles, and click beetles, are quite important as a trout food, mainly because of their abundance. Rotted logs, overhanging foliage, wooded areas, and grassy banks all provide a possible habitat for beetles. Many are deposited in the stream by high water or are blown in by the wind.

Even when they are present on the water in large numbers, it can be difficult for the occasional fisherman to detect them. Their low profile is not easy to detect unless you look really closely at the water. The increased activity of Japanese beetles has resulted in some excellent fishing in the affected areas. Patterns with opaque flat shapes and low-floating qualities are critical for proper simulation.

Japanese beetle

Black Beetle

Japanese Beetle

BODY: Green tying thread
HACKLE: Brown and grizzly palmered and trimmed top and bottom
WINGS: Three or four iridescent green neck feathers from a cock pheasant laid atop each other and lacquered

Black Beetle

BODY: Peacock herl
HACKLE: Black, palmered
WINGS: Black quill segment laid over whole body

ANTS

Ants belong to the order Hymenoptera, or "membrane wings," and have a complete life cycle. They vary considerably in size and have three distinct body regions. The four clear wings, when present, have simple venation, with the hind pair smaller than the front wings. Actually, ants are wingless except at swarming time, when they suddenly become of great interest to the angler. Some of the finest feeding activity of the season takes place when the swarming flights occur. In order to take advantage of the situation, one must stay alert and be prepared to swing into action quickly.

Several things can happen when ants begin to swarm, all of which could cause problems for the angler. First, if the ants float along with their wings

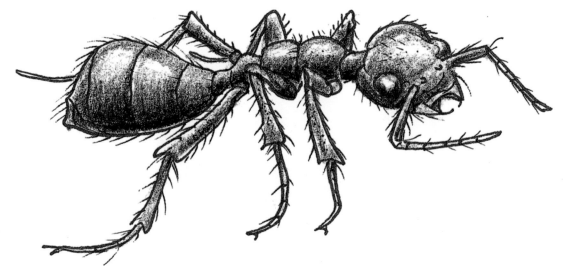

Black ant

in an upright position, they can be mistaken for mayflies and, unfortunately, mayfly patterns do not work very well when ants are on the water. Even if the mayfly imitation is of the proper size and coloration, it is not effective, because the shape of an ant body is vastly different from that of a mayfly. However, on the water this fact is difficult for the angler to perceive; he can see only upright wings, which normally would suggest mayflies. Many times we have wasted a good share of the flying-ant "hatch" by flailing water with a mayfly pattern.

If the ants have their wings in a spent position, then the problem is visibility. It is almost impossible to see spent-wing ants riding in the film. Their clear membrane wings and minute low-floating bodies can be detected only by close observation. This, of course, can quickly be solved by using a fine-mesh hand net to capture a sample. One other problem is that the swarm often descends very quickly, causing extraordinary but short-lived feeding activity. When this happens the angler must react immediately in order to take advantage of the situation.

Wingless ant imitations are very effective throughout the warmer months of the season. They are fished wet or dry, providing real excitement during some of the so-called dead periods of the day. Fishing the wingless pattern calls for a technique that is different from the one used for the winged variety. The fall of a swarm of flying ants results in casting for rising trout, which closely parallels the technique used when aquatic insects are emerging. However, wingless ants are not normally on the water in such great numbers as to cause either a general rise or extensive feeding activity. As a result, the creative angler must change his approach and cast to areas where ants might be falling into the water. These areas may be located under overhanging boughs near grassy shorelines, or around fallen logs. Fine leaders, a cautious approach, and delicate casting will contribute immensely to your success with this technique.

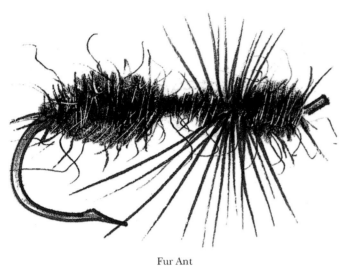

Fur Ant

Cinnamon and brown flying ant

Black Ant

BODY: Use black dubbing to form two lumps, larger one at rear of shank and smaller one behind eye, separated by a thin waist

HACKLE: High-quality natural black, very sparse, tied in right behind front lump

Cinnamon and Brown Flying Ant—Spent

BODY: Large lump at rear of shank out of dark to medium brown dubbing; front lump and thin waist out of cinnamon dubbing; use dark brown tying thread to form head

WINGS AND HACKLE: Bronze blue dun tied in immediately behind front lump and trimmed top and bottom

Large Cinnamon Flying Ant—Upright Wings

BODY: Rear lump and front lump out of cinnamon dubbing; use cinnamon tying thread to form head

WINGS: Light gray hackle tips or shaped light gray feather tied in immediately behind front lump in upright position, slightly spread

HACKLE: Bronze blue dun, sparse and trimmed on bottom

Flying Cinnamon Ant

The Black Ant dressing is a general pattern that can be tied in size #14 to #24, fished wet or dry. In the smaller sizes, #20 to #24, great care should be taken to keep the hackle small and sparse in order to maintain proper body silhouette. The small cinnamon and brown ant and the larger cinnamon ant are both specific flies that appear on Michigan's Au Sable River in later

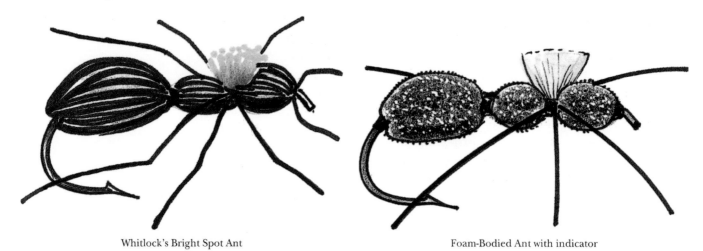

Whitlock's Bright Spot Ant   Foam-Bodied Ant with indicator

August and early September. A size #22 hook should be used for the cinnamon and brown pattern, whereas the larger all-cinnamon species is best imitated on a size #18. Each type should be tied with upright and spent wings.

On the Au Sable, both of these ants are on the water at the same time, producing a difficult situation. Things get further complicated, however, because at least one and sometimes two of the better mayfly hatches of the season are also occurring. On top of all this, the ants are often sporadic—that is, they will fall two or three times in one evening rather than all at once. These combined factors can produce a feeding situation that is constantly changing, so the angler must remain alert and extremely observant. When these conditions develop, the fish normally feed on the insects most numerous on the water. The effective fly fisherman must be able to detect any variation in feeding conditions and then quickly make the proper correction in pattern and presentation.

GREEN WORMS

Green worms build their nests in trees, and groups of them can be found in tentlike structures. During a 2-week period, usually in June, they come out and hang down by a silk thread, sometimes dangling over and falling

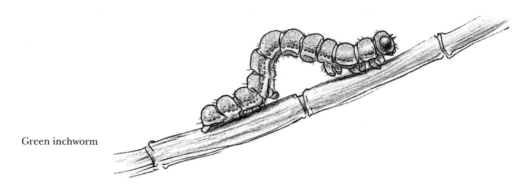

Green inchworm

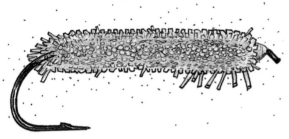

Deer-Hair Inchworm

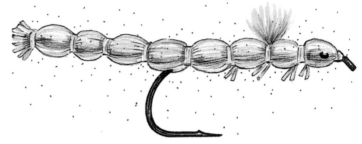

Whitlock's Bright Spot Green Inchworm

into the water. In locations where this phenomenon occurs, the trout (and often the largest ones) are on the lookout for these insects. They make a juicy morsel, according to our evidence. Autopsies performed by local guides show that stomachs of trout can be crammed full with green worms during the season.

Imitation Green Worm

BODY: Greenish yellowish deer body hair clipped, hook size #8 to #12

CHAPTER 14

The Super Hatches: Mayflies

IN AN ATTEMPT to keep the number of patterns to a minimum, we have devised the concept of "super hatches" for each section of the country. Probably 80 percent of all fly fishing to rising trout during a season would involve these insects, so it is logical that we should concentrate on these hatches. From our experience, we feel there are only eight mayflies of major significance in each area. In many cases, imitation of only one or two stages is necessary to fish a certain hatch properly, thus reducing the number of artificials to be carried in our already overloaded fishing vests. The charts list the super hatches of the East, Midwest, and West, along with peak emergence periods and patterns you will need for imitating the important stages of each species.

The corresponding dressings can be found in the master list of patterns, immediately following the charts. From this master list, an angler from any section of the country can, at a glance, determine which patterns he must carry. Fly tiers can also tie from this list.

You will see from the master list of patterns that only eight artificials are required for the Eastern super hatches, nine for the Midwest, and nine for the West. For the entire country, only eleven mayfly patterns are needed to fish all the species.

The master patterns will not only imitate the super hatches effectively, but they can also be used for many other hatches. The following list includes the master patterns and the species they simulate. (Caddisfly hatches are found in chapter 15; stonefly hatches are in chapter 16.)

EASTERN MAYFLY SUPER HATCHES

Genus and Species (Common Name) Size	April	May	June	July	August	Sept.	October	Nymph	Dun	Spinner	No.	Name
Epeorus pleuralis (Gordon Quill) #14 or #16	20	10						✓	✓		1 2	Slate/Brown Emerger Slate/Tan No-Hackle
Ephemerella subvaria (Hendrickson) #12 or #14	25	20						✓	✓	✓	1 2 11	Slate/Brown Emerger Slate/Tan Paradun Dun/Brown Hen Spinner
Ephemerella invaria, E. rotunda, E. dorothea (Sulphur Dun) #16 or #18		20		5					✓	✓	9 11	Gray/Yellow No-Hackle Dun/Brown Hen Spinner
Stenonema fuscum (Gray Fox) #10 or #12		25	15						✓		2	Slate/Tan Paradun
Ephemera guttulata (Green Drake) #8 or #10			1-10						✓	✓	9 13	Gray/Yellow Paradun Dun/Cream Hen Spinner
Drunella attenuata (Slate-Wing Olive Dun) #16 or #18			10	1					✓		8	Slate/Olive No-Hackle
Tricorythodes species (Tiny White-wing Black) #24 to #28				5	10					✓	14	White/Black Hen Spinner
Baetis species and *Plauditus dubios* (Blue-Winged Olive) #18 to #24	25						15		✓		7	Gray/Olive No-Hackle

Midwestern Mayfly Super Hatches

Genus and Species (Common Name) Size	Peak Emergence							Stage			No.	Patterns Required — Name
	April	May	June	July	August	Sept.	October	Nymph	Dun	Spinner		
Ephemerella subvaria (Hendrickson) #12 or #14	25	25						✓	✓	✓	1 2 11	Slate/Brown Emerger Slate/Tan Paradun Dun/Brown Hen Spinner
Ephemerella invaria, E. rotunda, E. dorothea (Sulphur Dun) #16 or #18	25			5					✓	✓	9 11	Gray/Yellow No-Hackle Dun/Brown Hen Spinner
Ephemera simulans (Brown Drake) #10 or #12			1-20						✓	✓	9 12	Gray/Yellow Paradun Dun/Yellow Hen Spinner
Plauditus punctiventris (Tiny Blue-Winged Olive) #24			20	20		1-30			✓	✓	6 11	Dun/Olive No-Hackle Dun/Brown Hen Spinner
Hexagenia limbata (Giant Michigan Mayfly) #4 to #8			25	20					✓	✓	9 12	Gray/Yellow No-Hackle Dun/Yellow Hen Spinner
Drunella lata (Slate-Wing Olive Dun) #18 to #20				5	5				✓	✓	8 11	Slate/Olive No-Hackle Dun/Brown Hen Spinner
Tricorythodes species (Tiny White-wing Black) #24 to #28				10		15				✓	14	White/Black Hen Spinner
Baetis species (Blue-Winged Olive) #18 to #24	25						15		✓		7	Gray/Olive No-Hackle

WESTERN MAYFLY SUPER HATCHES

Genus and Species (Common Name) Size	April	May	June	July	August	Sept.	October	Nymph	Dun	Spinner	No.	Name
Epeorus and *Paraleptophlebia* species (Slate-Wing Drakes) #12 or #16			1				5		✓		5	Slate/Brown Paradun
Ephemerella inermis group (Pale Morning Duns) #16 or #22			5				30	✓	✓	✓	1 9 11	Slate/Brown Emerger Gray/Yellow No-Hackle Dun/Brown Hen Spinner
Heptagenia and *Siphlonurus* species (Western Gray Drakes) #10 or #18			10			25			✓		2	Slate/Tan Paradun
Drunella grandis (Western Green Drake) #8 or #10			15	15				✓	✓		1 8	Slate/Brown Emerger Dun/Olive Paradun
Callibaetis species (Speckled Spinner) #14 to #16			20			30			✓	✓	2 13	Slate/Tan No-Hackle Dun/Cream Hen Spinner
Drunella flavilinea (Slate-Wing Olive Dun) #14 or #16			25		15			✓	✓	✓	1 8 11	Slate/Brown Emerger Slate/Olive No-Hackle Dun/Brown Hen Spinner
Tricorythodes species (Tiny White-wing Black) #22 to #28				20		30				✓	14	White/Black Hen Spinner
Baetis species and *Plauditus punctiventris* (Blue-Winged Olive) #18 to #24		1					30		✓	✓	7	Gray/Olive No-Hackle

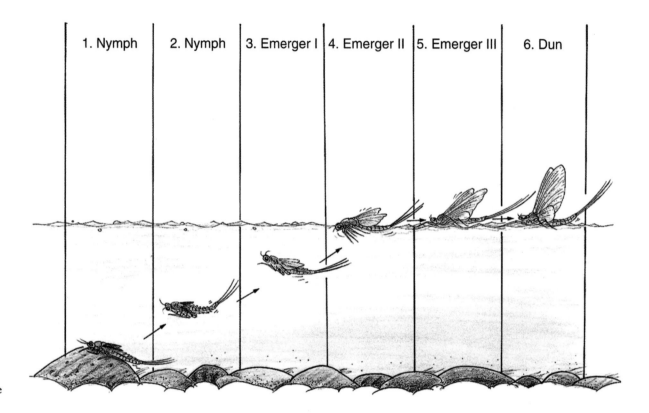

1. Nymph | 2. Nymph | 3. Emerger I | 4. Emerger II | 5. Emerger III | 6. Dun

Emergence

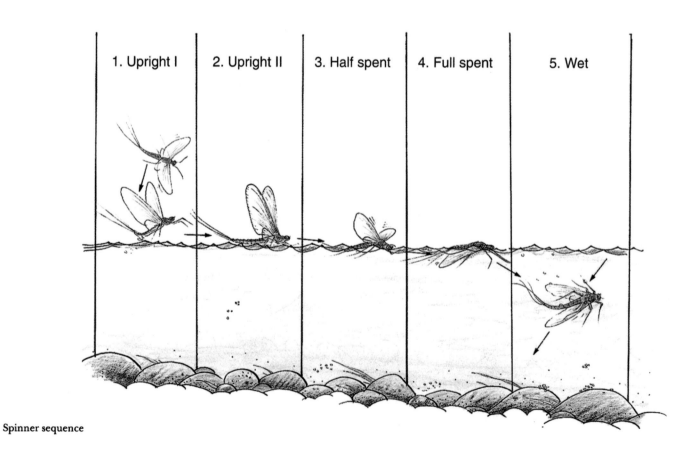

1. Upright I | 2. Upright II | 3. Half spent | 4. Full spent | 5. Wet

Spinner sequence

Master List of Patterns

No.	Wing/Body Type	Wings*	Body†	Tails	Hackle‡	East	Midwest	West
1	Slate/Brown Emerger	dark gray-hackle tips	brown fur	partridge or wood duck	partridge or wood duck	#12 to #16	#12 to #14	#8 to #10 #14 to #22
2	Slate/Tan Paradun	dark gray hen-hackle fibers	tan fur	gray hackle fibers	dark gray	#10 to #16	#12 to #14	#10 to #18
	Slate/Tan No-Hackle	dark gray duck shoulder	tan fur	gray hackle fibers	none			
3	Dun/Brown Paradun	light gray hen-hackle fibers	brown fur	gray hackle fibers	light gray			
	Dun/Brown No-Hackle	light gray duck shoulder	brown fur	gray hackle fibers	none			
4	Gray/Brown Paradun	gray hen-hackle fibers	brown fur	gray hackle fibers	gray			
	Gray/Brown No-Hackle	dark gray shoulder	brown fur	gray hackle fibers	none			
5	Slate/Brown Paradun	dark gray hen-hackle fibers	brown fur	gray hackle fibers	dark gray			#12 to #16
	Slate/Brown No-Hackle	dark gray duck shoulder	brown fur	gray hackle fibers	none			
6	Dun/Olive Paradun	light gray hen-hackle fibers	olive fur	gray hackle fibers	light gray		#24	
	Dun/Olive No-Hackle	light gray duck shoulder	olive fur	gray hackle fibers	none			
7	Gray/Olive Paradun	gray hen-hackle fibers	olive fur	gray hackle fibers	gray	#16 to #24	#18 to #24	#18 to #24
	Gray/Olive No-Hackle	gray duck shoulder	olive fur	gray hackle fibers	none			
8	Slate/Olive Paradun	dark gray hen-hackle fibers	olive fur	gray hackle fibers	dark gray	#16 to #18	#18 to #20	#8 to #10
	Slate/Olive No-Hackle	dark gray duck shoulder	olive fur	gray hackle fibers	none			#14 to #16
9	Grey/Yellow Paradun	gray hen-hackle fibers	yellow fur	gray hackle fibers	gray	#8 to #10 &	#4 to #12 &	#16 to #22
	Gray/Yellow No Hackle	gray duck shoulder	yellow fur	gray hackle fibers	none	#16 to #18	#16 to #18	
10	Cream/Yellow Paradun	cream hen-hackle fibers	yellow fur	gray hackle fibers	cream			
	Cream/Yellow No Hackle	cream duck shoulder	yellow fur	gray hackle fibers	none			

*For Paraduns size #12 and larger, use hair (such as elk or deer) for clump wings, replacing hackle fibers.
†Use Rabbit for all furs, except as otherwise noted.
‡For no-hackles, wings can also be paired duck-quill segments, partridge, or turkey breast.

MASTER LIST OF PATTERNS (continued)

No.	Wing/Body Type	Wings*	Body†	Tails	Hackle‡	East	Midwest	West
11	Dun/Brown Hen Spinner	light gray-hen tips	brown fur	gray hackle fibers	none	#12 to #18	#12 to #20	#14 to #22
	Dun/Brown Hen Partridge Spinner	gray partridge	brown fur	gray hackle fibers	none			
	Dun/Brown Hackle Spinner	light gray hackle	brown fur	gray hackle fibers	gray, sometimes clipped top and bottom			
12	Dun/Yellow Hen Spinner	light gray-hen tips	yellow fur	gray hackle fibers	sparse gray or none		#4 to #12	
	Dun/Yellow Hen Partridge Spinner	gray partridge	yellow fur	gray hackle fibers	sparse gray or none			
	Dun/Yellow Hackle Spinner	light gray hackle	yellow fur	gray hackle fibers	gray, sometimes clipped top and bottom			
13	Dun/Cream Hen Spinner	light gray-hen tips	German fitch	gray hackle fibers	sparse gray or none	#8 to #10		#14 to #16
	Dun/Cream Hen Partridge Spinner	gray partridge	cream fur	gray hackle fibers	sparse gray or none			
	Dun/Cream Hackle Spinner	light gray hackle		gray hackle fibers	gray, sometimes clipped top and bottom			
14	White/Black Hen Spinner	light gray-hen tips	dark mole fur	gray hackle fibers	none	#24 to #28	#24 to #28	#22 to #28
	White/Black Hen Partridge Spinner	gray partridge	dark mole fur	gray hackle fibers	none			
	White/Black Hackle Spinner	light gray hackle	dark mole fur	gray hackle fibers	gray, sometimes clipped top and bottom			

*For Paraduns size #12 and larger, use hair (such as elk or deer) for clump wings, replacing hackle fibers.

†Use Rabbit for all furs, except as otherwise noted.

‡For no-hackles, wings can also be paired duck-quill segments, partridge, or turkey breast.

Slate/Brown No-Hackle

Slate/Tan Paradun

NYMPHS

1. SLATE/BROWN EMERGER—EFFECTIVE FOR THE MAJORITY OF SPECIES

DUNS

2. SLATE/TAN PARADUN OR NO-HACKLE

Genus	*Ephemerella*	**Species**	*subvaria*
	Epeorus		*pleuralis*
			longimanus
	Stenonema		*ithaca*
			vicarium
	Heptagenia		*elegantula*
	Callibaetis		*fluctuans*

3. DUN/BROWN PARADUN OR NO-HACKLE

Genus	*Baetis*	**Species**	*tricaudatus*
			bicaudatus
			alexanderi

Dun/Brown Paradun

Baetis bicaudatus

Slate/Brown Paradun

4. GRAY/BROWN PARADUN OR NO-HACKLE

Genus		**Species**	
	Baetis		*cingulatus*
			phoebus
	Callibaetis		*fluctuans*
	Heptagenia		*criddlei*

5. SLATE/BROWN PARADUN OR NO-HACKLE

Genus		**Species**	
	Baetis		*tricaudatus*
			hiemalis
			parvus
	Callibaetis		*fluctuans*
	Isonychia		*bicolor*
	Epeorus		*nitidus*
			grandis
	Cinygmula		*ramaleyi*
	Rhithrogena		*jejuna*
	Leptophlebia		*johnsoni*
			cupida
	Paraleptophlebia		*adoptiva*
			debilis

6. DUN/OLIVE PARADUN OR NO-HACKLE

Genus		**Species**	
	Ephemerella		*extrucians*
	Pseudocloeon (now *Plauditus*)		*anoka* (now *punctiventris*)
			edmundsi (now *punctiventris*)

Slate/Olive Paradun

Gray/Yellow or Gray/Olive Paradun

7. GRAY/OLIVE PARADUN OR NO-HACKLE

Genus	*Baetis*	**Species**	*levitans*
			pygmaeus
			acerpenne

8. SLATE/OLIVE PARADUN OR NO-HACKLE

Genus	*Ephemerella* (now *Drunella*)	**Species**	*lata*
			attenuata
			walkeri
			needhami
			grandis
			flavilinea
	Paraleptophlebia		*packi*

9. GRAY/YELLOW OR GRAY/OLIVE PARADUN OR NO-HACKLE

Genus	*Ephemerella*	**Species**	*dorothea*
			inermis
			infrequens
			lacustris
			invaria
			rotunda
	Epeorus		*vitrea*
			deceptivus
	Heptagenia		*simplicioides*

10. CREAM/YELLOW PARADUN OR NO-HACKLE

Genus	*Stenacron*	**Species**	*canadense*
			frontale
			interpunctatum
			heterotarsale
	Potomanthus		*distinctus*

Cream/Yellow Paradun

11. DUN/BROWN HEN SPINNER, PARTRIDGE SPINNER, OR HACKLE SPINNER

Genus		**Species**	
	Ephemerella		*All*
	Baetis		*All*
	Callibaetis		*All*
	Isonychia		*All*
	Siphlonurus		*All*
	Heptagenia		*criddlei*
			elegantula
	Epeorus		*longimanus*
			nitidus
			grandis
			deceptivus
	Cinygmula		*ramaleyi*
	Rhithrogena		*jejuna*
	Leptophlebia		*All*
	Paraleptophlebia		*All*

12. DUN/YELLOW HEN SPINNER, PARTRIDGE SPINNER, OR HACKLE SPINNER

Genus		**Species**	
	Ephemera		*simulans*
	Hexagenia		*limbata*
	Potamanthus		*distinctus*

Dun/Brown Partridge Spinner

Yellow Hen Spinner

Dun/Cream Hen Spinner

13. DUN/CREAM OR DUN/YELLOW HEN SPINNER, PARTRIDGE SPINNER,
    OR HACKLE SPINNER

Genus	*Stenacron*	**Species**	*canadense*
	Ephemera		*guttulata*
			varia
	Heptagenia		*simplicioides*
	Epeorus		*pleuralis*
			vitrea
			albertae
	Callibaetis		*fluctuans*

14. WHITE/BLACK HEN SPINNER, PARTRIDGE SPINNER, OR HACKLE SPINNER

Genus	*Tricorythodes*	**Species**	*stygiatus*
			atratus
			minutus
	Brachycercus		*lacustris*
			prudens

Most of these imitations lack popular names, so we have given our favorite types the most general designations, such as Paradun, No-Hackle,
Hen Spinner, Partridge Spinner, and Hackle Spinner. Two colors appear in
front of these titles—the first indicating the shade of the wing and the second giving the general coloration of the body. In our system of classifying

wing color, slate is dark gray, gray is medium gray, and dun is light gray. Bodies are much more difficult to group, because of the multitude of colors found in many species. The body color used in our pattern names is the one that we feel is predominant, even though others may be present. For instance, the body colors in the spinners of *Ephemerella inermis* during the same fall vary from dark brown to olive tan, so a general matchup is usually effective.

PARADUN TYPE

These artificials usually have clump wings encircled with parachute hackle and are used to simulate freshly hatched duns, hence the name Paradun. For smaller flies, wing clumps are normally composed of webby fibers from a hen hackle feather, but for larger flies, either deer body hair, elk hair, or impala is more desirable. The parachute hackle is kept short, only two-thirds as long as the wings, and very sparse (two or three turns), so it does not obliterate the wing outline. It is normally the same general coloration as the wings.

Tails are constructed of stiff hackle fibers and spread widely for balance. Bodies are made of various kinds of fur such as mole, rabbit, and muskrat (or synthetic dubbing), either natural or dyed to the proper color. They are added to the tying thread by taking a small amount and spinning it with the thumb and forefinger, and then winding conventionally until the desired size and shape are achieved. For some hatches, a more realistic appearance is obtained by blending two or more colors. These furs are best for size #10 and smaller. For large flies, an extended deer or elk hair body is very effective.

HOW TO TIE AN EXTENDED-BODY PARADUN

1. Place the hook in the vise with the tails tied in and tying thread at the front of hook.
2. Take a bunch of hollow hair, such as deer or elk hair, and lay it parallel to and surrounding the hook shank.
3. Take the tying thread and wrap it around the hair, just as you would ribbing, to the length you desire the body to be.
4. Take a few turns around the end or tip of body and reverse the direction of the thread, tying back toward the head of the hook to give a criss-cross ribbing effect on the body.
5. Tie in a clump of elk hair or other wing material.
6. Wind some short stiff hackle three or four times around the base of the wing clump, and finish off.

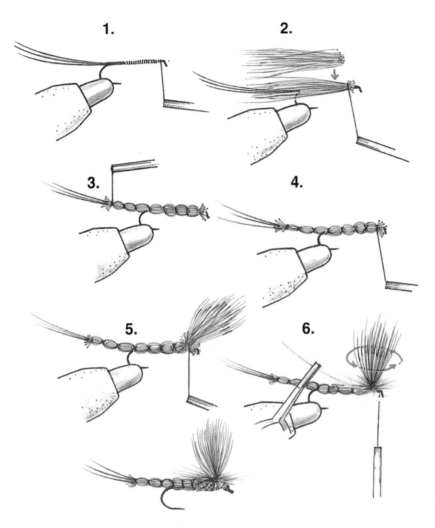

Tying the extended-body Mayfly Paradun

Stillborn Cul-de-Canard BWO

for Paradun
th, Ww=wing length=B, Ww=wing
rcent of B, T=tail length=B

Hair Wing Paradun

NO-HACKLE TYPE

Wings on our original No-Hackles were made of deer hair, either clumped or fanned. These are still very popular, as they float well and are extremely durable. When fish get really fussy, however, duck-quill segments and duck- or goose-shoulder feathers tied Sidewinder style are more effective. Wings of these materials present a more mayflylike silhouette, with a delicacy hard to achieve with coarse hair. For tiny microduns, we've found that hen-hackle fibers, turkey flats, fur, or CDC are all hard to beat. Tails are generally made of high-quality cock hackle fibers and are usually the color of the wings. Tails can easily be split by crimping the fibers into a ball of fur at the rear of the shank.

Mount the wings Sidewinder style, so they protrude from the sides of the body, and keep the tail fibers level and widely split. This will form four essential outriggers, which will ensure that the fly lands upright every time. If you use light-wire hooks, quality dubbing, and a good flotant, the No-Hackle will float just as well as a hackled fly. The most important factor contributing to the flotation of a fly is actually the buoyancy of the body. Without hackle, the wing outline is pure and the distorting effect of the hackle is eliminated.

NYMPH TYPE

We tie three basic types of nymphs: the conventional subsurface pattern, the wiggle type, and the floating nymph. All of these should have soft-dubbed bodies that look and feel realistic to the fish. Legs are best fashioned from partridge, wood duck, merganser, or hen-hackle fibers, all tinted the correct shade. Duck quill, fur, ostrich herl, and some of the new foams all make great wing cases.

Heavy-wire hooks should be used for the subsurface patterns, adding a few turns of wire when deeper drifts are desired. For wiggle nymphs, extra-light-wire hooks work better for the abdomen or rear half of the fly. The hinge can be made of monofilament, wire, rubber, or even thread.

For floating nymphs, use light-wire hooks and dub the body with a high-riding fur or synthetic. Splitting the tails and mounting the legs horizontally will add greatly to the flotation and proper orientation on the water. The expanding wing case can be imitated by spinning on a large ball of fur or tying in a mound of closed-cell foam. On larger patterns, such as size #14 and larger, tremendous flotation can be achieved by using rubber-mounted parachute hackle under the wing case. Here's a good tip on getting better buoyancy from long-fibered dubbing: Cut it into shorter lengths, ⅜ to ½ inch long, thus creating more "ends" protruding from the body. More ends mean more contact with the water, which results in better flotation.

STILLBORN DUN AND EMERGER TYPE: "CAPTIVES AND CRIPPLES"

Patterns for the stillborn dun are tied basically the same as they were 25 years ago, when we first discovered this phenomenon. These flies are designed to float on or in the surface film, so they should be dressed on dry-fly hooks with bodies of high-quality dubbing. The trailing shuck should be fashioned from opaque materials, because the outer covering of mayfly nymphs is opaque, usually dark brown to almost black. Synthetic fibers and yarns are our favorites at present. The shuck should be tapered at the end, with two or three fibers left long to simulate the tails.

Duck-quill segments and duck-shoulder feathers make tremendous-looking wings, but other materials such as partridge, hair, fur, turkey, CDC, and synthetics also work well. There are a number of options for wing style: both wings free, both trapped, or one up and one down. The patterns can be tied using either the hackle or no-hackle style. Hackled patterns work better if the hackle is clipped off top and bottom.

Cul-de-Canard Emerger

Cul-de-Canard Emerger with Shuck

Cul-de-Canard Dun

Stillborn Cul-de-Canard BWO

EMERGER TYPE

Bodies are made of dubbing and the emergent wings slant back and extend three-quarters the length of the body. The wings can be made of a variety of materials, including duck-quill segments, hackle tips, shoulder and body feathers, turkey flats, CDC, and partridge. Tails and legs are best imitated with partridge or wood duck. These artificials can be fished wet or dry depending on the weight of the hook and whether dressing is applied.

HEN SPINNER TYPE

These patterns are tied with hen-hackle tip wings. Normally they are fashioned in the full-spent position, but they can also be mounted fully upright or half spent. With spinners, the color is critical, but be sure to match the hen feather to the natural—wet and lying on the surface, not dry. Most tiers select a shade that is too light; it's better to err on the dark side. For better flotation and a more natural look on the water, the wings should be mounted with the *concave side up*. This also helps the aerodynamics and ensures that the flies land right-side up. When preparing the hackle tips, do not strip the butts, but clip them with scissors so they are not weakened.

Hen hackle is broader and more webby than rooster hackle, and when lying awash in the film it becomes translucent. This presents a supremely realistic outline. If well dressed, these wings absorb flotant and not water, so they actually help float the fly. Lightweight hooks, high-quality dubbing, and split tails all enhance the buoyancy and appearance.

HOW TO TIE THE EMERGER PATTERNS

1. Tie in three tail fibers (cock hackle wisps, wood duck fibers, or partridge breast fibers) and spin fur on tying thread.
2. Wind on tying thread with fur up to head of hook to form body.
3. Tie in wisps of partridge, wood duck, or hackle fibers for legs.
4. Tie in two short hackle tips, slanting back over body to form emerging wings, and then finish off.

HOW TO TIE THE HEN SPINNER

1. Spin tuft of fur on tying thread.
2. Wrap tuft of fur on rear of shank.
3. Tie in wisps of cock hackles on both sides of fur tuft so tails are widely spread, and then spin more fur on tying thread for body.
4. Wrap fur to head of hook to form body.
5. Tie in two hen hackle tips (either half spent or full spent, as desired). Do not strip butts of hackle feathers, as this weakens them. Clip butts with scissors.
6. Spin more thread on tying silk, wrap around wing to form thorax, and then finish. Tails on spinners should be much longer than on dun imitations.

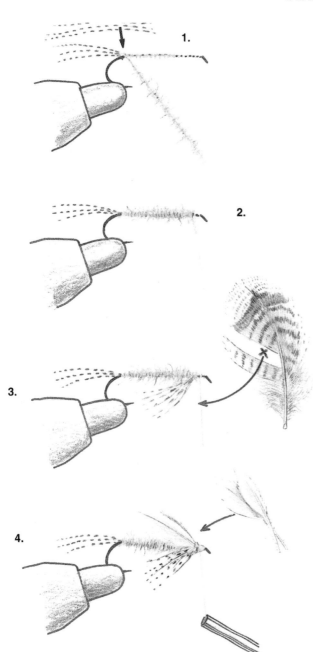

How to tie emerger patterns

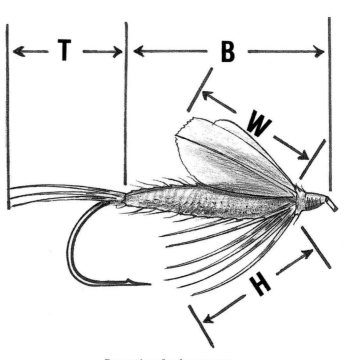

Proportions for the emerger
B=body length, W=wing length = ¾ B, H=hackle length= ¾ B,
T=tail length = ½ to ¾ B

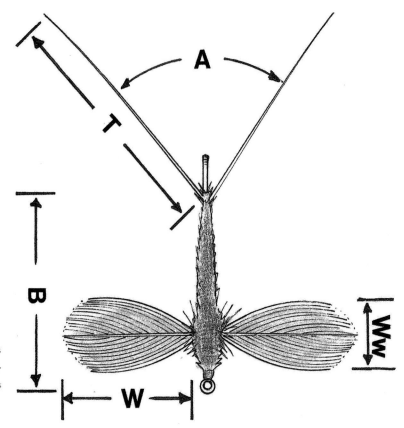

No-Hackle Hen Spinner proportions
B=body length, W=wing length=B, Ww=Wing width=30 percent of B, T=tail length= 1½ B, A=tail-split angle=90 degrees

PARTRIDGE SPINNER TYPE

This is also a no-hackle type of pattern, similar to the Hen Spinner, except that the wings are made of light partridge and tied either half or full
spent. The fibers take on a translucent, speckled appearance when wet, resembling the hyaline wings of most spinners.

HACKLE SPINNER TYPE

Wings for these spinners are constructed of one or more hackles, which
are wound on in the conventional style and trimmed top and bottom. The
remaining fibers protruding out the sides represent the hyaline wings.
They can also be trimmed half spent or left full, if a high-floating imitation
of the start of the spinner fall is desired. Another version that is often very
deadly is to trim just on the bottom. The same effect can be realized by
criss-crossing the body material over and under the hackle so that all the
fibers protrude out the sides.

PARACHUTE SPINNER TYPE

Our "rubber post" mounting system has resulted in some very effective
spinner patterns, especially for the smaller species, such as *Baetis* and *Tricos.*
The basic pattern consists of hackle-fiber tails, either bunched or split; a

dubbed body; and parachute hackle that is wrapped around one or more strands of tightly stretched rubber. A rigid gallows tool is very helpful for holding the rubber in proper position, although it can be held by hand. Rubber with a diameter in the .035 to .045 range is good for most flies, even as small as size #28. In the stretch position, the diameter will be halved. After wrapping and tying off, the rubber is cut just above the hackle. The resulting expansion forms a rivet head, or what we call a "button." It completely locks the hackle in place, making these flies incredibly durable.

There are many variations of this fly. For anglers who want more visible flies, materials such as synthetic yarn, partridge, CDC feathers, or snowshoe rabbit may be tied in with the rubber. An easier and more subtle method is simply to put a drop of Hi-Vis acrylic paint on the "button." Then the fish can't see it, but you can. An even simpler method is to leave a white rubber post ¼ inch long, which will be quite visible on a sunny day. For darker days, paint the top half of the post black.

Our most recent version involves mounting the parachute hackle on top of the wings, which can be made of hackle tips, partridge, turkey, hair, synthetic, or many types of body and wing feathers. Although a little harder to tie, these flies are very realistic. The hackle can be mounted below the wings, but this does not look as natural on the water.

Another style is to wrap two or more different types of feathers around the round rubber, using partridge feathers and grizzly cock hackle, for example. You can create some unbelievable effects by combining various types of wet and dry hackles. Remember that partridge feathers and hen body feathers float beautifully when treated with a water-repellent liquid such as Scotch Guard. And this rubber post parachute can also be used to imitate craneflies and midges.

PARTRIDGE DRAKE

These are used to represent the larger duns. The wing is light partridge breast feathers, usually dyed dark gray and tied on as fan wings. Bodies can be made of spun fur or extended elk or deer hair. They can be no-hackle types or parachute or V-hackle.

THE V-HACKLE

Any of the dun patterns can be changed to V-hackle by winding a short cock hackle in the normal manner and clipping all fibers top and bottom so that only the fibers on the side remain. These act as outriggers, allowing this pattern to land upright amazingly well. It is the same principle as a Paradun, but easier to tie. This V-hackle pattern is one of our favorite dun imitations. It is what Orvis calls its thorax pattern.

CHAPTER 15

The Super Hatches: Caddisflies

BECAUSE THE CADDISFLY is such an essential element of fly fishing, it's worth considering the ones that are of prime importance in each area of the country. We define "super caddis" as a species of Tricoptera that emerges in good numbers and upon which the trout feed actively for at least 1 week. These species all live in running water, although many also live in still water. These lists are purely subjective, of course, but we have read most of the literature on the subject and we share more than a hundred years of experience between us. Even so, we certainly have not fished every trout stream in the country. Your own river may well have a caddis emergence you consider "super" that we do not list as such. For this reason, we describe many of the more common species under "Emerging and Egg-Laying Habits of the Caddis Families." Our rating system of up to four *'s next to the species name indicates the relative importance of these flies. A note on imitations: The first color given is the wing color. The second color, when listed, is the color of the body. Complete recipes are given in chapter 11, including the color of feathers, such as light or dark partridge. Other feathers may be substituted if they are the correct color, as described in chapter 10.

TYPES OF FORMS FOR CADDIS LARVAE

1. Free-living forms: Rhyacophilidae
2. Saddle case makers: Glossosomatidae
3. Purse case makers: Hydroptilidae
4. Tube case makers: Phryganeidae (giant case makers), Brachycentridae (humpless case makers), Limnephilidae and Uenoidae (northern case makers), Lepidostomatidae (tube case makers), Odontoceridae (strong case makers), Molannidae (hood case makers), Helicopsychidae (snail case makers), Leptoceridae (long-horned case makers).
5. Net spinners: Hydropsychidae (common net spinners), Philopotamidae (finger-net spinners), Psychomyiidae (net-tube spinners), Polycentropidae (trumpet-net and tube-making caddisflies).

EASTERN SUPER CADDIS

Little Black Caddis****
(Also known as grannom)

GENUS AND SPECIES:	*Brachycentrus numerosus, Brachycentrus appalachia, Brachycentrus solomoni*
FAMILY:	Brachycentridae
SIZE:	8 to 10 mm (#16 to #18 hook size)
COLOR:	Body is dusky brownish gray with a green or tan lateral line; wings are tawny with a series of pale spots, making them look light gray when flying; legs are paler than body. Females of *Brachycentrus appalachia* have straw-colored bodies and gray wings.
IMITATION:	Partridge and Dark Mole Caddis

Extremely important in the early spring for a few weeks, with an explosive daytime emergence.

Little black caddis

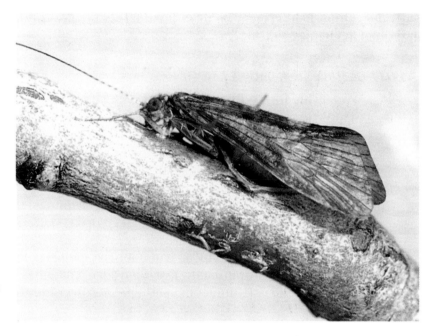

Spotted sedge

Spotted Sedge****
(Also known as cinnamon sedge, window wing sedge)

GENUS AND SPECIES:	*Ceratopsyche bronta, Ceratopsyche sparna, Ceratopsyche morosa*
FAMILY:	Hydropsychidae
SIZE:	8 to 11 mm (#16 to #18 hook size)
COLOR:	Body is cinnamon brown; wings are brownish gray with tan spots; legs are cinnamon brown.
IMITATION:	Quail and Cinnamon Sedge

The most important genus of all Tricoptera all season. Usually an evening emergence, but they can come at noon.

Little olive sedge

Little Olive Sedge****
(Also known as little sister sedge)

GENUS AND SPECIES:	*Cheumatopsyche pettiti* and *harwoodi*
FAMILY:	Hydropsychidae
SIZE:	7 to 9 mm (#18 to #22 hook size)
COLOR:	Body is olive green; wings are brownish gray, usually with tan markings; legs are brown.
IMITATION:	Early season, Quail and Olive Sedge; late season, Partridge and Olive Sedge (insects get lighter as the season progresses)

Second most important genus of all Tricoptera all season, with a morning and an evening emergence.

Little black short-horned sedge

Little Black Short-Horned Sedge***

GENUS AND SPECIES: *Glossosoma negrior*
FAMILY: Glossosomatidae
SIZE: 6 to 7.5 mm (#20 to #22 hook size)
COLOR: Grayish black.
IMITATION: Black Hen and Dark Mole Sedge

Important during June evenings.

Dark Blue Sedge***

GENUS AND SPECIES: *Psilotreta labida*
FAMILY: Odontoceridae
SIZE: 12 to 14 mm (#14 to #16 hook size)
COLOR: Body is green to almost black; wings are dark grayish brown, with very small scattered light spots; legs are almost black.
IMITATION: Dun Hen and Green Sedge

Very important from New England to midsouth from late April to June in the evening.

Grannom**

GENUS AND SPECIES: *Brachycentrus americanus*
FAMILY: Brachycentridae
SIZE: 11 to 13 mm (#16 to #18 hook size)
COLOR: Body is grayish brown; wings are grayish brown with pale flecks, especially around the apex; legs are brown.
IMITATION: Quill and Brown Sedge

These caddisflies are related to *Brachycentrus numerosus* but have a longer, less explosive emergence in the morning after *Brachycentrus numerosus*.

Green sedge larva

Green Sedge**

GENUS AND SPECIES:	*Rhyacophilia manistee, R. melita*
FAMILY:	Rhyacophilidae
SIZE:	8 to 13 mm (#14 to #18 hook size)
COLOR:	Body is green; wings are mottled dark gray and brown; legs are olive.
IMITATION:	Partridge and Green Sedge

Can be important on fast, cool rivers on summer evenings.

Plain Red-Brown Long-Horned Sedge**

GENUS AND SPECIES:	*Oecetis inconspicua*
FAMILY:	Leptoceridae
SIZE:	10 to 11 mm (#16 to #18 hook size)
COLOR:	Body is yellow brown to reddish brown to olive; wings are light brown; legs are tan.
IMITATION:	Red-Brown and Tan Sedge, Olive and Tan Sedge

Important during midsummer evenings.

Plain Brown Scaly-Wing Sedge**

GENUS AND SPECIES:	*Ceraclea transversa* most common, but many other species
FAMILY:	Leptoceridae
SIZE:	11 to 13 mm (#16 to #18 hook size)
COLOR:	Bodies and wings are reddish brown to almost black.
IMITATION:	Brown Hen and Red-Brown Sedge, Dark Gray and Mole Sedge

Brown scaly-wing sedge

Important on summer evenings.

Small dot-wing sedge

Small Dot-Wing Sedge**

GENUS AND SPECIES: *Neophylax fuscus*
FAMILY: Uenoidae
SIZE: 9 to 12 mm (#16 to #18 hook size)
COLOR: Body is dark grayish brown; wings are brown with many translucent tan spots; legs are tan.
IMITATION: Mottled Hen Saddle and Dark Mole Sedge

Very important in late fall, October to November, late morning and afternoon.

MIDWESTERN CADDIS SUPER HATCHES

Little Black Caddis****
(Also known as grannom)

GENUS AND SPECIES: *Brachycentrus numerosus, B. lateralis*
FAMILY: Brachycentridae
SIZE: 11 to 12.5 mm (#16 to #18 hook size)
COLOR: Body is dusky brownish gray with a green or tan lateral line; wings are tawny, with pale spots that make them look light gray in flight; legs are paler than body.
IMITATION: Partridge and Dark Mole Caddis

Extremely important in early spring for a few weeks, with explosive daytime emergence.

Spotted Sedge****
(Also known as cinnamon sedge, window wing sedge)

GENUS AND SPECIES: *Ceratopsyche bronta, sparna, bifida, slossonae, recurvata; Hydropsyche phalerata*
SIZE: 8 to 11 mm (#16 to #18 hook size)
COLOR: Body is cinnamon brown; wings are brownish gray with tan spots; legs are cinnamon brown.
IMITATION: Quail and Cinnamon Sedge

The most important genera of all Tricoptera all season. Usually an evening emergence, but they can come in the morning and even at noon.

Little Olive Sedge****
(Also known as little sister sedge)

GENUS AND SPECIES:	*Cheumatopsyche petti, speciosa, lasa, campyla*
FAMILY:	Hydropsychidae
SIZE:	7 to 9 mm (#20 to #22 hook size)
COLOR:	Body is olive green; wings are brownish gray, usually with tan markings; legs are brown.
IMITATION:	Early season, Quail and Olive Sedge; late season, Partridge and Olive Sedge (insects get lighter as the season progresses)

Second most important genus of all Tricoptera all season, with a morning and an evening emergence.

Little Black Short-Horned Sedge**

GENUS AND SPECIES:	*Glossosoma negrior*
FAMILY:	Glossosomatidae
SIZE:	6 to 7.5 mm (#20 to #22 hook size)
COLOR:	Grayish black.
IMITATION:	Black Hen and Dark Mole Sedge

Important during June evenings.

Grannom**

GENUS AND SPECIES:	*Brachycentrus americanus*
FAMILY:	Brachycentridae
SIZE:	11 to 13 mm (#16 to #18 hook size)
COLOR:	Body is grayish brown; wings are grayish brown with pale flecks, especially around apex; legs are brown.
IMITATION:	Quail and Brown Sedge

These caddisflies are related to *Brachycentrus numerosus* but have a longer, less explosive emergence in the morning, after *Brachycentrus lateralis*.

Plain Red-Brown Long-Horned Sedge**

GENUS AND SPECIES:	*Oecetis inconspicua*
FAMILY:	Leptoceridae
SIZE:	10 to 11 mm (#16 to #18 hook size)
COLOR:	Body is yellow brown to reddish brown to olive; wings are light brown; legs are tan.
IMITATION:	Red-Brown and Tan Sedge, Olive and Tan Sedge

Important during midsummer evenings.

Tan spotted-wing long-horned sedge

Tan Spotted-Wing Long-Horned Sedge

GENUS AND SPECIES:	*Oecetis avara*
FAMILY:	Leptoceridae
SIZE:	10 to 11 mm (#16 to #18 hook size)
COLOR:	Body is yellow brown to olive; wings are light brown with a few dark spots; legs are tan.
IMITATION:	Red-Brown and Tan Sedge, Olive and Tan Sedge

Important during midsummer evenings.

Plain Brown Scaly-Wing Sedge**

GENUS AND SPECIES:	*Ceraclea transversa* most common, but many other species
FAMILY:	Leptoceridae
SIZE:	11 to 13 mm (#16 to #18 hook size)
IMITATION:	Brown Hen and Red-Brown Sedge, Dark Gray and Mole Sedge

Important during summer evenings.

Little Grannom**

GENUS AND SPECIES:	*Microsema rusticum*
FAMILY:	Brachycentridae
SIZE:	6 to 9.5 mm (#20 hook size)
COLOR:	Very dark gray, almost black.
IMITATION:	Black Sedge

Important in June and July during evenings.

Green Sedge**

GENUS AND SPECIES:	*Rhyacophilia manistee, R. melita*
FAMILY:	Rhyacophilidae
SIZE:	8 to 13 mm (#14 to #18 hook size)
COLOR:	Body is green; wings are mottled dark gray and brown; legs are olive.
IMITATION:	Bobwhite and Green Sedge

Can be important on fast, cool rivers on summer evenings.

Yellow Sedge***

GENUS AND SPECIES:	*Potama flava*
FAMILY:	Hydropsychidae
SIZE:	10 to 11 mm (#16 to #18 hook size)
COLOR:	Body is yellow; wings are very light tan with almost no markings; legs are straw colored.
IMITATION:	Tan and Yellow Sedge

Can be important on large midwestern and southern rivers.

White Miller**

GENUS AND SPECIES:	*Nectopsyche albida, N. exquisita*
FAMILY:	Leptoceridae
SIZE:	14 to 15 mm (#14 to #16 hook size)
COLOR:	Body is light green with ginger thorax; wings are white with slight tan mottling; legs are ginger.
IMITATION:	White and Green Sedge

Very important in the Midwest in midsummer, late evening.

White miller

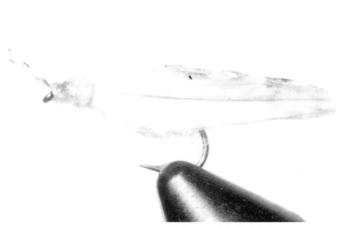

White Miller

Small Dot-Wing Sedge***

GENUS AND SPECIES:	*Neophylax fuscus*
FAMILY:	Uenoidae
SIZE:	9 to 12 mm (#18 hook size)
COLOR:	Body is dark grayish brown; wings are brown with many translucent tan spots; legs are tan.
IMITATION:	Mottled Hen Hackle and Dark Mole Sedge

Very important in late fall, October to November, late morning and afternoon.

WESTERN SUPER CADDIS

Little Black Caddis****

GENUS AND SPECIES:	*Brachycentrus occidentalis*
FAMILY:	Brachycentridae
SIZE:	Males 7 to 8 mm, females 9 to 10 mm from head to wing tip (#16 to #18 hook size)
COLOR:	Body is dark brownish gray, almost black, with a green lateral line; wings are gray with black veins; legs are paler gray.
IMITATION:	Black Hen and Dark Mole Caddis

Brachycentrus occidentalis is very important for a short time in the spring, usually before runoff in the daytime.

Spotted Sedge****

GENUS AND SPECIES:	*Hydropsyche cockerlli, occidentalis, oslara,* and *placoda*
FAMILY:	Hydropsychidae
SIZE:	8 to 12 mm (#16 to #18 hook size)
COLOR:	Body is cinnamon brown; a few species may be olive but all turn some shade of brown after emergence; wings are brownish gray with small tan spots; legs are cinnamon brown.
IMITATION:	Quail and Cinnamon Sedge

Most important genus of all Tricoptera (by a wide margin) during the entire season, usually emerging at evening.

Little Green Sedge****

GENUS AND SPECIES:	*Cheumatopsyche petti, Cheumatopsyche lasa,* and *Cheumatopsyche campyla*
FAMILY:	Hydropsychidae
SIZE:	7 to 10 mm (#18 to #22 hook size)
COLOR:	Body is olive; wings are brownish gray with tan markings; legs are brown.
IMITATION:	Early season, Quail and Olive Sedge; late season, Light Partridge and Olive Sedge (these species get lighter as the season progresses)

Cheumatopsyche adult

Second most important genus of all Tricoptera all season, morning and evening emergences.

Little Black Short-Horned Sedge**

GENUS AND SPECIES:	*Glossosoma montana*
FAMILY:	Leptoceridae
SIZE:	10 to 12 mm (#16 to #18 hook size)
COLOR:	Body of male is blue green; females are yellow; wings are light gray; legs are tan.
IMITATION:	Gray Hen and Yellow Sedge

Important in late June at peak emergence in late afternoon and evening.

Speckled Peter**

GENUS AND SPECIES:	*Helicopsyche borealis*
FAMILY:	Helicopsychidae
SIZE:	5 to 7 mm (#20 to #22 hook size)
COLOR:	Body is amber; wings are light brown with a heavy speckling of dark brown; legs are brown.
IMITATION:	Dark Gray Hen and Dark Mole Sedge

Important from mid-June to early July.

Tan Spotted-Wing Long-Horned Sedge**

GENUS AND SPECIES:	*Oecetis avara*
FAMILY:	Leptoceridae
SIZE:	10 to 12 mm (#16 to #18 hook size)
COLOR:	Body is yellow olive; wings are light brown with a few dark spots; legs are ginger.
IMITATION:	Tan Hen and Olive Tan Sedge

Important at mid-July peak emergence.

Little Brown Sedge**

GENUS AND SPECIES:	*Lepidostoma pluviale*
FAMILY:	Lepidostomatidae
SIZE:	8 to 10 mm (#18 hook size)
COLOR:	Body is olive; wings are brown (males have a dark gray recurve on leading edge of wings, an easy method of identification).
IMITATION:	Brown Hen and Olive Green Sedge

Important mid-June to late September at times of peak emergence.

Little Grannom***

GENUS AND SPECIES: *Microsema bactro*
FAMILY: Brachycentridae
SIZE: 6 to 7.5 mm (#20 to #22 hook size)
COLOR: Body is green; wings are black; legs are dark gray.
IMITATION: Black Hen and Green Sedge

Important in late June in the evening.

Black Wing Long-Horned Sedge***
(Also known as black dancer)

GENUS AND SPECIES: *Mystacides alafimbriata*
FAMILY: Leptoceridae
SIZE: 8 to 9 mm (#16 hook size)
COLOR: Body is dark green to dull amber; wings are black.
IMITATION: Black Hen and Dark Green, Amber, or Black Sedge (color depends on river)

Very important late June to early July in the morning.

Grannom**

GENUS AND SPECIES: *Brachycentrus americanus*
FAMILY: Brachycentridae
SIZE: 11 to 13 mm (#16 to #18 hook size)
COLOR: Body is grayish brown; wings are grayish brown with pale flecks, especially around apex; legs are brown.
IMITATION: Quail and Brown Sedge

These caddisflies are related to *Brachycentrus occidentalis* but have a longer, less explosive emergence on midsummer mornings.

Giant Orange Sedge****

GENUS AND SPECIES: *Discosmoecus atripes, D. gilvipes,* and *D. jucundus*
FAMILY: Limnephilidae
SIZE: 20 to 30 mm (#4 to #8 hook size)
COLOR: Body is reddish orange; wings are mottled gray and black brown; legs are light brown to black.
IMITATION: Orange and Tan Sedge

Extremely important on Pacific Coast rivers in the fall during afternoons and evenings.

Giant Orange Sedge

EMERGING AND EGG-LAYING HABITS OF THE CADDIS FAMILIES

Understanding the particular habits of the caddisflies to which you are fishing is vital for success. For that reason we include the descriptions of other species that live in trout streams but are not listed as super hatches. These insects may well be important in your favorite stream. We urge you to use the "Keys to the Families and Genera of Caddisflies" in appendix B to identify insects you find plentiful in your area. These keys are easy to use. With very little practice, you should be able to identify most Tricoptera to the family level. Once you know the family, you can go to the descriptions in this section and in the super hatch lists and almost certainly be able to figure out the genus and in many cases the species.

Hydropsychidae

Ceratopsyche	(Cinnamon sedge, or spotted sedge)	Super hatch
Cheumatopsyche	(Little green sedge, or little sister sedge)	Super hatch
Arctopsyche	(Great gray spotted-wing sedge)	West
Macrostemum	(Zebra-wing caddis, or black and tan pattern-wing sedge)	East, Midwest

The pupae of the Hydropsychidae emerge by swimming to the surface. The downstream drift is longer than that of most caddis species, and the trout feed on the pupae long before surface activity is apparent. The pupae also take longer to struggle out of the shuck. As a result, pupal imitations are most effective, although trout do feed on the emergers and adults. Most of the emergence activity is in the evening, but it can occur in the morning or even at midday. In the Midwest, *Cheumatopsyche analis* is an evening emerger in August but switches to mornings in September.

With most Hydropsychidae, egg laying has morning and evening peaks but occurs sporadically all day. To lay eggs, females crawl underwater and sprawl or bounce on the surface. A wet fly works well at these times. A spent Quad Wing imitation is very useful in the late evenings, after ovipositing.

Zebra Sedge

Macrostemum

Macrostemum zebratum

LENGTH: 11 mm
COLOR: Body is black with lighter rings; wings are black with distinctive tannish yellow pattern; legs are ginger; antennae are very long (41 mm) and black.
EMERGENCE: Early to late August on eastern and midwestern tailwater rivers and warmer trout streams.

Genus *Macrostemum* has only one significant species, *Macrostemum zebratum*, which is important on eastern and midwestern tailwater rivers, warmer trout streams, and smallmouth bass streams. It is called the zebra caddis because of its distinctive black and yellow striped wings. This is a very large caddisfly. On some rivers it can be extremely important, even reaching super hatch status.

Arctopsyche

Arctopsyche grandis

LENGTH: 17 to 20 mm
COLOR: Body is bright olive to brownish olive depending on the river; wings are grayish brown with lighter brown speckles; antennae are brown with darker rings; legs are brown.
EMERGENCE: Late June to early July at night.

Genus *Arctopsyche* has only one important species, *Arctopsyche grandis*. This western species is mostly nocturnal, but because it is so large you can use an adult imitation as a daytime searching pattern. Because the larvae are sizable and active, any imitations fished on the bottom can catch a lot of fish. These are the great gray spotted sedges. (The other genera in this family are described in the super hatch lists.)

Brachycentridae

Brachycentrus	(Little black caddis, or grannom)	Super hatch
Microsema	(Little weedy water sedge, or tiny grannom)	Super hatch

Although the hatches last only 1 to 2 weeks, the species of these genera generally emerge in the spring in explosive numbers. This makes them the most important group for fly fishermen at this time. The hatches begin soon after opening day in many areas, just when the weather is becoming pleasant. The insects fly in the early afternoon; egg laying takes place in the late afternoon to evening, although it can coincide with the emergence. The pupae emerge in midstream and drift for about 10 to 20 feet while struggling out of the pupal shuck. Once out of it, two flaps of their wings take them off the water quickly. Ovipositing is done by sprawling on the water and by crawling underwater. Note that the males are smaller than the females by one hook size.

The one species in this group that is an exception to these early and explosive emergences is *Brachycentrus americanus*, which hatches a little later in the year, with fewer numbers but over a longer time. The major spring species on the Au Sable River is *Brachycentrus lateralis*. The hook size is #16 to #20, and the larval type is classified as humpless tube case makers. The important species are described in the super hatch lists.

Other Species

Seven species of *Brachycentrus,* other than those listed in the super hatch list, are of local importance to fishermen. *Brachycentrus nigrosoma* is an eastern species very similar to *Brachycentrus numerosus. Brachycentrus eco,* limited to California and Utah, is smaller, 5.5 to 8 mm. *Brachycentrus incanus* is an eastern and midwestern species, similar to *Brachycentrus numerosus. Brachycentrus fuliginosus* is quite rare, known only from northern Michigan and Canada. *Brachycentrus chelatus* is a southern species known from Alabama, Florida, Georgia, and South Carolina (and similar to *Brachycentrus numerosus). Brachycentrus spinae* is limited to the southern Appalachian region and is similar to *Brachycentrus numerosus. Brachycentrus etowahensis* is similar to *Brachycentrus numerosus* and is also limited to the southern end of the Appalachians.

Philopotamidae

Chimarra	(Tiny black caddis)	East
Dolophilodes	(Tiny black gold speckled-wing caddis)	East, Midwest
	(Medium evening sedge)	West
Wormaldia	(Little autumn sedge)	East, Midwest, West

Chimarra

The species in this genus come in the spring, at about the same time as *Brachycentrus* and often on the same day. *Chimarra* is a morning-noon emerger, with ovipositing in the afternoon. The pupae crawl out of the water and emerge on land. Females dive or crawl underwater to lay their eggs. According to the literature, these are supposed to be common on the Au Sable River in Michigan, producing clouds of insects with heavy trout feeding. We have not found it important in this area but have noted it in Tennessee. The insect that anglers have been calling *Chimarra* is actually *Brachycentrus lateralis.* The hook size is #20 to #22; the larval type is classified as finger-net caddis.

Tiny black gold speckled-wing caddis

Chimarra aterrima	(Tiny black caddis, common in the Midwest)	East, Midwest
Chimarra obscura	(Common in southern tailwaters)	East, Midwest
Chimarra socia	(Common in the Northeast)	East

LENGTH: 6 to 8 mm

COLOR: Body is very dark brown, almost black; sides of abdomen and parts of femora are white; wings are black; antennae and legs are dark brown.

EMERGENCE: First of May to the middle of June; often mixed with *Brachycentrus*.

Dolophilodes

Dolophilodes distinctus emerges as a pupa in the stream and crawls over the surface of the water to shore, at least in the spring. The females are wingless in winter and spring. When fishing to an emergence, the adult and emerger imitations are useless. The angler must use a hackled pupa skated over the water toward shore. The egg-laying flight is important for both species. Later in the summer, pupae swim or crawl to shore or emerge in the stream.

Dolophilodes aequalis	(Medium evening sedge, common in Montana in small streams and rivers such as Rock Creek)	West
Dolophilodes distinctus	(Tiny gold flecked-wing sedge, common in Michigan from April to fall; widespread from Northeast to North Carolina; prefers cold streams.)	East, Midwest

LENGTH: *Dolophilodes aequalis* 7 to 12 mm; *Dolophilodes distinctus* 8 mm (#20 to #22 hook size)

COLOR: *Dolophilodes aequalis* earlier in the season is dark, almost black, becoming lighter (light brown) and smaller as the season progresses. *Dolophilodes distinctus* is very dark brownish gray; wings have small gold spots or scales; legs and antennae are almost black.

EMERGENCE: *Dolophilodes aequalis* is most important in evenings in July. *Dolophilodes distinctus* emerges year-round; winter females are wingless; midsummer evening emergers all have wings. In the spring there is a transition period when some have wings and some do not. This period occurs in late April and early June, just before and during the Hendrickson and grannom hatches. The emergence is in the morning and afternoon. This species does not come in large numbers, but emerges almost every day during the entire season.

Wormaldia

These insects are most common in cold, fast trout streams and uncommon in tailwaters and spring creeks.

Wormaldia anilla	(Little autumn sedge, common in small streams in the Northwest)	West
Wormaldia gabriella	(Found in larger streams than *anilla*)	West
Wormaldia moesta	(Widespread)	East, Midwest

LENGTH: 8 to 10 mm

COLOR: Body is olive brown; wings are gray; some western species are mottled brown; legs are brown.

EMERGENCE: *Wormaldia anilla* from April to June, and September to November; *Wormaldia gabriella* from August to October; *Wormaldia moesta* in March and April.

Leptoceridae

Oecetis	(Long-horned sedge)	Super hatch
Ceraclea	(Scaly-wing sedge)	Super hatch
Nectopsyche	(White miller)	Super hatch
Mystacides	(Black dancer)	Super hatch

The species of this family are summer fliers. They have very long antennae, two and a half times the length of their bodies. The wings are slimmer than those of most caddis, and the bodies are shorter and slimmer in relation to the length of the wings. The pupae crawl or swim to the surface to emerge, then sprawl on the surface or dive underwater to lay their eggs. Emergence is in the afternoon and evening, except for the white millers, which emerge at dusk and just after dark. The black dancer emerges in the morning in the West.

Helicopsychidae

Helicopsyche	(Speckled Peter)	Super hatch

Emergence and egg laying of these small caddis occur in the evening. During egg laying, the females float in the surface close to the banks, crawl underwater, and flop on the surface to oviposit. Then they ride the water serenely in the normal resting position, and trout take them with gentle rises. The hook size is #20 to #22 and the larval type is snail case makers.

Glossosomatidae

Glossosoma	(Little black short-horned sedge)	Super hatch
Protophilia	(Pseudo-microcaddis)	Super hatch

Glossosoma

These caddis are afternoon emergers in the early spring, and evening fliers as the season progresses. The emergence is usually more important than the egg laying. Females dive underwater to oviposit. Pupae swim to the surface to emerge, and at least some swim on the surface to shore, where they take about 2 minutes to crawl out of their pupal shucks. The hook size of *Glossosoma* is #20 to #24; for *Protophilia*, it is #24 to #28.

Protophilia

There are many species of these very small caddis, appearing in almost any color. They are between 2.5 and 5 mm long, yet can be important even though they are tiny because they often emerge in huge numbers. The most common colors in the rivers we fish are all black, with a gray wing and a cinnamon body. They emerge and oviposit mainly in midsummer, during the afternoon and evening.

Lepidostomatidae

Lepidostoma	(Little gray sedge, little black sedge)	Super hatch (some species)

These caddis are evening emergers and egg layers, with the pupae swimming to the surface to emerge. The emergers ride the water longer than most caddis, and pupae, emergers, and adults will all be taken by fish. Adults ride the water quietly during egg laying. There are more than twenty-five species in the Nearctic region (Michigan), but their distribution is very localized. This genus has been called the little plain brown sedge and described as having a plain brown wing and a brown body. However, the two most important species (at least in our experience)—*Lepidostoma pluviale* and *Lepidostoma togatum*—have green or olive bodies. *Lepidostoma togatum* and *Lepidostoma sommermane* (Ohio) have two black spots on a gray wing. We have not seen any completely brown species, but it is entirely possible that some do exist. The hook size is #18 to #20. The larval type is tube case makers.

Lepidostoma pluviale	(Little gray sedge, little black sedge)	West
Lepidostoma togatum		East, Midwest
Lepidostoma costalis		East, Midwest
Lepidostoma bryanti		Midwest
Lepidostoma costalis		East, Midwest
Lepidostoma strophis		East, Midwest, West

LENGTH: 9 to 11 mm
COLOR: The body is olive or green with a darker dorsal; wings are grayish brown or grayish, whereas some species have patches of hair that may be light or dark and look spotted or patterned; legs and antennae are grayish brown, with dark bands on the antennae. Some males of *Lepidostoma pluviale* have a distinctive dark gray recurve on the top of the wings that can be used for identification.
EMERGENCE: Mid-June to late September in the evenings in the West. Last of June to mid-August in the East and Midwest; some may come in the mornings. They inhabit small, cool, woodland streams. Adults ride the surface for a long time at emergence, so trout will take the pupae and dry adults at egg laying. In the Midwest, *Lepidostoma bryanti* begins in June, followed by *Lepidostoma costalis* in late July, then *Lepidostoma togatum* from August to September.

Psychomyiidae

Psychomyia	(Dinky purple-breasted sedge)	East, Midwest, West
Lipe	(Dark eastern woodland sedge)	East

The pupae of these Tricoptera swim to the surface to emerge in the river. The females dive underwater to oviposit. The eastern woodland sedges fly in the afternoon; females start egg laying in the early evening. The purple-breasted sedge emerges just at dark, except on overcast days, when emergence can occur at any time. The hook size is #20 to #22. The larval type is classified as net-tube caddisflies.

Psychomyia flavida	(Dinky purple-breasted sedge)	East, Midwest, West

LENGTH: 5 to 6 mm
COLOR: Body is yellow with a purple cast; wings are brown; antennae and legs are yellow.
EMERGENCE: June to August, usually after dark.

Lipe diversa	(Dark eastern woodland sedge)	East, Midwest

LENGTH: 6 to 7 mm
COLOR: Body is very dark brown; wings are uniformly very dark gray, almost black; legs and antennae are very dark brown.
EMERGENCE: May and June in afternoon and evening from small, cool, woodland streams.

Rhyacophilidae

The bright green larvae of this caddis are sometimes more important than the adults to trout fishermen. The family is widespread and abundant, but on some rivers they do not emerge in a sufficiently coordinated fashion to cause selective feeding. The larvae, on the other hand, are free living, of good size, and readily available to trout all season long. These are a fast-water caddis; the larvae live in rapids and riffles, and the adults emerge and oviposit in the same riffles. The pupae are fast emergers; the females enter the water to lay their eggs. Some individuals of this genus run to shore after emergence and/or egg laying, so a dry fly skittered from the riffles to shore can be effective. Emergence and egg laying occur in the afternoon-to-dusk period in calm weather (they do not like wind). The hook size is #14 to #18; the larval type is classified as free-living worms.

Rhyacophilia bifila	(Green sedge)	West
Rhyacophilia coloradensis		West
Rhyacophilia melita	(common on the Au Sable)	Midwest
Rhyacophilia manistee		East, Midwest
Rhyacophilia fuscula		East, Midwest

LENGTH: As long as 16 mm, but most species 8 to 13 mm
COLOR: Body is green; wings are mottled light and dark gray and brown; legs are ginger; antennae are gray with darker rings.
EMERGENCE: April through October in the West, May to July in the East and Midwest.

Hydroptilidae

Agraylea	(Salt and pepper microcaddis)	East, Midwest, West
Hydroptila	(Varicolored microcaddis)	East, Midwest, West
Leucotrichia	(Ring-horned microcaddis)	East, Midwest, West
Oxyethira	(Cream and brown microcaddis)	East, Midwest, West

These very small caddisflies generally range from 2 to 5 mm, (#36 to #24 hook size), which is why we do not list them in the true super hatch category. However, at times they can be important and create selective feeding when they are on the water in great numbers. They are more important on slow rivers and gentle spring creeks, where trout can sip them without expending much energy. The pupae swim or crawl to the surface; the females dive or crawl underwater to lay their eggs. The hook size is #24 to #36 and the larval type is classified as purse case makers.

Agraylea multipunctata	(Salt and pepper microcaddis)	East, Midwest, West

LENGTH:	4 to 5 mm
COLOR:	Body is green; wings are black and white mottled to almost black; legs and antennae are black.
EMERGENCE:	June and July at dawn.

Hydroptila species   (Varicolored microcaddis)   East, Midwest, West
About 60 species

LENGTH:	3 to 4 mm
COLOR:	Bodies can be almost any color; wings are gray to brown, and can be spotted or unspotted; legs and antennae are tan to black. Colors vary even within the same species.
EMERGENCE:	All summer at any time of day.

Leucotrichia pictipes   (Ring-horned microcaddis)   East, Midwest West

LENGTH:	4 to 4.5 mm
COLOR:	Body and appendages are dark brown to black; wings have a few scattered light spots; antennae and tarsi are banded with white.
EMERGENCE:	Summer, usually at midday.

Oxyethira michiganensis,   (Cream and brown   East, Midwest, West
serrata, pallida   microcaddis)

LENGTH:	2 to 3 mm
COLOR:	Body is greenish yellow; wings are cream and brown mottled; antennae and legs are yellow.
EMERGENCE:	Summer, usually in the evening.

Molannidae

Two species of this family can be important to trout fishermen. Both species are found in the East and Midwest. The pupae swim to the surface and emerge; the females crawl or dive underwater to oviposit and prefer quiet streams. They take a long time to cast their shucks. The hook size is #14 to #16, and the larval type is classified as hood case makers.

Molanna tryphena   (Gray checkered sedge)   East, Midwest
Molanna uniophila   East, Midwest

LENGTH:	15 to 16 mm
COLOR:	Body is brown; wings are gray with a mottled checkered pattern of light and dark areas, mostly in the middle; legs and antennae are brown.
EMERGENCE:	Mid-July to early September.

Phryganeidae
Phryganea (Rush sedge)

These large pupae crawl or swim to the bank to emerge on shore. Females lay their eggs on the water's surface and run across the water to return to shore. These are large insects, so they attract big trout. Generally they prefer quiet streams and lakes. Fishing tactics are different from most other Tricoptera. Pupal imitations should be crawled to shore in quiet backwaters; adult imitations should be skittered to shore during ovipositing. The egg-laying flights are in the evening. The hook size is #10 to #12, and the larval type is classified as giant case makers.

Phryganea cinera	(Rush sedge)	East, Midwest, West
Phryganea sayi		East, Midwest

LENGTH: 21 to 25 mm
COLOR: Body is reddish brown; wings are gray and brown, with an irregular pattern of shades of brown with light gray patches along the posterior margin. These form triangular marks when the wings are folded. Legs and antennae are yellow to brown.
EMERGENCE: May and June (*Phryganea sayi* 2 weeks later than *Phryganea cinera*).

Ptilostomis

Ptilostomis ocellifera	(Giant rusty sedge)	East, Midwest, West
Ptilostomis semifasciata		East, Midwest, West

LENGTH: 21 to 25 mm
COLOR: Body is yellowish brown; wings are light reddish brown with some irregular and obscure darker markings; legs are light reddish brown; antennae are darker reddish brown with dark rings.
EMERGENCE: June and July after dark from lakes and slow weedy streams.

Odontoceridae

The pupae of this family swim and crawl to the surface to emerge; females drop on the surface, where they flop and flutter while extruding the egg mass. Emergence and egg laying take place in the evenings. The hook size is #14 to #16, and the larval type is classified as strong case makers.

Psilotreta

Psilotreta labia,	(Dark blue sedge)	East
P. frontalis		

LENGTH:	12 to 14 mm
COLOR:	Body is green or almost black, with legs and mouthparts showing lighter areas of grayish brown; wings are very dark grayish brown, with very small, irregularly scattered lighter dots; legs and antennae are almost black.
EMERGENCE:	Late July to mid-June in the evening. (*Psilotreta frontalis* inhabits smaller streams; there is, however, some overlap.)

Polycentropidae

These caddis live in the quieter areas of streams. The pupae swim to the surface to emerge in the evening during the summer. Females swim to the bottom of the stream to oviposit. The hook size is #18 to #20, and the larval type is classified as trumpet-net and tube-making caddisflies.

| *Polycentropus cinereus* | (Brown checkered summer sedge) | East, Midwest, West |

LENGTH:	7 to 9 mm
COLOR:	Body is yellowish brown to brown; wings have light and dark brown mottling; legs and antennae are brown.
EMERGENCE:	Mid-June to mid-July, much more common in lakes and streams in Michigan.

| *Nyctiophylax moestus* | (Dinky light summer sedge) | East, Midwest, West |

LENGTH:	5 to 7 mm (#22 to #24 hook size)
COLOR:	Body is yellowish brown; wings are brown; legs and antennae are yellowish brown.
EMERGENCE:	Late afternoon and evening in June; egg laying and emergence take place at the same time.

Limnephilidae

This very diverse family has species of all sizes and colors. The habits of the various genera are also diverse, so it must be handled a little differently from the other families. We will explain some of the habits under the genus listings rather than the family listings.

Emergence is accomplished by swimming to the surface or crawling to shore. Egg laying is achieved by diving or crawling underwater in most of the species. About half of the subfamily Limnephilinae lay their eggs on shoreside objects, but even here some individuals may crawl underwater. The hook size is #2 to #24, and the larval type is classified as tube case makers.

Limnephilus (Summer Flier)

When the adults emerge in the spring they are not sexually mature. They become mature during the summer and oviposit in the fall. Females lay eggs on objects near the water or crawl into the water. Some species have two generations each year. The hook size is #14 to #16.

Limnephilus sericeus	(Summer flier)	East, Midwest, West
Limnephilus submonilifer		East, Midwest
Limnephilus thorus		West

LENGTH: 13 to 16 mm

COLOR: Body is brown and slender with a darker dorsal; wings are brown, variegated with irregular light and darker spots; legs and antennae are tan to brown.

EMERGENCE: Mid-April to mid-June; sometimes has two generations each year, one in the spring and one in the fall. *Limnephilus thorus* is common on Montana's Big Horn River in late September and October, although it is not known elsewhere. (This was a new find for the authors in 1995.)

Apatania (Early Smoky-Wing Sedge)

This is a very important Tricoptera in southern New England. Emergence and egg laying occur all day in the spring. The hook size is #18 to #20.

Apatania incerta	(Early smoky-wing sedge)	East

LENGTH: 7 to 8.5 mm

COLOR: Body is grayish brown; wings are smoky gray; legs and antennae are grayish brown.

EMERGENCE: Mid-April to late May during the day.

Frenessa (Dot-Wing Sedge)

These caddisflies emerge late in the season in the East and Midwest. They are very important in November and December (when not much else is hatching) and continue through February, especially on unseasonably warm days. Pupae crawl and swim to the shallows to emerge in the late morning and afternoon. Egg laying probably occurs near shore. The hook size for *Frenessa missa* is #16 and for *Frenessa difficilis* is #14 to #16.

Frenessa missa	(Dot-wing sedge)	East, Midwest
Frenessa difficilis		East

LENGTH:	*Frenessa missa* 11 to 13 mm, *Frenessa difficilis* 14.5 to 15.5 mm
COLOR:	Body is dark grayish brown with a light yellowish lateral line; wings are brown with uniform tan translucent dots; legs are ginger; antennae are light brown.
EMERGENCE:	November and December on warm afternoons.

Geora (Little Gray Sedge)

These little caddis emerge from riffles. *Geora stylata* is very common in the Midwest. The hook size is #18.

Geora stylata	(Little gray sedge)	Midwest
Geora calcarata		East, Midwest, West

LENGTH:	8 to 10 mm
COLOR:	Body is pale yellow; wings are tannish gray; legs are tannish gray; antennae are dark gray.
EMERGENCE:	Late May to early June from small, cold, gravel-bottomed streams.

Neophylax (Autumn Mottled Sedge or Small Dot-Wing Sedge)

These caddis can be important in the fall, emerging in the daytime in good numbers when not much else is going on. *Neophylax fuscus* is a very important hatch in the Midwest. (Note that this genus has recently been moved to the family Uenoidae, but the key to this genus was made before the move and these insects do not conform well to the new key.)

Neophylax concinnus=autumnus	(Autumn mottled sedge)	East, Midwest
Neophylax rickeri		West
Neophylax splendens		West
Neophylax fuscus	(Small dot-wing sedge)	Midwest

LENGTH:	*Neophylax concinnus* 9 to 12 mm, *Neophylax rickeri* and *Neophylax splendens* 16 to 18 mm
COLOR:	Body is brownish yellow to dark gray; wings are mottled light and dark brown. *Neophylax concinnus* has a light brown double-diamond design on the top of the folded wings. Legs and antennae are brownish yellow. The body of *Neophylax fuscus* is very dark gray with a yellowish lateral line.
EMERGENCE:	Autumn.

Pycnopsyche (Great Brown Autumn Sedge)

The pupae emerge and the adults oviposit mostly at night, but some activity occurs at dusk and dawn. Large trout are certainly on the lookout for this meaty insect. The pupae migrate to the banks to emerge, and then

 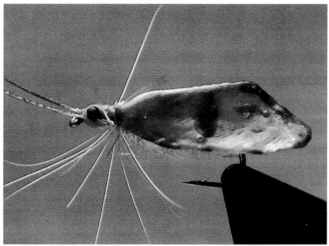

Great brown autumn sedge

crawl underwater to lay their eggs. A large pupal imitation is effective when fished slowly on the bottom. *Pycnopsyche guttifer* is supposed to be rare in the West, but the Big Horn River has a good population. Imitations produce big fish in September and October. The hook size is #12 to #14.

Pycnopsyche guttifer	(Great brown autumn	East, Midwest, West
Pycnopsyche lepida	sedges)	East, Midwest
Pycnopsyche scabripennis		East, Midwest

LENGTH: 19 to 20 mm

COLOR: Body is cinnamon; wings are yellow to brown with two conspicuous brownish black marks in the middle and a black border at the apex; legs and antennae are cinnamon; antennae have dark bands.

EMERGENCE: Mid-July to October.

Discosmoecus (Giant Orange Sedge)

The larvae, pupae, and adults are all important stages of this huge caddisfly. The larvae exhibit behavioral drift in the summer and, unlike most aquatic insects, they drift in the afternoon. The pupae migrate to the shallows before emerging in the late afternoon and evening. When egg laying takes place at dusk, the females make a commotion that the fish certainly notice. Fishing a pupa and a dry on a dropper in the shallows with a twitching retrieve can be deadly. The hook size is #4 to #8.

Discosmoecus atripes	(Giant orange sedges)	West
Discosmoecus gilvipes		West
Discosmoecus jucundus		West

LENGTH:	18 to 30 mm
COLOR:	Body is orange; wings are gray and brown mottled with heavy veins; antennae and legs are tan.
EMERGENCE:	September and October.

Hesperophylax (Silver Striped Sedge)

These insects emerge at night, but they are so large that trout are on the lookout for this summer emerger. The hook size is #12 for *Hesperophylax designatus* and #6 to #8 for *Hesperophylax incisus*.

| *Hesperophylax designatus* | (Silver striped sedges) | East, Midwest |
| *Hesperophylax incisus* | | East, Midwest, West |

LENGTH:	17 to 20 mm for the eastern species; 30 to 34 mm for the western species
COLOR:	Body is yellow to cinnamon; wings are cream and light brown with a long silver stripe; legs and antennae are ginger.
EMERGENCE:	Mid-summer.

Hydatophylax (Giant Cream Pattern-Wing Sedge)

These caddis emerge in the mornings. Trout feed mostly on the pupae; egg laying is not important to anglers. The hook size is #4 to #6.

| *Hydatophylax argus* | (Giant cream pattern-wing sedges) | East, Midwest |
| *Hydatophylax hesperus* | | West |

LENGTH:	30 to 34 mm
COLOR:	Body is yellowish tan; wings are light brown with cream patterns, *Hydatophylax argus* has a Z-pattern; head is yellow; antennae are dark grayish brown; legs are tannish.
EMERGENCE:	Late May to fall for eastern species; August to October for western species.

Platycentropus (Chocolate and Cream Sedge)

These large caddis are nocturnal emergers in midsummer, but some big trout can be taken early in the morning on dry adult patterns. The hook size is #12 to #14.

| *Platycentropus radiatus* | (Chocolate and cream sedge) | East, Midwest |

LENGTH:	20 to 33 mm
COLOR:	Body is yellow to brown; wings are shades of cream to dark brown; legs and antennae are dark yellow.
EMERGENCE:	July and August.

Emergence Table for Eastern Caddisflies

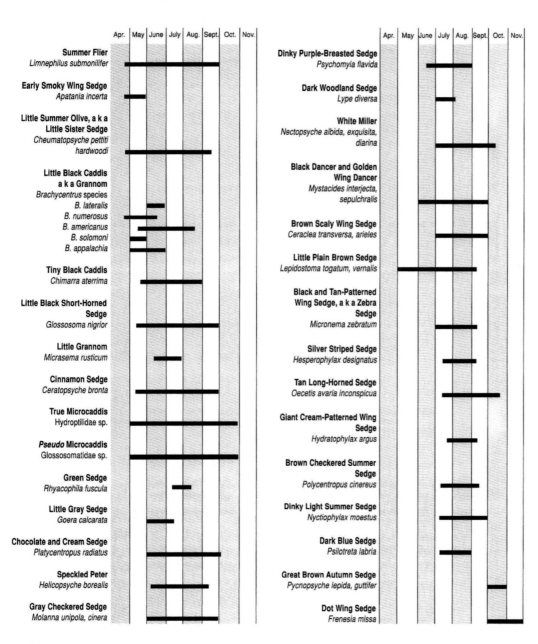

	Apr.	May	June	July	Aug.	Sept.	Oct.	Nov.
Summer Flier *Limnephilus submonilifer*		▬▬▬▬▬▬▬▬▬						
Early Smoky Wing Sedge *Apatania incerta*		▬▬						
Little Summer Olive, a k a Little Sister Sedge *Cheumatopsyche pettiti hardwoodi*		▬▬▬▬▬▬▬						
Little Black Caddis a k a Grannom *Brachycentrus species*								
B. lateralis			▬					
B. numerosus		▬▬						
B. americanus		▬▬▬▬						
B. solomoni		▬						
B. appalachia		▬▬						
Tiny Black Caddis *Chimarra aterrima*		▬▬▬▬▬						
Little Black Short-Horned Sedge *Glossosoma nigrior*		▬▬▬▬▬▬▬▬						
Little Grannom *Micrasema rusticum*		▬▬						
Cinnamon Sedge *Ceratopsyche bronta*		▬▬▬▬▬						
True Microcaddis *Hydroptilidae sp.*		▬▬▬▬▬▬▬▬▬						
Pseudo Microcaddis *Glossosomatidae sp.*		▬▬▬▬▬▬▬▬▬						
Green Sedge *Rhyacophila fuscula*		▬▬						
Little Gray Sedge *Goera calcarata*		▬▬▬						
Chocolate and Cream Sedge *Platycentropus radiatus*		▬▬▬▬▬▬						
Speckled Peter *Helicopsyche borealis*		▬▬▬▬▬						
Gray Checkered Sedge *Molanna unipola, cinera*		▬▬▬▬▬▬						
Dinky Purple-Breasted Sedge *Psychomyia flavida*			▬▬▬					
Dark Woodland Sedge *Lype diversa*			▬▬					
White Miller *Nectopsyche albida, exquisita, diarina*			▬▬▬▬					
Black Dancer and Golden Wing Dancer *Mystacides interjecta, sepulchralis*			▬▬▬▬▬					
Brown Scaly Wing Sedge *Ceraclea transversa, arieles*			▬▬▬▬▬					
Little Plain Brown Sedge *Lepidostoma togatum, vernalis*		▬▬▬▬▬▬▬▬						
Black and Tan-Patterned Wing Sedge, a k a Zebra Sedge *Micronema zebratum*			▬▬▬					
Silver Striped Sedge *Hesperophylax designatus*			▬▬					
Tan Long-Horned Sedge *Oecetis avaria inconspicua*			▬▬▬▬					
Giant Cream-Patterned Wing Sedge *Hydratophylax argus*			▬▬					
Brown Checkered Summer Sedge *Polycentropus cinereus*			▬▬▬					
Dinky Light Summer Sedge *Nyctiophylax moestus*			▬▬					
Dark Blue Sedge *Psilotreta labria*			▬▬					
Great Brown Autumn Sedge *Pycnopsyche lepida, guttifer*							▬▬	
Dot Wing Sedge *Frenesia missa*							▬▬▬▬	

Emergence Table for Midwestern Caddisflies

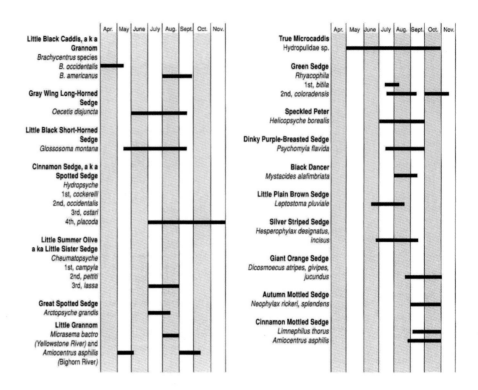

Emergence Table for Western Caddisflies

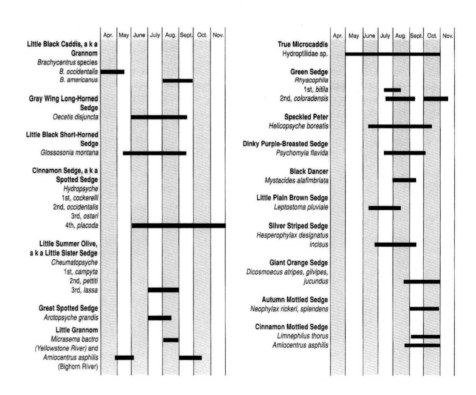

CHAPTER 16

The Super Hatches: Stoneflies

MOST FLY FISHERMEN prefer to fish during a hatch. At these times the trout are prompted to rise to floating naturals that ride the surface of the water. During certain times of the day, stoneflies can produce this hatch scenario for the angler, although it is really a spinner fall or egg-laying flight. Stoneflies will create significant hatches during the cold months of January, February, and March. Many of their winter flush emergences are confined to small and medium-sized freestone streams and rivers. This winter emergence falls outside the legal fishing season in many states, not to mention outside the enthusiasm of many anglers who are unwilling to be on the streams so early in the year. In addition, the metabolism of the trout does not peak until the water temperature reaches the 50-degree mark.

Springtime is the season to begin fly fishing earnestly. It marks the emergence of legions of eager anglers trekking toward their favorite rivers. They will probably begin the season with well-oiled reels, clean fly lines, exuberant spirits, and high hopes for the coming season. The winter stoneflies that continue into spring will unknowingly play an important role in satisfying these expectations.

Stoneflies are a much smaller order of insects than caddisflies and mayflies. In fact, there are only six major types of stoneflies on which the angler needs to focus, making these insects much easier to study and imitate. The simplicity of the emergence and the egg-laying processes also reduces the need for a large number of imitations. Since the habits of stoneflies are so uncomplicated, picking the right imitation is easy, and there are many effective patterns available. It helps to be aware of the few species that are important to anglers. Here is our basic list, along with their descriptions.

SPRING ACTIVITY

Tiny Winter Blacks (Capniidae, Nemouridae, and Leuctridae)

These are 4 to 10 mm long and range in color from black to dark reddish brown. The emergence occurs from late winter to the middle of spring. *Allocapnia granulata* is the most common and abundant species of Capniidae in the East. *Capnia gracilaria* is its western counterpart.

Early Brown and Black Stones (Taeniopterygidae)

These stoneflies range in length from 9 to 14 mm. *Taeniopteryx navalis* is the most prevalent black species in the East. It emerges at midday from late February to mid-March. Steelhead in Michigan and Wisconsin feed on the nymphs, and imitations of them have accounted for many hookups. *Strophopteryx fasciata* is the eastern brown species. It ranges from 9 to 11 mm and emerges in the last week of March and the first 2 weeks of April at midday. The emergence coincides with the opening of the trout season in New York, so it is a very important eastern stonefly.

Salmonflies (Pteronarcidae)

These are huge flies, so the large fish feed on them voraciously. In the West, *Pteronarcys* and *Pteronarcella* constitute the salmonfly hatch. Respectively, these are 23 to 40 mm and 20 to 24 mm long. The adults are black with dark orange thoraxes. Emergence is from the late spring to the early summer. The East and Midwest have an equivalent emergence of *Pteronarcys dorsata*, which not many anglers notice because it is nocturnal. *Pteronarcys dorsata* emerges at the same time as the Hex hatch but from a different type of water. The Hex hatch comes from slow areas with muck banks; the stones come from the fast, deep riffles. Note that the eastern species has a yellowish underside.

Salmonfly nymph

Salmonfly adult

SUMMER ACTIVITY

Big Goldens (Perlidae complex)

The big goldens exhibit a mosaic network of conspicuous yellow markings on a background of either black or brown. They are the first to appear in summer and are mostly nighttime emergers. The eastern species in order of importance are *Phasganophora capitata*, *Acroneuria carolinensis*, and *Parahgentina immarginata*. *Phasganophora capitata* is an early-morning emerger, laying its eggs at dusk in June and July. *Acroneuria carolinensis* emerges from midsummer to August from small to medium-sized streams. *Parahgentina immarginata* emerges at the same time of year as *Phasganophora capitata* from a similar type of water.

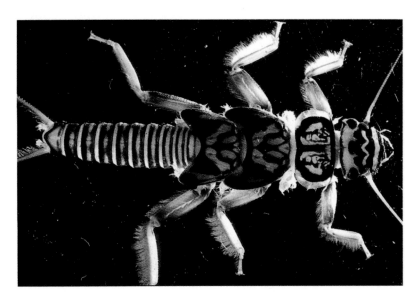

Big golden stonefly nymph

The midwestern species are *Parahgentina media, Acroneuria lycorias,* and *Peresta placida. P. media* emerges from the last week in June until the last week of July from all types of water. Emergence occurs in the first 3 hours of darkness, and egg laying is at dusk. *A. lycorias* emerges 2 weeks before *P. media,* early in the morning. *P. placida* arrives during the first week of July to the middle of August, an hour after dark.

The western species are *A. pacifica, A. californica,* and *Classenia sabulosa. A. pacifica* emerges during June and July. *A. californica* is most abundant in the Pacific states and comes in July and August. Both are a favorite of summer steelhead. *C. sabulosa* is a huge insect, 32 mm in length, and is a late-season emerger from August to September. It comes at any time of day.

Medium Browns and Yellows (Perlodidae)

The eastern olive brown species that are most important to fishermen are *Isogenus olivacenus* and *Isoperla bilineata. I. olivacenus* emerges during May and June at midday. *I. bilineata* emerges during May and June at midday. *I. bilineata* emerges from 10:00 p.m. until midnight, but it has an evening egg-laying flight. The yellow species are *Isogenus decisus* and *Isoperla signata.* These are the common pale yellow stoneflies of summer. The emergence is after dark, while the egg-laying flight is at dusk.

The important western species of the browns are *Isoperla fulva* and *Isogenus tostonus.* The yellow species are *Isoperla patricia* and *Isoperla mormona.* They are common during the latter half of the season.

Little Yellows and Greens (Chloroperlidae)

These small stoneflies are important from the middle to the end of summer. The most important eastern species are *Alloperla caudata,* a delicate yellow species, and *Alloperla imbecilla,* a bright green species.

In the West, *Alloperla delicata* and *A. severa* are common green species. *A. pallidula, A. coloradensis,* and *A. pacifica* are all common yellow species. *Alloperla* are 7.5 to 10 mm in length; *Chloroperla* are less than 7 mm. The little yellows and greens emerge from 8:00 a.m. until 10:00 a.m. The greatest ovipositing activity occurs in the late afternoon and evening.

In the East and Midwest the seasonally waning tiny winter blacks and early brown stones will be most effective. In the West, because of the effects of the higher altitudes, the little winter stoneflies will still be emerging abundantly, with the early brown stones not peaking until late April or May. Both of the winter types will eventually disappear for the season, and the trout waters will be dominated by much larger stoneflies (such as the *Pteronarcys,* or salmonfly). These, in turn, will be succeeded by the nocturnal stoneflies of summer.

The summer stonefly activity is brought about by three types: the big goldens, the medium browns, and the little yellows and greens. These flies exhibit a strong tendency to emerge and become active between late afternoon and early morning. Hence, their hatches complement the daytime

Little yellow stonefly nymph

hatches of the mayflies and caddisflies. Night anglers and early-rising anglers will benefit from this "off-hours" activity. This is fortunate for those anglers because big browns in particular like to feed at night.

There are, however, many notable and important summer stoneflies that are morning and dusk emergers. (We have emphasized these types in previous chapters.) Many of the stoneflies' impressive hatches and egg-laying activities have gone largely unnoticed by anglers. Because of increasing competition for outdoor "space" among anglers and canoeists, campers, and hikers, these off-hour stonefly activities will probably gain importance in the future for fly fishermen who are looking for solitude.

SEASONAL EMERGENCES OF STONEFLIES

Stoneflies display certain unmistakable changes in their appearance and streamside habits as the season progresses. Here we will only discuss those transformations that are relevant to fly fishing. We will continue to split the stoneflies into two groups, spring and summer, although the spring season certainly overlaps with winter.

SPRING STONEFLIES

These flies are comprised of three types. The first begin to emerge in January and will continue doing so through April and even May in some locales. They are tiny (4 to 7 mm) and dark, which is obviously why we named them tiny winter blacks. These little forms are found throughout the country. Late-winter emergers are abundant and are considerably larger in size (10 to 15 mm). A more common and appropriate name for them is early black stones *(Taeniopteryx)*, of importance primarily in eastern and midwestern waters.

The last to emerge are the early brown stones *(Brachypteras)*, whose geographical range includes the entire country. Their growth is continued well into the spring—either April, May, or June—depending on the area, when the hatches of the gigantic salmonflies *(Pteronarcys)* make their seasonal debut. These are the largest stoneflies (32 to 40 mm)—actually the largest aquatic insects on North American waters. They are abundant and significant on western rivers. All of these winter-spring types exhibit certain parallel characteristics. Of greatest relevance to the fly fisherman is that they are all midday emergers, and their adult forms can live for 3 or 4 weeks after the actual emergence.

Stoneflies must leave their aquatic habitat in order for the nymph-to-adult metamorphosis to take place. The cycle's completion is dependent not only on the nymphs reaching the rocks or logs along the edge of the stream, but also on the ability of the adults to break the nymphal shucks in order to escape. Hardening of this nymphal shuck, caused by either the direct sun or exceedingly dry hot air, can prove fatal. However, bright sunny days of winter and spring seem ideal for the midday emergence of stoneflies. It is at such time that the tiny winter blacks, early black stones, and early brown stones will come out of the water.

The salmonflies, which emerge during spring and even into early summer in many areas, exercise more caution. In the West, because of the cooler temperatures of the higher elevation, *Pteronarcys*, like their seasonal predecessors, continue to emerge at midday. Their best hatches are during overcast days that afford them some protection from the sun. Eastern specimens of this stonefly, the *Pteronarcys dorsata,* which emerge from the latter part of April until early June, hatch both earlier and later in the day during the second half of their seasonal cycle. Their hatches at such times are missed by most anglers who are not accustomed to fishing before 8:00 a.m. or after dusk.

After actual emergence takes place, winter-spring stoneflies demonstrate the remarkable ability to live in the adult stage as long as 4 weeks before completing the mating-ovipositing phase of the life cycle. This is because the adults are able to feed on the algal growth on rocks, bark, and streamside vegetation. Some stonefly adults are nonfeeders. Encountering these stoneflies at streamside usually means that hatching is taking place in the stream nearby. However, it is also possible that the hatch is currently located well upstream from where they are found.

Stonefly hatches move upstream because each species must experience a certain number of days with water temperatures that are conducive to growth (between 35 and 65 degrees) in order to hatch. This first occurs in the lowest sections of a river system, farther from the cold headwaters. The water in these lower sections has been exposed longer to the warming rays of the sun. Thus, the hatches of a particular species will first appear in the lower reaches and progressively move upstream. In some cases, it will require as long as a month and a half to complete the emergence cycle in a particular river. No better example exists than that of the salmonfly hatches in western rivers. They travel upstream approximately 4 or 5 miles each day.

We have seen that these early stoneflies can exist for weeks after their emergence and that the hatches move upstream at a regular pace. These facts should warn the angler that the mere presence of adults along a stream does not mean that the hatches are still taking place. If the adults are already copulating, it is usually an indication that the hatch may have expired. The egg-laying activity of the adults will now be of most concern to the angler.

The summer stoneflies are also comprised of three principal types. The first emergences feature what is probably the most important stonefly to the fly fisherman, the big golden. Its seasonal occurrences begin in the wake of the slightly larger salmonfly. Its proportions range from 22 to 28 mm, but it is the big golden's abundance in most trout streams that makes it so significant. The smaller and paler medium brown is a second summer stonefly that appears from June until early August. The third type, the little yellow and green, is at its best during August, September, and even October, although many species appear in late May, June, and July.

When we consider the entire year, we find that stoneflies will peak in size with the emergences of the spring hatches of the salmonflies. Then they will begin to reverse the process toward winter. In coloration, they get paler as the season progresses.

The three summer types also exhibit certain common traits. In contrast to the spring stoneflies, they emerge between early evening and the morning hours. The adults live for only a short time—3 to 5 days. The hot temperatures of summer discourage their hatches from taking place during the day, so most species hatch during the cooler times, and many hatch at night. The fact that the adults live briefly would imply that when an angler encounters them in the vegetation along the stream, he can expect their actual emergences still to be occurring nearby in the stream.

It is interesting to note that many summer stoneflies have short, nonfunctional wings in the adult stage, whereas the females emerge with already developed eggs. Apparently, nature wants to ensure that they do not venture too far from their point of origin. This facilitates the quick completion of the mating-fertilization-ovipositing processes of the life cycle and the greatest chance for survival of the species.

DISTRIBUTION

Separate groups of the stonefly species obviously inhabit both halves of the country. However, the seasonal distribution shows a similar chronological order of their appearance. Each stonefly group, either in the East and Midwest or in the West, tends to follow the other in appearing at certain times of the year.

Even when we consider that the emergence cycle of each group is really the result of more than one species, there are certain time factors involved. Each species tends to reach maximum abundance one at a time, usually for a period of only a few days. However, their hatches cannot help but overlap. Time factors among stonefly groups, even among species *within* each group, are also evident in species of other aquatic insects—mayflies and caddisflies included.

Why such a grand design of nature? Perhaps it is best understood when we stop to consider that each species has to occupy an available niche in the scheme of nature. This causes direct competition to be reduced. In the confined world of the trout, such competition would be for the limited amount of food available along the bottom of the stream, of which the nymphs and larvae of each species must make quick use just before maturity. Often, when two closely related species must share a river system, they will "split" it between themselves. A classic case is the two *Pteronarcys* species that produce the salmonfly hatch in western rivers. *Pteronarcys californica* and *princeps* share the same waters, but the first species is the most important to the angler because it lives in rivers located at elevations to 7,000 feet. *Pteronarcys princeps* will be found most commonly in higher elevations.

DEVIATIONS OF SEASONAL EMERGENCES

The effect of the *average* altitude and longitude of a given area of the country may advance or delay the overall emergence of stoneflies. For the dates cited in the eastern-midwestern timetable, we have chosen the times of the season when stoneflies hatch out of northern trout streams. These are the streams of southern New York and northern Pennsylvania, Michigan, and Wisconsin. Western emergence times are applicable to southern Montana and the uppermost parts of Wyoming, and also to Idaho and Oregon. Lower longitudinal zones in the East, such as Maryland and Virginia and west to Missouri, will experience the hatches 3 to 4 weeks sooner. Colorado, Utah, and northern California will experience the hatches that much earlier than the times stated in the western emergence table.

Local altitudinal differences, even in a specific area, have the effect of advancing or delaying a seasonal cycle. Such local deviations are most relevant to the western angler, whose rivers may vary drastically in altitude throughout their long courses. Any differences in altitude or longitude will influence all groups of aquatic insects by approximately the same degree. The nearly predictable sequence of seasonal emergence of the stonefly groups will be preserved in most cases.

Climatic deviations from year to year can also have a noticeable effect on when the entire cycle will take place in a specific locale. This is seen in mountainous areas capable of holding snowpacks, where a delay in the spring melt may contain the water at a temperature much colder than usual. This might delay the time of hatches for as long as 3 weeks.

The two factors that enable a stonefly to emerge during a specific time of the season or at a particular time of day are the water temperature and the photoperiod (length of daylight). To what degree either of these factors influences the emergence of each stonefly species is apparently complex. However, there are enough consistencies in most of the species to allow us to make some generalizations.

In order for the nymphs of any species to emerge, they must reach full maturity. Growth to maturity in stoneflies occurs during times when the water temperature passes the freezing point. This enables them to emerge during winter. The tiny winter blacks begin to reach full maturity when the temperature of the water hits 33 to 37 degrees, whereas early black and early brown stones do so in the lower-40-degree range. The downstream sections of a river will almost always be first to experience emergences, and the hatching activity will slowly travel upstream. In western mountains this progression may take some considerable time to be completed.

A drastic example of this pattern is found in the common little species *Capnia gracilaria*, which first appears at 4,000 to 5,000 feet in January and will not emerge until April at 7,000 feet. Yet a closely related species, *Capnia brevicaudata*, which follows it in seasonal succession, will appear *at all altitudes* during the first 3 weeks of April, in waters that may differ in temperature as much as 25 degrees. Its seasonal emergence is dependent solely on photoperiod, namely those first 20 to 25 days of the year attaining a specific number of daylight hours.

The point of this example is certainly not to give you the impression that you must be aware of all the biological facts about each species in order to encounter their hatches. Rather, it is to show that wherever you choose to fish, in any part of the country, you stand to find some type of stonefly. In those various waters there are different species that depend for seasonal emergence on either water temperature, photoperiod, or a combination of both. Often, when none of the hatches or adult activity is taking place in one stretch of a river, it may be doing so in either direction, upstream or down.

The time of emergence for winter-spring stoneflies occurs at midday, with some exceptions. These early-season emergers appear to be in search of warmth; thus their hatches take place approximately between 11:00 a.m. and 4:00 p.m. The members of the summer fauna appear to be more preoccupied with escaping the hottest part of the day. With the cool and overcast days, they will usually emerge during the evening, night, or early-morning hours. On the other hand, their adult activity, which is of concern to the angler, is not confined to such an irregular timetable.

So far we have made many generalizations concerning the eastern, midwestern, and western stoneflies—about the domination of certain types and the specific times of the day and year when they emerge. The accompanying charts will help to summarize and clarify some of these details.

Stoneflies   EMERGENCE TABLE FOR MIDWEST AND EAST

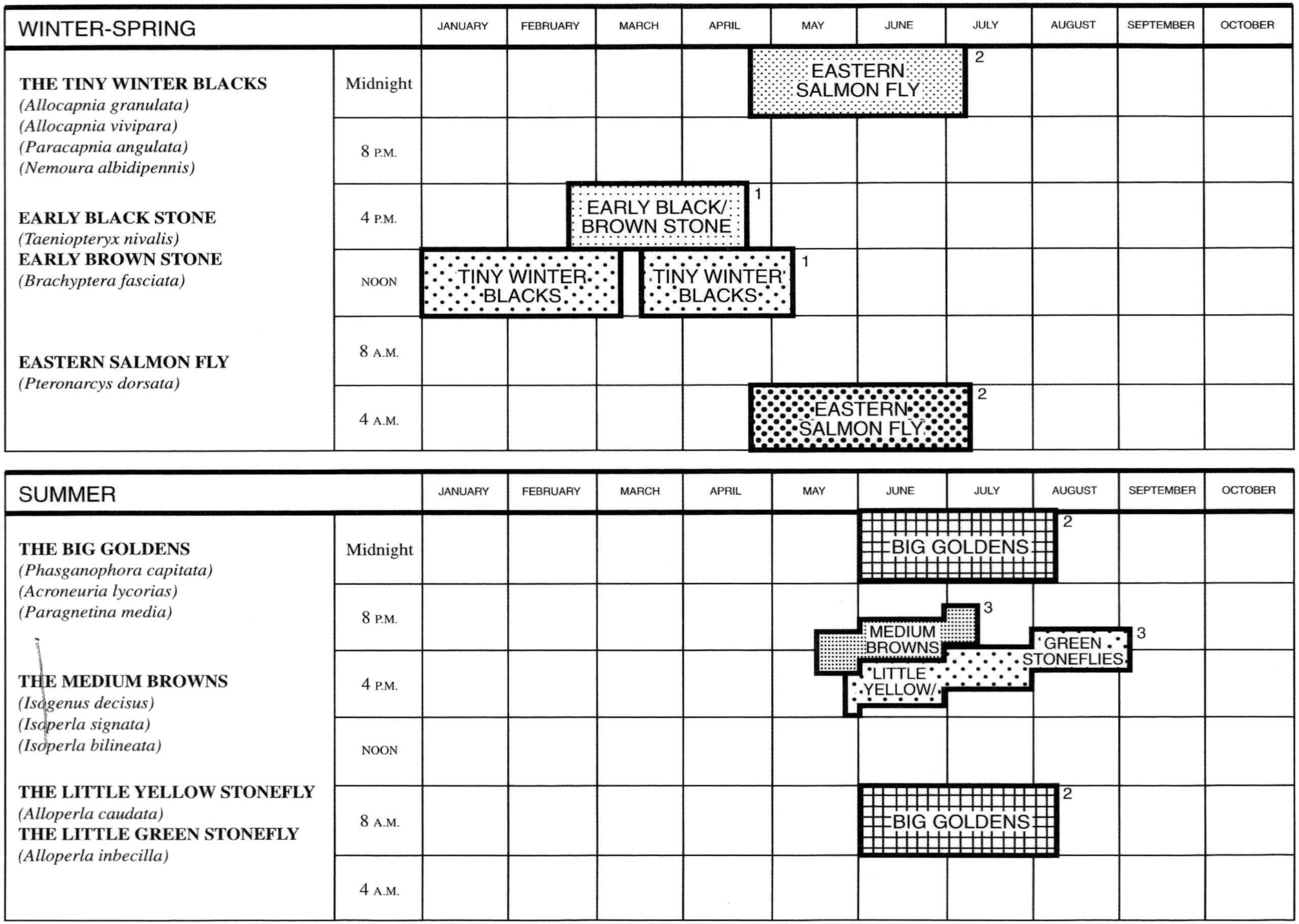

WINTER-SPRING

Time of day (rows): Midnight, 8 P.M., 4 P.M., NOON, 8 A.M., 4 A.M.
Months (columns): January, February, March, April, May, June, July, August, September, October

Species	Emergence
THE TINY WINTER BLACKS (*Allocapnia granulata*) (*Allocapnia vivipara*) (*Paracapnia angulata*) (*Nemoura albidipennis*)	EASTERN SALMON FLY — 2 (April–June, at Midnight/8 P.M.); TINY WINTER BLACKS (January–March, at NOON)
EARLY BLACK STONE (*Taeniopteryx nivalis*) **EARLY BROWN STONE** (*Brachyptera fasciata*)	EARLY BLACK/BROWN STONE — 1 (February–April, at 4 P.M.); TINY WINTER BLACKS — 1 (March–April, at NOON)
EASTERN SALMON FLY (*Pteronarcys dorsata*)	EASTERN SALMON FLY — 2 (April–July, at 4 A.M.)

SUMMER

Time of day (rows): Midnight, 8 P.M., 4 P.M., NOON, 8 A.M., 4 A.M.
Months (columns): January, February, March, April, May, June, July, August, September, October

Species	Emergence
THE BIG GOLDENS (*Phasganophora capitata*) (*Acroneuria lycorias*) (*Paragnetina media*)	BIG GOLDENS — 2 (May–August, at 8 P.M.); BIG GOLDENS — 2 (June–August, at 8 A.M.)
THE MEDIUM BROWNS (*Isogenus decisus*) (*Isoperla signata*) (*Isoperla bilineata*)	MEDIUM BROWNS — 3 (June–July, at 4 P.M.)
THE LITTLE YELLOW STONEFLY (*Alloperla caudata*) **THE LITTLE GREEN STONEFLY** (*Alloperla inbecilla*)	LITTLE YELLOW/GREEN STONEFLIES — 3 (June–September, at 4 P.M.)

Stoneflies   EMERGENCE TABLE FOR WEST

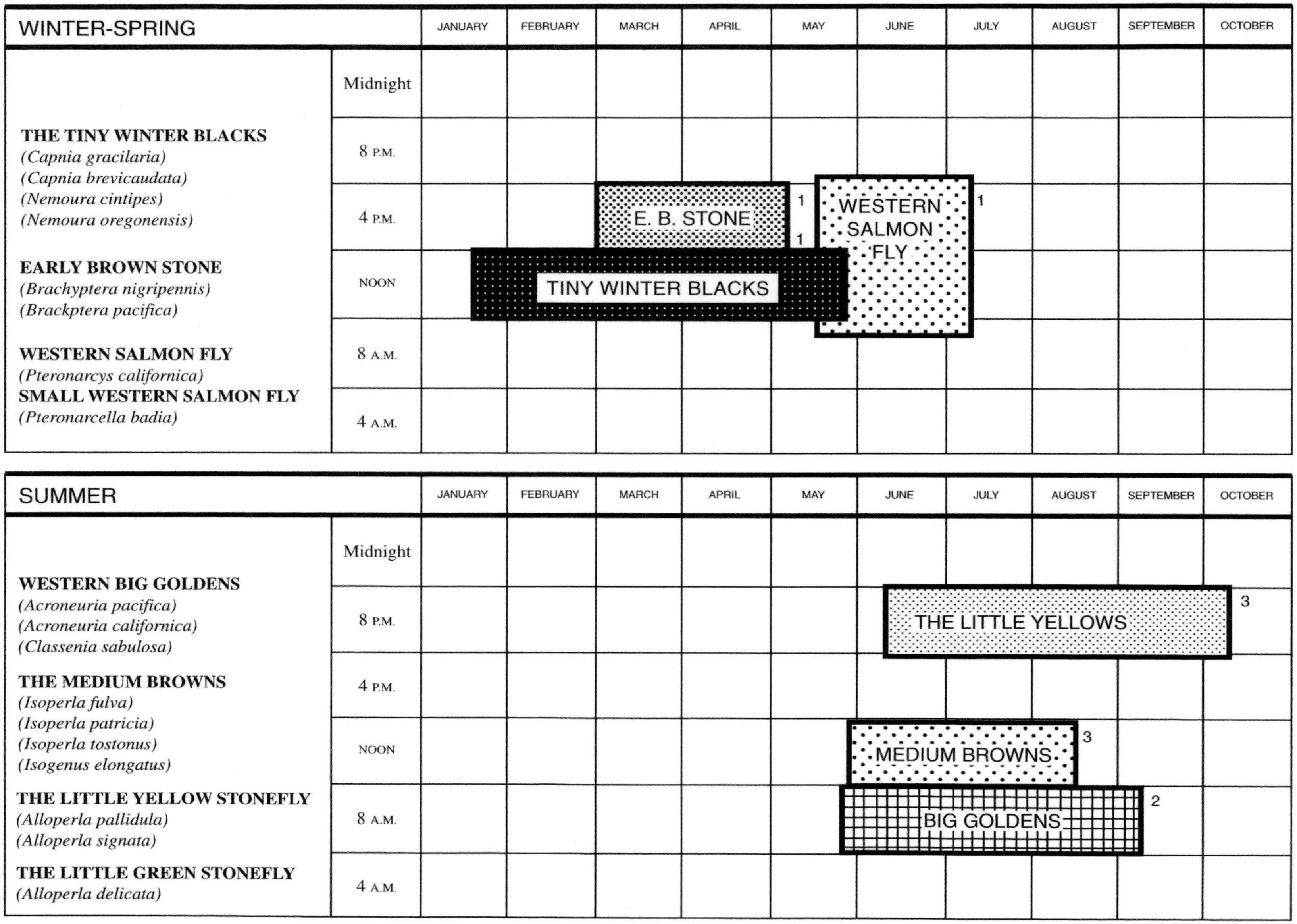

WINTER-SPRING

	JANUARY	FEBRUARY	MARCH	APRIL	MAY	JUNE	JULY	AUGUST	SEPTEMBER	OCTOBER
Midnight										
8 P.M.										
4 P.M.			E. B. STONE (1)		(1)					
NOON		TINY WINTER BLACKS			WESTERN SALMON FLY (1)					
8 A.M.										
4 A.M.										

THE TINY WINTER BLACKS
(*Capnia gracilaria*)
(*Capnia brevicaudata*)
(*Nemoura cintipes*)
(*Nemoura oregonensis*)

EARLY BROWN STONE
(*Brachyptera nigripennis*)
(*Brackptera pacifica*)

WESTERN SALMON FLY
(*Pteronarcys californica*)
SMALL WESTERN SALMON FLY
(*Pteronarcella badia*)

SUMMER

	JANUARY	FEBRUARY	MARCH	APRIL	MAY	JUNE	JULY	AUGUST	SEPTEMBER	OCTOBER
Midnight										
8 P.M.						THE LITTLE YELLOWS				(3)
4 P.M.										
NOON						MEDIUM BROWNS		(3)		
8 A.M.						BIG GOLDENS			(2)	
4 A.M.										

WESTERN BIG GOLDENS
(*Acroneuria pacifica*)
(*Acroneuria californica*)
(*Classenia sabulosa*)

THE MEDIUM BROWNS
(*Isoperla fulva*)
(*Isoperla patricia*)
(*Isoperla tostonus*)
(*Isogenus elongatus*)

THE LITTLE YELLOW STONEFLY
(*Alloperla pallidula*)
(*Alloperla signata*)

THE LITTLE GREEN STONEFLY
(*Alloperla delicata*)

CHAPTER 17

Night Fishing

NIGHT IS THE time when you may expect to catch large trout, especially browns, on flies. Usually these large fish are unwilling to leave their hiding places during the day for fear of their archenemies—fish-eating birds and mammals. However, after dark they can roam the shallows in search of food with little or no threat of danger from most of their predators. A river that seems dead in the heat of the day often becomes alive at night, with both large and small fish ranging all over the stream in search of food.

Fishing a river in daylight, and fishing the same stretch at night, are vastly different experiences. A wide, smooth, quiet stretch of river seems to become larger, faster, deeper, and more frightening at night. The unexpected explosion of a huge brown trout out of the eerie darkness can be a spine-chilling experience. Huge trout that would never venture forth in the sun can be found in the most unlikely places after dark, and often they are willing to strike at the most outlandish creations of a fly tier's imagination. Baby muskrats and ducklings have been found in autopsies of brown trout.

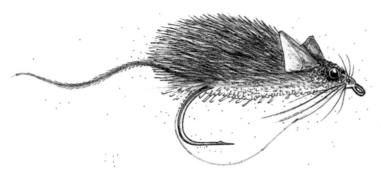

Whitlock's Mouserat with snapguard

As a result, you can use flies that would make a daytime dry-fly purist cringe. These concoctions will be not only effective but also enthusiastically received by the fish.

There are four main types of night fishing. The first, fishing to a spinner fall, usually occurs from dusk until an hour after dark. The second, fishing to a hatch of emerging duns, can come sporadically off and on all night long. The third type of night fishing is surface fishing to trout that are not feeding actively on a specific insect. This would include insects that are found in the water by accident, such as large beetles, night moths, spiders, and craneflies. The fourth type is wet-fly and streamer fishing either just below the surface or deep in holes and runs with a sinking line.

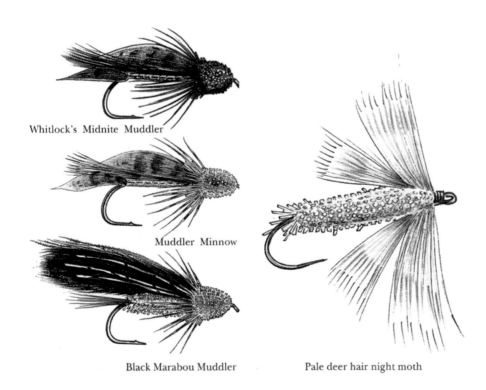

Whitlock's Midnite Muddler

Muddler Minnow

Black Marabou Muddler

Pale deer hair night moth

Night moth or giant caddis or stonefly adult:
impala wing, mohlon body, palmer hackle

Dry-fly fishing to a fall of spinners usually begins just *before* dusk. Since the fish can be extremely selective at these times, it is essential that you use a good pattern. The size and outline are a little more important after dark than is the color, but do not ignore shades of color completely. Sometimes even a slight discrepancy in size or shape will make a pattern almost useless during these spinner falls, because returning spinners fall en masse or in a much more concentrated group than duns that are hatching or emerging. An emergence of duns takes place over 2 to 3 hours, whereas the spinner fall is condensed into 30 to 45 minutes. There are far more flies on the water at a given time, and these great numbers of flies falling into the water excite the trout into feeding voraciously during these times.

It is often difficult after dusk to tell exactly where your artificial is among groups of naturals. Sometimes when you think a fish is striking the artificial, it is actually taking a natural. And other times when a fish is really taking your fly, you might think your imitation is a bit off the line and not react quickly to the rise. One of the best ways to offset this disadvantage is to get close to the rising trout. This is possible at dusk because the fish do not seem to be bothered as much by the closeness of the angler if he wades in quietly.

One of our favorite patterns for the dusk spinner-fall fishing is the Hen Spinner. Spinner falls can range from very small insects, as small as #24 *Plauditus (Pseudocloeon)*, to an extremely large *Hexagenia limbata* or giant Michigan mayfly. Of course, the larger the insect, the larger the trout that can be expected to feed on the fall, although even the smaller flies at dusk may entice larger fish. At this time, fish usually adopt lines of drift where large numbers of insects are carried to them. They do not move far off these lines to feed, so your casting must be accurate. Hence the need to wade as close as possible in order to keep your casts short and accurate.

After dark, the fish often continue to feed on spent spinners, and the rise form becomes almost unnoticeable. If the moon is out, you can wade into position so that its reflection lines up with the rising trout. On the water you will then see tiny dimples, which may well be large fish feeding quietly to these spinners. This type of fishing usually does not last longer than an hour, but it is very fast and intense. Because it is so brief, it pays to have the right pattern. These fish are aware of the correct size and form because so many of the naturals are passing over their heads. They quickly "get the color," as the English would say. If you think you know what is going on and you have a good pattern that does not work within 3 or 4 minutes, check the water discreetly with a flashlight and hand net to see what is on the surface. Often the hatch or spinner fall will change just at dusk, as small flies become invisible to the eye. This is the only way to be certain that you have the correct pattern.

The second type of night fishing is also for active rising trout and it concentrates on fishing to a hatch of emerging duns. Some of our largest mayflies, such as the giant Michigan mayfly of the Midwest, the brown drake of the Midwest and West, as well as some of our smaller mayflies, such as *Ephemerella dorothea*, hatch after dark later in the season. Here again, the size, shape, and floating ability are usually more important than color, but a

Leadwing Coachman   Gold-Ribbed Hare's Ear   Hair-Wing Stonefly

good representation of the naturals is necessary. Some of our larger species will start hatching at dark and will continue on and off throughout the night. When you know a hatch is in progress, do not stop fishing an hour after dark. It is quite possible that you will have spurts of great activity later that night. Extremely large fish will move from their holes to range widely over the river. We have seen browns and rainbows move 400 to 500 feet from their hiding places to feed on these large night-hatching duns, and studies on the south branch of the Au Sable have shown they will move 2 miles.

At night, you will not need long, fine leaders. However, 15-pound browns are not unheard of at night on large dry flies, so it is best to be equipped with large, strong, sharp hooks and the heaviest leaders practical for the size of fly you are using. You should check your flies often at night to make sure they have not picked up small pieces of grass and that they are dry and floating well. Sometimes a small tangle can develop at night at the end of the leader, which you will not notice unless you check periodically. It is usually impossible to tell if your fly is dragging after dark. Indeed, sometimes it does not seem to matter, although often it does, and various positions should be tried when casting to an extremely wary fish.

Large fish can be found at night in some of the most unlikely spots imaginable, particularly rocky shallows, muddy shallows, and gravel bars. On warm nights, trout often prowl these areas for crayfish, baitfish, large beetles, or anything else that might come their way. This third type of fishing is especially good after the spinner fall is over and also when no aquatic insects are actually hatching out of the water. It can be effective from dark until dawn. Short, heavy leaders are in order here, as large fish are often encountered. The hooks on these flies should also be very sharp because large fish frequently have hard, bony mouths. These large dry flies are cast straight across and then allowed to swing in a dead drift. Here again, if you wade quietly, long casts are not necessary. Many strikes are missed in this type of fishing by casting downstream at too great an angle. Casting at 45 degrees from the trout produces many more hooked fish on the strike. In this type of fishing, if the moon is out, work the dark side of the river in the shadows.

Our favorite types of patterns for this type of fishing are large night moths, either tied with a clipped deer hair body and impala wings with no hackle, or a night moth with a body of mohlon, a short hackle tied palmer, and a deer hair or impala wing. The two colors of the most common naturals are light cream and tan; fish seem to show a definite preference for the lighter variety. Large salmon-type dry stoneflies are often very effective. Many of our streams have large stoneflies returning to lay their eggs after dark. Often they swim across the river in the expelling operation. The patterns we use are also good imitations of the large caddisflies that one encounters periodically at night. Often extremely large western patterns, such as #6 or #8 Irresistibles or Goofus Bugs, are good when fished in midwestern or eastern rivers at night. Usually with this kind of fishing you are covering a lot of water, so it is important to know the holes you are fishing. Remember: *It is dangerous not to be well prepared when you go night fishing.*

The fourth type of night fishing uses wet flies and streamers. You can be just under the surface with a floating line or deep with a high-density sinking line. Fur-bodied Squirrel Tails are effective when fished shallow to imitate the nymphs and adults of adult stoneflies, either ready to crawl out of the water to hatch or in the egg-laying process. Large wet flies such as the Gold-Ribbed Hare's Ear and Leadwing Coachman in sizes #2, #4, #6, and #8 are very effective. These imitate caddisflies and stoneflies. A yellow body with a gray squirrel wing and brown hackle is good, as is an orange body with a fox squirrel wing.

Our favorite pattern, however, on which we have caught more large trout at night than any other streamer, is a fox squirrel wing with a red wool body, gold ribbing, and brown hackle. It is best when tied in sizes #2 to #10 3X long; the smaller sizes are used at dusk and just before dark, whereas the larger sizes are good later on as the night progresses. This type of fishing consists mainly of casting slightly down and across stream and letting the streamer swim dead, drawing it slowly back, or stripping back as fast as you can. All three methods work well—you'll just have to experiment to see which one works best on a particular night. These flies are also fished in deep holes and runs with a high-density line. When the water is extremely fast and deep, they may also need to be weighted.

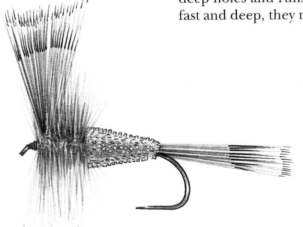

Irresistible Dry Fly

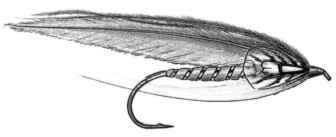

Gray Ghost Streamer

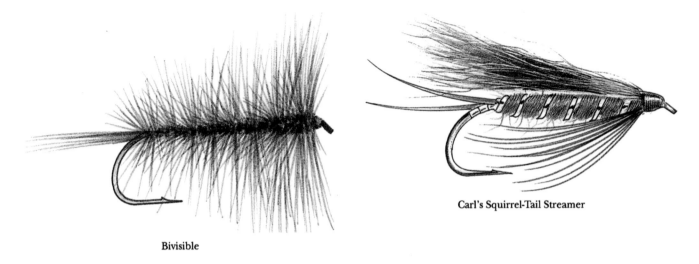

Bivisible

Carl's Squirrel-Tail Streamer

Remember that many fish will cruise the shallow gravel bars and riffles, sometimes with their dorsal fins and backs completely out of the water. They do this while grubbing for crawdads that are kicking out of their skins or shells in order to undergo the next cycle, much as the mayfly nymph sheds its outer skin many times in order to grow. Or these large fish may cruise around looking for the minnows and baitfish that inhabit the shallows. The stonefly nymphs are also in the shallows at night before they crawl out on the bank to hatch. A light Squirrel Tail fished with a floating line can often produce explosive action in such situations.

Finally, here are few more suggestions. Fishing blind in shallow water often leads to snags, so a fly tied upside down with the hook riding up is a great help. It is best if you can learn to change flies without the use of a flashlight. Bright lights will scare large trout and ruin a good pool for a long time. But in spite of these handicaps, night fishing can add a new dimension to your trout fishing. And it may well land you the largest trout of your life.

CHAPTER 18

A Barbless Hook

TRADITION IS, OF course, something handed down from the past. It's an inherited culture, belief, practice, or attitude. And very few fields of endeavor have more tradition associated with them than the sport of fly fishing. Only in recent years have trends toward scientific improvement and advancements been fully realized. Equipment, for example, has changed tremendously in the past few decades, including the development of such items as better-floating and longer-casting fly lines, rods with outstanding action, and leaders with increased strength and fineness of diameter. Flies by many more tiers are being produced that are based on common sense and not just tradition—and they are much more realistic. In fact, a major theme of this book has been to reexamine traditional ideas and advance some new concepts. We hope we have instilled the idea of using common sense and close observation as criteria for devising effective patterns.

There is one area of our sport in which we *must* continue to adjust our thinking and depart from tradition: the choice of killing or releasing. For some illogical reason, our trout-fishing tradition used to demand that we kill our catch. This probably originated with our forefathers, who had to depend on wildlife to survive and who never imagined that our natural resources would get depleted. Today our attitudes are changing, but some fishermen still need to prove their prowess by displaying creels and freezers full of dead fish. In our opinion, this characteristic is not very admirable.

The true angling enjoyment comes from the challenge of imitating and appreciating the environment—*and not from killing trout*. The amount of satisfaction and enjoyment gained is the real measure of success. Good fishermen recognize the fact that they can seriously jeopardize their sport, and normally they make an effort to limit their kill. They realize that the whole idea of fly fishing is the deception of *live* trout, and that by killing their catch they kill the sport. They also know that each time a trout is released it becomes a little more leader shy and sophisticated. Trout that are smarter and more sophisticated create a greater challenge for deception. And this, of course, improves our sport. These are the kinds of trout we enjoy fishing over. One of this variety is worth half a dozen out of the hatchery.

With the mounting problems of overpopulation, pollution, and the ever-decreasing amount of good trout water, we must soon make some meaningful decisions about our sport. In the end, it comes down to the choice of fishing with regulations or not fishing at all. On this basis, it's quite obvious what must be done. We must maintain stringent size and creel limitations, as well as our no-kill and trophy-fish regulations. This sounds like a simple solution, but when these recommendations are made there are still howls from certain quarters. (It has been our experience that some of those who yell loudest are also the ones who damage their sport by killing every fish they catch.)

What we need to encourage is a new breed of angler who is truly interested in the improvement of our sport. We must all work through any means at our disposal to promote and improve the quality of fly fishing everywhere. Sportsmen's clubs, fly-fishing federations, and fly-tying organizations all provide excellent venues for learning about our sport and promoting the need for conservation. These groups must work closely with the state departments to promote the necessary regulations that will safeguard our sport.

The future of fly fishing is contingent on our ability to reverse the past trends of stream pollution, dam building, careless regulations, and generally uneducated anglers. And reversal of these tendencies will only continue through the actions of concerned individuals. Since fly fishermen represent a minority group, the best procedure has been to sell the concept of clean water to the public—rather than to promote only the sport of trout fishing. Similarly, the great dam builders can still be regulated by putting pressure on our legislators, both state and federal.

As for regulations themselves, our conservation agencies need to be continually reminded that "harvest" does not necessarily mean "dead fish." Harvest also means "a reward for exertion," and what better reward is there for the true angler than a released *live* trout that is free to rise again? It takes a bigger and better person to release a trout than to kill one. In fact, perhaps we can all take a small but admirable step and begin to fish with a barbless hook. We will all reap the rewards.

Keys to the Families
of Mayflies

THE ANATOMY OF MAYFLIES

Semi-diagrammatic drawings of a mayfly male imago (spinner), and a mayfly nymph showing characters used in the keys.

KEYS, DESCRIPTIONS, AND DISTRIBUTION OF THE FAMILIES, GENERA, AND SPECIES OF EPHEMEROPTERA (MAYFLIES)

Note: Red signifies that the family, genus, or species is very important to fly fishermen; blue signifies that the family, genus, or species can be of local importance; green signifies that the family, genus, or species is of little importance.

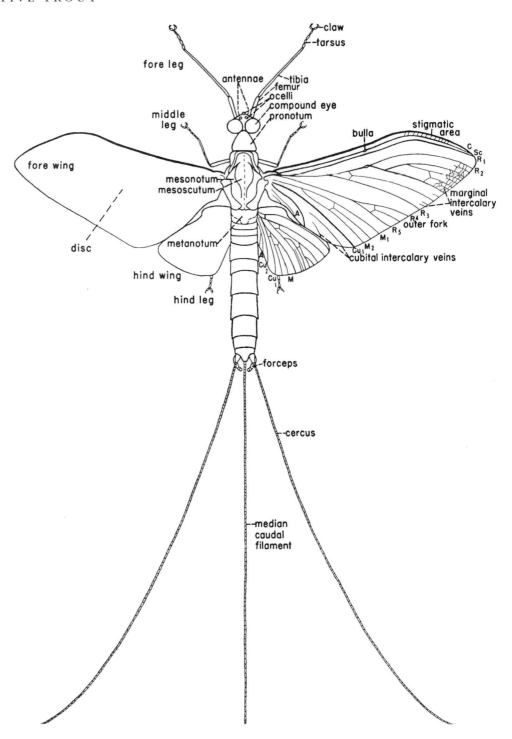

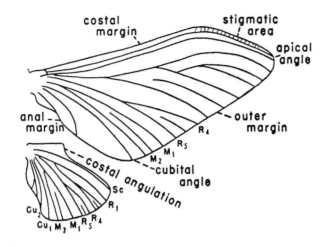

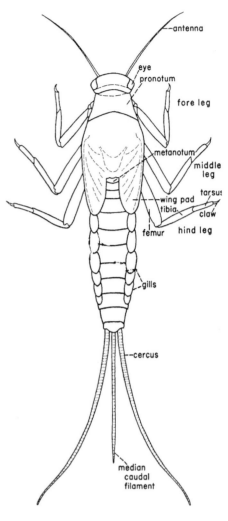

NYMPHS

1. Mandibles bearing long tusks (see figure 1), overall length from
10mm to 40mm (Brown Drakes, Green Drakes, Yellow Drakes, Hex,
White Fly) . . . . Ephemeridae, Potamanthidae, Polymitarcidae

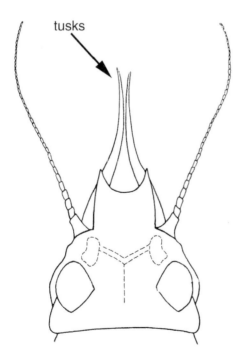

Figure 1 tusks

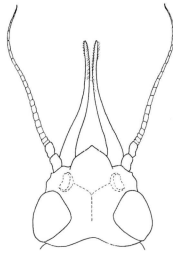

Figure 2

Figure 3

Figure 4

a. Frontal process deeply forked (see figure 1): *Ephemera;* or broadly rounded (see figure 2): *Hexagenia* or *Litobrancha;* tusks of head curve outward and upward . . . . Ephemeridae

This family has three genera, *Ephemera, Hexagenia,* and *Litobrancha.*

Ephemera Species

Ephemera simulans (Brown Drake): 10mm to 15mm long; distribution E, M, AS, W.

E. guttulata (Green Drake): 15mm to 26mm long; distribution E, AS.

E. varia (Golden Drake): 13mm to 17mm long; distribution E, AS.

E. blanda, (Golden Drake): 12mm to 16mm long; distribution AS.

Hexagenia Species

Hexagenia limbata (Giant Michigan Mayfly): males 18mm to 25mm long; females 20mm to 30mm long; distribution E, M, AS, W; widespread and abundant.

H. astrocaudata: 18mm to 26mm long; distribution E, M; abundant in cold beaver-impoundment waters.

H. ridida: 22mm to 29mm long; distribution E, M; widespread but only fairly abundant; avoid cold spring-fed waters.

H. bilineata: 18mm to 25mm long; distribution SE, M; common on large rivers.

H. munda: 17mm to 30mm long; distribution E, M; of main importance in SE.

Litobrancha Species

Litobrancha has one species, *L. recurvata* (Great Dark Green Drake): males 20mm to 40mm long; females 21mm to 32mm long; distribution E, M; most numerous in cold, spring-fed streams of small to moderate size.

Note: *Litobrancha* can be differentiated from *Hexagenia* and *Ephemera* by the short setae on the antennae (*Hexagenia* and *Ephemera* have long setae), and the small gills on segment 1 single in *Litobrancha.*

b. Frontal process appears to be lacking, tusks curve inward and downward from the base (see figure 3), (Cream and Golden Drakes) . . . . Potamanthidae

The single genus *Anthopotamus* which has been changed from *Potamanthus* (Cream and Golden Drakes) has about eight species; 8mm to 15mm long; distribution E, M, AS. Important species: *A. distinctus,* most abundant in the East and Midwest; *E. myops,* fairly common in the Midwest.

c. Frontal process narrowly rounded, tusks curve inward at the tips (see figure 4), (White Fly) . . . . Polymitarcidae

The single important genus, *Ephoron* (White Fly): 8mm to 12mm long; distribution E, M, AS, W. Important species: *E. leukon;* E, M; and *E. album;* E, W.

Mandibles without long tusks: Go to **2.**

2. Gills of abdominal segments 2 operculate, almost entirely covering remaining gills (see figure 5), overall length 3mm to 6mm, (Angler's Curse, Tricos) . . . . Caenidae, Leptohyphidae

a. Gills of segment 2 triangular-shaped (see figure 5) . . . . Leptohyphidae

This family has one genus, *Tricorythodes* (Tricos): 3mm to 6mm long; important species, *T. atratus, T. stygiatus* (E, M), *T. minutus* (W).

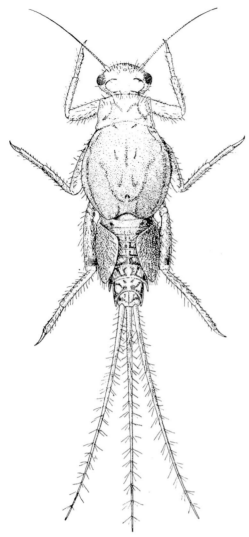

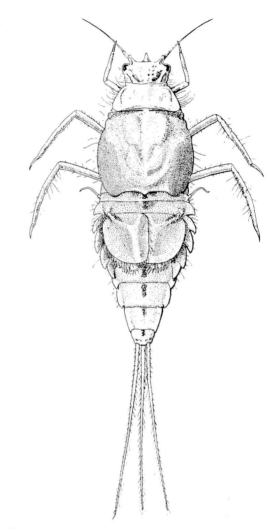

Figure 5: *Tricorythodes stygiatus* nymph

Figure 6: *Brachycercus lacustris* nymph

b. Gills of segment 2 nearly rectangular
    in shape (see figure 6) .... Caenidae
    This family has two genera, *Caenis* (Angler's Curse), and *Brachycercus* (no common
    name, uncommon on trout streams). *Caenis* are 2.5mm to 4mm in length and are
    buff- to pale-yellow to whitish in color, and are more common in lakes than
    streams. Most important species are *C. simulans* (E, M, W) and *C. anceps* (E, M).
    Brachycercus are larger and darker than *Caenis* (6mm to 7mm), with dark-brown
    to brown bodies and whitish wings, and are found on trout streams but are
    uncommon. *Caenis* lacks the prominent tubercles that *Brachycercus* possess on
    its head.

Gills of abdominal segment 2 absent, or if present, not operculate: Go
to **3.**

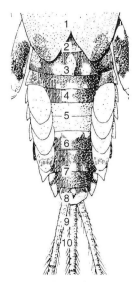
Figure 7

3. No gills on segments 1 or 2; in some cases 1, 2, and 3 (see figure7); overall length 5mm to 15mm: (Hendricksons, Sulphurs, Slate Olive Duns, Western Green Drakes) . . . . Ephemerellidae

> This is the most important family for trout fishermen. It previously had only one genus, *Ephemerella*, which has been split into seven genera. See chapters 7, 8, 9, and 14 for complete descriptions of the important genera and species.

Gills on segments 1 to 7 or 1 to 6: Go to **4.**

4. Gills on abdominal segments 1 to 6 largely concealed by carapace-like extension of mesonotum (see figure 8), overall length 10mm to 12mm (no common name) . . . . Baetiscidae

> This family has only one genus, *Baetisca*, widespread and though you may encounter them they do not seem to have a swarming emergence as with other mayflies, and do not cause trout to feed on the surface. Length 10mm to 12mm, some species are smaller. Dun bodies are very dark brown with an olive sheen, wings heavily black and white spotted. Species *B. laurentina, B. obesa* (E, M).

Gills on segments 1 to 7: Go to **5.**

5. Body strongly flattened, eyes on dorsal surface of head (see figure 9), overall length 8mm to 17mm . . . . Heptageniidae

> This family contains ten genera, *Stenonema* (March Browns and Light Cahills), *Stenacron* (Cream Cahills and Orange Cahills), *Epeorus* (Quill Gordons), *Rhithrogena* (Dark Blue Quill, Western Red Quill), *Heptagenia* (Pale Evening Dun and Gray Fox), *Cinygmula* (no common name), *Cinygma* (Western March Brown), *Leucrocuta* (Pale Evening Dun), *Nixe* (Pale Evening Dun), and *Ironodes nitidus* (Slate Maroon Dun). See chapters 7, 8, 9, and 14 for complete descriptions of the important genera and species.

Body not strongly flattened: Go to **6.**

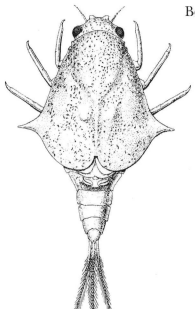
Figure 8: carapace

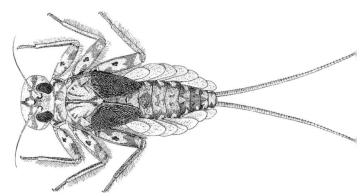
Figure 9: *Epeorus sp.* Nymph the only genera in the family with only two tails as a nymph

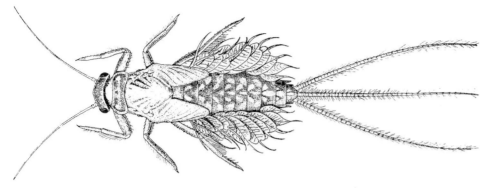

Figure 10: *Leptophlebia cupida* nymph, 10mm to 14mm

6. Tails clothed with hairs on both sides (see figure 10), length 10mm to 14mm, (Mahogany Duns, also known as Black Drakes, length 7mm to 9mm (see figure 11, Little Mahogany Duns) . . . . Leptophlebiidae

> This family contains two genera, *Leptophlebia* (Mahogany Duns, also known as Black Drakes), 10mm to 14mm long; and *Paraleptophlebia* (Little Mahogany Dun), 7mm to 9mm long. Important species: *L. cupida* (E, M), *L. nebulosa* (E, M, W), *P. debilis* (E, M, W), *P. bicornuta* (W), *P. adoptiva* (E, M), *P. mollis* (E, M). There are many other species that may be locally abundant and produce good hatches. See chapters 7, 8, 9, and 14 for complete descriptions of the important genera and species.

Outer pair of tails with short hairs on inner side only: Go to **7.**

7. Minnow-like nymphs, front tarsal claw double, length 14mm to 19mm (Pseudo-Gray Drakes) . . . . Metretopodidae

> The one species, *Siphloplecton basale,* is of slight interest to fishermen, producing small hatches on Eastern and Midwestern rivers in early spring. The nymphs crawl out of the water to emerge in late April to early June, and look like Gray Drakes. They may create fishable spinner falls on a few large rivers.

Minnow-like nymphs,

front tarsal claw single . . . . Baetidae, Isonychiidae, Siphlonuridae, Ameletidae

> These families were all in the family Baetidae until recently.

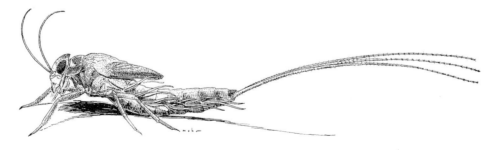

Figure 11: *Paraleptophlebia adoptiva* nymph, 7mm to 9mm

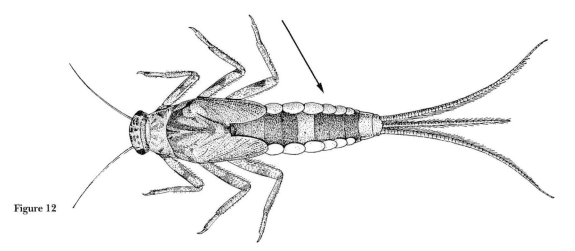

Figure 12

a. Streamlined bodies, 3mm to 12mm long, platelike gills are present on abdominal segments 1 to 7, or 1 to 5, or 2 to 7. Posterior abdominal sements usually lack posterolateral spines (see figure 12) but rarely have moderately-developed spines (see figure 13). Antennae long, two or three times more than the width of the head, or antennae shorter than twice than the width of the head, but labrum with notched distal margin . . . . Baetidae

> Ten genera in this family are found in trout streams; there are many other genera that are not. The ten are *Acentrella, Baetis, Plauditus, Diphetor, Acerpenna, Heterocloeon, Barbaetis, Labiobaetis, Centroptilum,* and *Callibaetis. Pseudocloeon* was in this family but was transferred to *Apobaetis, Acentrella, Baetis,* and *Barbaetis.* In 1998 all eleven species transferred to *Baetis* and *Barbaetis cestus* was put into a new genus, *Plauditus. Baetis* and *Plauditus* are by far the most important genera in the family. **Note:** Species in this family are under constant study and reclassification. Entomologists often have difficulty with exact species identification; the latest change was the creation of the new genus *Plauditus.* Some of the more important name changes are: *B. brunicolor* and *B. hiemalis* are now regarded as synonymous although they are different colors and the nymphs have different body patterns; *B. tricaudatus* and *B. vagans* are synonymous. *B. phoebus* and *B. flavilistriga* are synonymous; the genus *Diphetor* now contains the species *D. hageni* and *D. devinctus* (both previously in *Baetis*); *Baetis pygmaeus* is now in the genus *Acerpenna (A. pygmae); Labiobaetis propinquus* is the new classification for *Baetis propinquus.* This re-

Figure 13: *Callibaetis* nymph. The only important genus in the family with poorly developed spines.

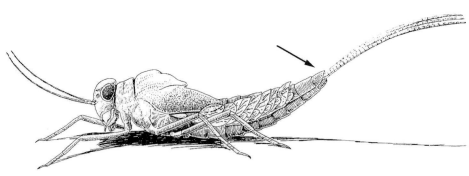

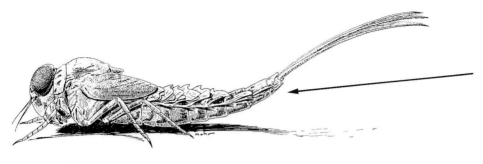

Figure 14: *Siphlonurus* nymph. Sharply developed posterolateral spines and platelike gills.

classification is almost certainly not over. From an angler's point of view it makes more sense for us to simply call them all *Baetis* (Small Blue Winged Olives, size 16 to 20), and *Plauditus* (Tiny Blue Winged Olives, size 22 to 26).

b. Streamlined forms, length 6mm to 20mm, antennae no more than twice the width of the head, platelike gills on abdominal segments 1 to 7, posterior abdominal segments with sharp posterolateral spines (see figure 14) .... Siphonuridae

One genus, *Siphlonurus* (Gray Drakes), 9mm to 17mm long. Important species: *S. occidentalis,* 12mm to 16mm long (M, W); *S. alternatus,* 13mm to 16mm long; *S. quebecensis,* 12mm to 15mm long; *S. rapidus,* 9mm to 12mm long (E, M).

Figure 15

c. Streamlined forms with two rows of conspicuous long hairs along inner surface of forelegs (see figure 15), length 8mm to 17mm (Slate Drakes) .... Isonychiidae

One genus, Isonychia (Slate Drake or White Gloved Howdy); 12mm to 17mm long. The most important species are *I. bicolor* (W, M, AS) and *I. velma* (W).

d. Maxillae with crown of pectinate splines (see figure 16), gills with single lamella, more or less oval with a sclerotized band along lateral margin (see figure 17), and usually with a similar band on near mesial margin (see figure 18) (Pseudo-Gray Drake) .... Ameletidae

One genus, *Ameletus,* 9mm to 14mm long, two species, *A. cooki* (W), *A. ludens* (E), emerges in April and looks like a Gray Drake.

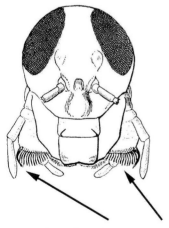

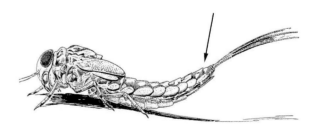

Figure 16 pectinate spines   **Figure 17**   **Figure 18**   **Figure 19:** *Ameletus* nymph with broad band on tails

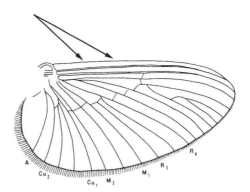

Figure 20: *Tricorythodes stygiatus* forewing and cross veins

ADULTS

1. Length 3mm to 7mm; lateral ocellus nearly half as large as compound eye; cross veins numerous (see figure 20); male claspers three segmented and the last segment rounded (Tricos); common, widespread, and important . . . . **Leptohyphidae;** *Tricorythodes*

   ### Description of the Species
   Three important species: *T. minutus,* 5mm to 7mm, (E, M, W); *T. allectus* and *T. stygiatus,* 3mm to 5mm, (E, M). These insects have three tails and two wings, the duns' wings are light gray and spinners' wings are clear. Female duns have an olive abdomen and dark brown thorax. Male duns have dark brown bodies. Female spinners have a pale to dark green abdomen and a dark brown thorax, male spinners are almost black.

   ### Emergence
   Emergence is from June through September. Duns emerge at night and very early in the morning, spinners fall in midmorning in high numbers. Spinner fall is usually much more important than the emergence.

   Cross veins few, male clasper one segmented and sharply pointed, uncommon and unimportant on trout streams . . . . **Caenidae**

   ### Description of the Species
   This family has two genera, *Caenis* (Anglers Curse) and *Brachycercus* (no common name). *Caenis* are very small—2.5mm to 3mm—with a cream abdomen and tan thorax. *Brachycercus* are a little larger at 3mm to 6mm, and have brownish bodies. This family prefers warmer and slower water, so they are seldom of importance to trout fishermen.

   Lateral ocellus only one-tenth to one-fourth as large as compound eye: Go to **2.**

2. Abdominal segments 6 and 7 wider, longer, and higher in profile view than segments 5 and 8, 10mm to 12mm long: uncommon and unimportant . . . . **Baetiscidae;** *Baetisca*

   ### Description of the Species
   Duns have dark brownish olive bodies and heavily black and white spotted wings, no common name, you will find these on trout streams but they do not produce good rises.

Abdominal segments 6 and 7 not wider and higher in profile view than segments 5 and 8: Go to **3**.

3. Hind tarsus with five clearly differentiated movable segments (see figure 21), length 7mm to 17mm, (March Browns, Yellow Cahills, Light Cahills, Quill Gordons) widespread, common, and important. . . . . **Heptageniidae**

There are ten genera in this family but the most important for fishermen are *Epeorus* (Quill Gordon), *Stenonema* (March Brown), and *Stenacron* (Yellow and Orange Cahill).

Hind tarsus with only three or four clearly differentiated, movable segments: Go to **4**.

4. Vein M1 of forewing sharply bent near the wing base (see figure 22); length 12mm to 40mm; if three tails *(Ephemera* and *Litobrancha)*, then middle tail is of equal length to outer tails. (Brown Drakes, Green Drakes, Yellow Drakes, Hexes) widespread, common, and important . . . . **Ephemeridae**

Description of the Genera

The *Ephemera* species have heavily spotted wings and three tails. They are the Brown Drakes, Green Drakes, and Yellow Drakes. The genus *Hexagenia* does not have heavily spotted wings and only two tails. The genus *Litobrancha* was in *Hexagenia,* but now has its own genus.

Emergence

These insects generally emerge at dusk or after dark from late spring to summer.

Vein M1 of forewing sharply bent near the wing base (see figure 22); most common species 12mm to 15mm; middle tail is about one half the length of outer tails (Golden Drakes); common in the East and Midwest, but emerges on warmer streams marginal for trout . . . . **Potamanthidae;** *Anthopotamus*

Description of the Species

The most important species are *A. distinctus,* 12mm to 16mm long (E, M); and *A. myops,* 13mm to 18mm long. The duns have a yellowish to golden body and yellow wings. The spinners have hyaline wings with no mottling.

Figure 21: Hind tarsus of Heptageniidae species (adult)

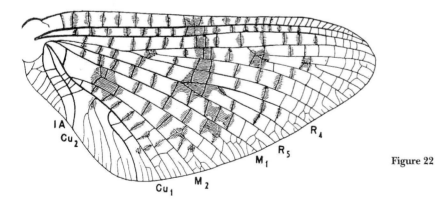

Figure 22

Emergence

Mid- to late June until mid-August in the evening, in the slower sections of streams.

Vein M1 of forewing sharply bent near the wing base (see figure 22); length 6mm to 21mm; wings and bodies whitish (White Fly); common and widespread but restricted to warmer sections of trout streams . . . . **Polymitarcidae;** *Ephoron*

Descriptions of the Species

Ephoron album, 11mm to 13mm (E, M); *E. leukon*, 9mm to 12mm (M, W); duns have yellowish white wings and bodies, spinners have white bodies and hyaline wings.

Emergence

Emerge from mid-August to mid-September in the evenings; the number of insects can be enormous. Spinners fall the same day at dusk and after dark.

Vein M2 of forewing not bent near the wing base: Go to **5.**

5. Forewing with one or two long intercalary veins between M2 and Cu1 (see figure 23); length 6mm to 15mm. (Hendricksons, Sulphurs, Slate Olive Duns, Western Green Drakes, Pale Morning Duns) widespread, common, and most important . . . . **Ephemerellidae**

> By far the most important genus in this family is *Ephemerella* (Hendricksons, Sulphurs, Pale Evening Dun, and Pale Morning Dun). The second most important genus is *Drunella*, the western Green Drake and the eastern Slate Olive Duns. For descriptions of the numerous important species and emergence data, see chapters 7, 8, 9, and 14.

Forewing without long intercalary veins between M2 and Cu1: Go to **6.**

6. Three tails; length 7mm to 14mm. (Large and Small Mahogany Duns). Widespread, common, and important . . . . **Leptophlebiidae**

> For complete descriptions of the genera, species, and emergence data, see chapters 7, 8, and 14.

Two tails: Go to **7.**

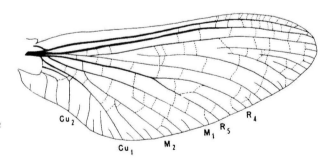

Figure 23 Cu$_1$, long intercalary vein M$_2$

7. Forewings heavily spotted with one or two pairs of long parallel cubital intercalary veins and without free marginal veinlets; hind wings spotted and relatively large; 16mm to 20mm; (E, M). (No common name). Uncommon and rarely important . . . . **Metretopodidae;** *Siphloplecton basale*

> ### Description of the species
> These species are found in the East and the Midwest, are generally uncommon, and resemble Gray Drakes.

Forewings with a series of short, slightly sinuate veinlets between Cu1 and inner margin of wing: Go to **8.**

Forewings with one or two long, basally detached cubital intercalary veins accompanied by free marginal veinlets; hind wings may be small or absent; length 3mm to 10mm. (Speckled Spinner, Small Blue Winged Olive, Tiny Blue Winged Olive). Common, widespread, and very important . . . . **Baetidae**

> The most important genera in this family are *Baetis* (Small Blue Winged Olive) and *Plauditus* (Tiny Blue Winged Olive). *Plauditus* was formerly in *Pseudocloeon*, and was just recently designated *Baetis*. For complete descriptions of the many important genera, species, and emergence data, see chapters 7, 8, 9, and 14.

8. Gill remnants present on base of foreleg; length 12mm to 18mm. (Slate Drakes, also known as White Gloved Howdy). Common and important, distributed in the East and Midwest; uncommon in the West . . . . **Isonychiidae;** *Isonychia bicolor*

> ### Description of the Species
> Duns have slate wings and dark brown to black bodies. Spinners are similar with hyaline wings. Most important species is *Isonychia bicolor.*
>
> ### Emergence
> Emergence is from late spring to fall in afternoon to dusk. Nymphs usually crawl out on shore to emerge but sometimes emerge in midriver.

Gill remnants absent on base of foreleg and hind taursus possesses four well-defined segments; claws of each foot sharp; length 9mm to 19mm. (Gray Drakes). Common, widespread, and important . . . **Siphlonuridae;** *Siphlonurus*

> ### Descriptions of the Species
> Duns are not important as they emerge on land. Spinners are conspicuously marked with purplish-gray and shades of reddish-brown. Eyes in life are reddish brown with horizontal bands of pale, purplish gray. Important species: *Siphlonurus Occidentalis,* (W); *S. colombianus* (W); *S. spectabilis* (W); *S. alternatus,* (E, M, W); *S. rapidus,* (E, M); *S. quebecensis,* (E, M).
>
> ### Emergence
> Emergence is from shore. Spinner falls can be massive. In the East and Midwest, the peak activity is from mid-May to Mid-June. Western spinner falls can occur from April to September.

Gill remnants absent on base of foreleg; hind tarsus with four well-defined segments; claws of each foot one sharp, one blunt; length 9mm to 11mm. (Brown Duns). Of minor importance in the West, rare in the East . . . . **Ameletidae;** *Ameletus cooki*

Description of the Species
Spinners are large brown to yellowish-brown insects.

Emergence Data
Duns are not important because they emerge on land. Spinner falls are of minor interest on some high-altitude western streams.

Keys to the Families and Genera of Caddisflies

ADULTS

These keys are intended for the caddisfly families, genera, and species found on trout streams in numbers sufficient to cause good rises by trout. Many uncommon species, species found only in warm water or still water have been eliminated for simplicity's sake. In some cases an 8X to 10X magnifying glass is necessary for examination of the insects. These can be obtained at camera shops in the form of slide viewers. Occasionally 20X to 30X magnification will be needed for very small species. These lenses are inexpensive and can be obtained from BioQuip Products. In cases where this increased magnification is necessary but unavailable (sections 1 and 2), suggestions are given so the angler who lacks more than 8X magnification can still identify the insect.

Size in millimeters means the overall length of the insect from head to the tip of the wing.

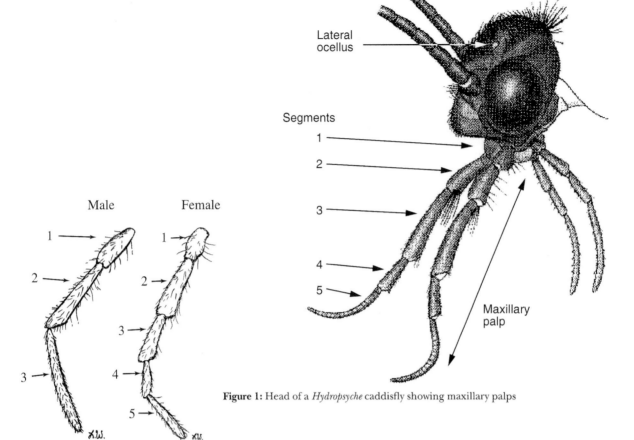

Figure 1: Head of a *Hydropsyche* caddisfly showing maxillary palps

Figure 2: Brachycentridae maxillary palps

Figure 3: *Rhyacophilia* maxillary palp

A. Caddisflies with maxillary palps 5 segmented and segment 5 is twice as long as segment 4 (see figure 1): **The Net Spinners**—*Go to Section 1.*

B. Caddisflies with male maxillary palps 3 segmented and female maxillary palps 5 segmented, (see figure 2): **The Tube Case Builders**—*Go to Section 2.*

C. Caddisflies with antennae more than twice as long as bodies—*Go to Section 3.*

D. Very small caddisflies from 2.4mm to 5.5mm: **The Microcaddisflies and Pseudo-Microcaddisflies**—*Go to Section 4.*

E. Very large caddisflies from 17mm to 34mm: **The Great and Giant Caddisflies**—*Go to Section 5.*

F. Caddisflies with segment 5 of the maxillary palp not much longer than segment 4 and segments 1 and 2 are much shorter than segments 3, 4, and 5 (see figure 3): **The Free Living Caddisflies**—*Go to Section 6.*

G. Small caddisflies (5mm to 7mm) with anterior margin of hindwing with a row of modified hairs in the basal half and a slight concavity in

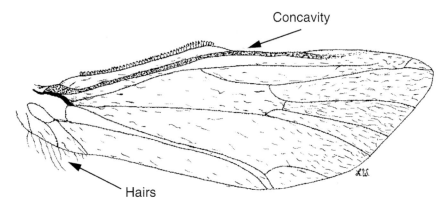

Concavity

Hairs

Figure 4: Hindwing of *Helicopsyche borealis*

the distal half (see figure 4), bodies bright amber with dark gray wings which have a heavy freckling of dark brown, distribution in the East, Appalachian South, Midwest, and West: **Speckled Peter, Snail Case Makers-Helicopsychidae;** *Helicopsyche borealis.*

H. Medium-sized caddisflies (12mm to 15mm) with dark gray wings which have small scattered light spots and dark-green to almost-black bodies. These insects always have maxillary palps 5 segmented, a single narrow transverse wart on the scutellum (see figure 5), and are found only in the East and Appalachian South: **Dark Blue Sedge, Strong Case Makers—Odontoceridae;** *Psilotreta labia* and *P. frontalis.*

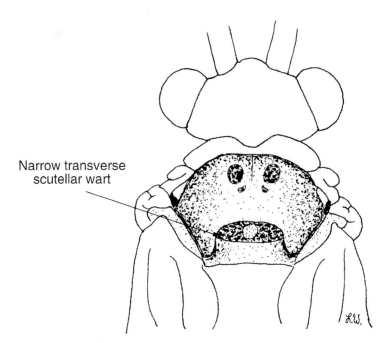

Narrow transverse scutellar wart

Figure 5: Narrow transverse scutellar wart

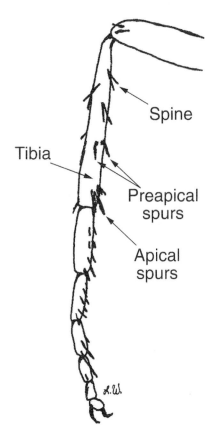

Figure 6

I. Large caddisflies (15mm to 17mm) with brown bodies and whose wings are grey with a checkered pattern of light and dark areas. *Molanna blenda* (from Ohio) appears almost black with long slender wings and very thick antennae. Tibia of middle legs with a pair of preapical spurs and a row of six to ten spines on the back side (see figure 6). Distribution in the East, Appalachian South, and the Midwest: **Gray Checkered Sedge, Hood Case Makers—Molannidae;** *Molanna uniophila, M. tryphena, M. blenda.*

SECTION 1: THE NET SPINNERS

This group includes Hydropsychidae (The Common Net Spinners), the most important group of caddisflies for fly fishermen.

a. Maxillary palps 5 segmented and segment 5 is more than twice as long as segment 4 (see figure 1); ocelli, scutal warts, and preapical spurs of foreleg all absent, unique wing shape (see figure 7): **The Super Caddisflies—Hydropsychidae.**

Cinnamon Sedges, aka Spotted Sedges, length 8mm to 15mm, wings brownish-gray with many tiny tan spots, bodies from yellow to orange, to cinnamon brown (the latter most common), distribution in the East, the Appalachian South, the Midwest, and the West—*Hydropsyche* and *Ceratopsyche* spp.

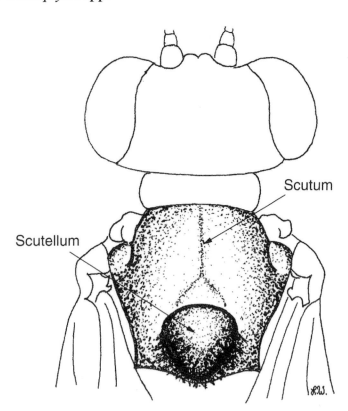

Figure 7: Dorsal view of head and thorax of Hydropsychidae

Little Olive Sedges, aka Little Sister Sedges, length 7mm to 12mm, wings brownish-gray, usually with some irregular tan markings (much lighter in fall), bodies olive green, distribution in the East, the Appalachian South, the Midwest, and the West—*Cheumatopsyche* **spp.**

For the other important genera in the family, *Macrostemum zebratum* **(Zebra Sedges),** *Arctopsyche grandis,* and *A. irrorata,* (**Great Gray Spotted Sedges**), see Sections 3 and 5.

b. Maxillary palps 5 segmented and segment 5 is more than twice as long as segment 4, (see figure 1), ocelli absent, scutum possesses warts (see figure 8), tibia of foreleg has a preapical spur (see figure 8). Length: 5mm to 11mm. **Small Yellow Brown Summer Sedges** and **Brown Checkered Sedge—Polycentropidae.**

This family has three genera: *Neureclipsis crepuscularis* (Little Red Twilight Sedge), 8mm to 9mm long, body and legs yellow, wings reddish-brown, distribution in the East, Appalachian South, and Midwest; *Nyctiophylax celta, N. afinis, N. moestus* (Little Yellow Brown Summer Sedges), 5mm to 7 mm long, bodies and legs are yellow, wings brown, distribution in the East, Appalachian South, and Midwest; *Polycentropus cinereus* (Brown Checkered Summer Sedge), 10mm to 11mm long, yellow body, checkered light and dark brown wings, dis-

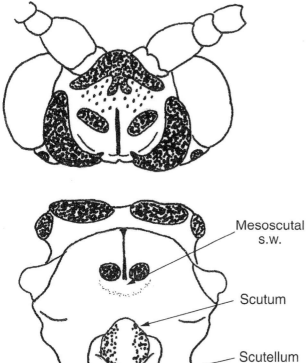

Mesoscutal s.w.

Scutum

Scutellum

Figure 8: Dorsal view of head and thorax of Polycentropidae, *Polycentropus* sp.

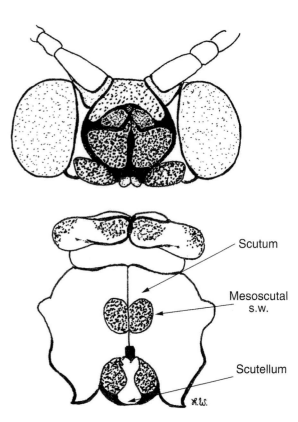

Figure 9: Dorsal view of head and thorax of Psychomyiidae, *Psychomysis* sp.

Scutum

Mesoscutal s.w.

Scutellum

tribution in the East, Appalachian South, Midwest, and West, (*Polycentropus confusus* is common on the Mad River in Ohio).

c. Five mm to 7mm long, maxillary palps 5 segmented and segment 5 is more than twice as long as segment 4 (see figure1), ocelli absent, scutum possesses warts, (see figure 9), tibia of foreleg lacks a preapical spur: **Tiny Dark Eastern Woodland Sedge** or **Tiny Yellow Brown Sedge** (aka **Tiny Purple Breasted Sedge**)—**Psychomyiidae.**

The two genera in this family are *Lipe* and *Psychomyia*. *Lipe diversa* (6mm to 7mm long) is the important species in the first genus, and is found in the East, the Appalachian South, and the Midwest. They emerge on summer evenings and have dark brown bodies with almost black wings. *Psychomyia flavida* is the important species in the second genus (5mm to 6mm long), and is found in the East, the Midwest, the Appalachian South, and the West. The bodies are yellow with a purplish cast, the wings are brown, and they emerge at dark on summer evenings.

d. 5.5mm to 10mm long, maxillary palps 5 segmented and segment 5 is more than twice as long as segment 4, (see figure 1). Ocelli present, scutum possesses warts, tibia of foreleg has a preapical spur (see figure

10): **Little Black Caddis** (6mm to 8mm), **Brown Evening Sedge** (6mm to 8mm), **Autumn Stream Sedge.**

This family has three genera that are important to trout fishermen. The first is *Chimarra* (Little Black Caddis). They are a small black species 5.5mm to 8mm long. They emerge in the spring. The pupae crawl to shore by skating over the surface of the water. Anglers in Michigan have been calling *Brachycentrus lateralis,* (which emerges from mid-stream in huge numbers), *Chimarra. Chimarra* do not emerge in huge numbers and are not as important as *Brachycentrus,* but trout do feed on them during early spring mornings. The most important species are *Chimarra aterrima,* found in the East, the Midwest, and the Appalachian South; *C.socia,* in the East; and *C. obscura,* in the East, Appalachian South, and Midwest.

The second genus in the family is *Dolophilodes.* They are 5.5mm to 8mm long and are also a small dark species, very dark brown, almost black. *Dolophilodes distinctus* is found in the East, Appalachian South, and Midwest, and is easily recognized by the tiny golden spots in the wings. This species emerges all year long, and in the winter and spring, the females are wingless. The pupae swim to the surface and then to shore where they emerge on land. *Dolophilodes aequalis* is a Western species, which is important in small Western streams such as Rock Creek in Montana, and emerge on evenings in July. Early emergers are almost black but later shift to light brown.

The third Genera in the family is *Wormaldia=Dolophilus.* These are larger (to 10mm) and they have olive-brown bodies with gray or mottled-brown wings. *Wormaldia anilla* is from the West and emerges in the spring and again in the fall. *W. gabriella* is also a western species which emerges from August to October. *W. moesta* is the Eastern species and emerges during the spring.

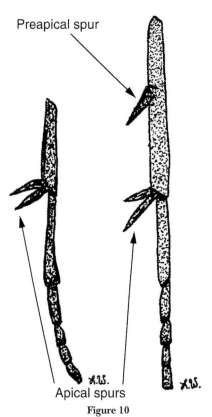

Preapical spur

Apical spurs

Figure 10

A note on the group of caddisflies whose fifth maxillary palps are segmented and twice as long as segment 4. This key involves the presence or absence of ocelli, warts, and spurs. These can be difficult to see, especially on the small dark species without more magnification than a slide magnifier will provide. The palps can be seen on all but the smallest species. If you do not have a more powerful means of examining the insect there is a way to identify it. The most important family in the group is Hydropsychidae. These can be easily recognized by their size, color, and unique wing shape. The Polycentropidae are somewhat similar but to Hydropsychidae but do not have the unique wing shape. The Psychomyiidae are very small, the Philopotamidae are a little larger than the Psychomyiidae. When one compares the colors, sizes, range, and time of year of emergence, one should be able to differentiate the genera without a microscope.

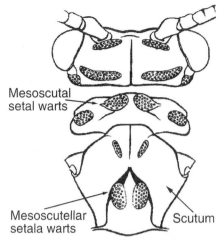

Mesoscutal
setal warts

Mesoscutellar
setala warts

Scutum

Figure 11: Dorsal view of head and thorax of
Brachycentrus sp.

SECTION 2: THE TUBE AND CHIMNEY CASE MAKERS

This group includes the Little Black Caddis, which are very important in the spring.

a. Male maxillary palps 3 segmented and female maxillary palps 5 segmented. Ocelli are absent, scutum possesses a pair of small separated warts (see figure 11), the tibia of the middle leg has an irregular row of spines. The preapical spur or spurs on the middle tibia are 1/3 of the way up from the apex of the tibia (see figure 12), or without preapical spurs. The abdomen has gland openings on venter v in a pair of rounded sclerotized lobes (see fig 13). **Mother's Day Caddis, Little Black Caddis, American Grannom, Little Weedy Water Sedge—Brachycentridae.**

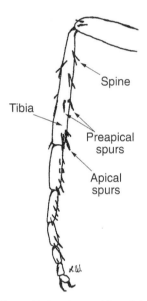

Tibia

Spine

Preapical
spurs

Apical
spurs

Figure 12: Brachycentridae adult
male leg row of spines preapical
spur, if present, 1/3 of the way up
from the apex apical spurs

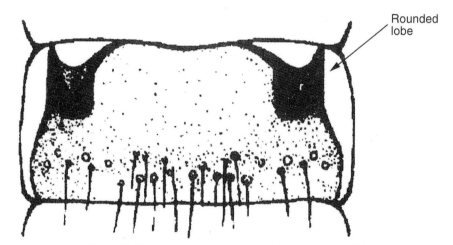

Rounded
lobe

Figure 13: Brachycentridae segment 5 of abdomen, ventral view

This family has three very important genera that often produce swarming hatches, especially in the spring. The first and most important genus is *Brachycentrus*. These insects are 7mm to 13mm long, have almost-black bodies (with green lateral lines when freshly emerged), and light gray wings. The other two genera, *Amiocentrus* and *Microsema* are smaller (6mm to 8mm long), and are similar to **Brachycentrus,** except that their wings are darker, and they come a little later in the season. Some species have another brood in the fall.

b. Same as a., above, but the male maxillary palp 1 may appear segmented, the tibia of the middle leg lacks a row of spines, and the preapical spurs of middle leg are one half the way up from the apex and are hairy (see figure 14). **Little Green Bodied Brown Wing Sedge** aka **Little Plane Brown Sedge**—Lepidostomatidae.

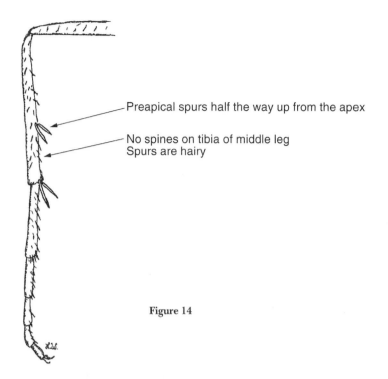

Preapical spurs half the way up from the apex

No spines on tibia of middle leg
Spurs are hairy

Figure 14

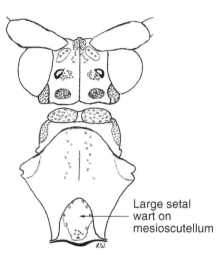

Large setal
wart on
mesioscutellum

Figure 15: Dorsal view of head and thorax
of *Limnephilus* sp.

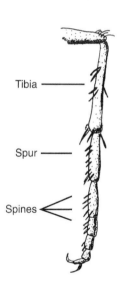

Tibia

Spur

Spines

Figure 16: Adult foreleg

This family has one genus, *Lepidostoma,* disrtributed in the East, Appalachian South, Midwest, and the West. They are 9mm to 10mm long. Many species have green bodies and dark grayish-brown wings, sometimes with a few dark spots. *Lepidostoma pluviale* is the important western species which has a yellow body and light brown wings. There are many species of local importance whose colors may vary from species to species. Males of some species have hairy maxillary palps.

c. Male maxillary palps 3 segmented, and female maxillary palps 5 segmented (see figure 3); mesioscutellum with a single large setal wart (see figure 15); tibia of foreleg has fewer than two spurs (figure 16) or if more, then the scutellum has a single oval wart; tibia of middle leg with one or no preapical spurs (see figure 17); hind wings usually much wider than fore wings (see figure 18): **The Diverse Caddisflies—**Limnephillidae.

This is a very diverse family with fourteen genera, but most species are not very important to fly fishermen.

A note on this group of caddisflies with male maxillary palps 3 segmented and female maxillary palps 5 segmented. As with Section 4, this key involves the presence or absence of structures which may be hard to see with a slide magnifier. The angler should be able to discover the family by looking at the palps with an 8X or 10X glass and comparing the size, color, distribution, and time of emergence for the insect. For instance, if the cad-

one preapical spur

Spines

Figure 17: Middle tibia and tarsus of *Limnephilus* sp.

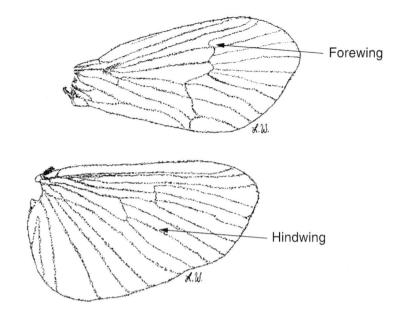

Forewing

Hindwing

Figure 18: Wings of *Discomoecus* sp.

disfly is 6mm to 13mm long, has a black body with green lateral lines, and light gray or black wings, it is probably a Brachycentridae. If the insect is 9mm to 10mm long, has a green body with brown or dark gray wings (or in the West, a yellow body with light brown wings), and the wings have a distinctive recurve, it is most likely a Lepidostomatidae. All others will probably be Limnephilidae.

SECTION 3: THE LONG HORNED SEDGES AND THE ZEBRA SEDGES

With the exception of the White Miller, these caddisflies emerge in midsummer. The White Miller generally emerges in late August and early September. All species oviposit in the evenings.

a. Wings cream with faint tan markings; body light green; thorax and legs ginger; 10mm to 17 mm long; distributed in the East, Appalachian South, and Midwest: **White Millers—Leptoceridae;** *Nectopsyche albida, N. exquisita, N. diarana.*

b. Wings dark gray to dark brown, often with light patches of scales; bodies dark gray to dark brown; 11mm to 17mm long; distributed in the East, Appalachian South, Midwest, and West: **Dark Long Horned Sedges** aka **Scaly Wing Sedges—Leptoceridae;** *Ceraclea* sp.

c. Wings and bodies black (*Mystacides alafimbriata* can have amber bodies); 9mm long; distributed in the East, Appalachian South, Midwest, and West (*M. alafimbriata* in the West only): **Black Dancer—Leptoceridae,** *Mystacides sepulchraliis, M. alafimbriata.*

d. Wings tan; bodies olive or ginger; 7mm to 12mm long; distributed in the East, Appalachian South, Midwest, and West: **Tan Long Horned Sedge—Leptoceridae;** *Oecetis inconspicua, O. avara, O. cinera, O. osteni.*

e. Wings gray, bodies males bright blue green, females golden yellow, 9mm to 11mm long, distribution in the West: **Gray Winged Long Horned Sedge—Leptoceridae;** *Oecetis disjuncta.*

f. Wings black with distinctive yellow pattern; bodies greenish-olive with black rings in freshly emerged insects; body darkens with age; 15mm to 18mm long; distributed in the East, Appalachian South, and Midwest: **Zebra Sedge—Hydropsychidae,** *Macrostemum zebratum.*

SECTION 4: THE MICROCADDISFLIES AND PSEUDO-MICROCADDISFLIES

a. Tiny caddisflies; always less than 6mm long and usually 2mm to 4.5mm long; very hairy; wings are narrow with long fringes of hair; antennae shorter than forewings (see figure 19); distributed in the East, Appalachian South, Midwest, and West: **True Microcaddisflies— Hydroptilidae.**

> Note: There are four important genera in this family. *Leucotrichia pictipes* (Ring Horned Microcaddis) is very dark brown to black, its wings have a few scattered light spots, the antennae have white bands around them, and is 3mm to 4.5mm long. *Agraylea multipunctata* (Salt and Pepper Microcaddis) has a green body, dark brown legs, speckled gray and white wings, and is 3mm to 4.5mm long. *Oxyethira pallida, O. serrate, O. michiganensis* (Cream and Brown Microcaddis) have light greenish-yellow bodies, yellow legs, cream and brown mottled wings, and are 2mm to 3mm long. *Hydroptila* sp. (Varicolored Microcaddis) have yellow, orange, or various brown-shaded bodies, gray or brown wings (spotted or plain), and are 2.5mm to 4mm long.

b. Tiny caddisflies, 3mm to 5.5mm long, not hairy, wings not narrow, distributed in the East, Appalachian South, Midwest, and West: **Pseudo-Microcaddisflies—Glossosomatidae;** *Protophilia* **sp.**

> Note: There are many species in this genus and colors vary considerably. The most common colors are gray wings with cinnamon legs and black bodies. Although small, this genus can be very important due to huge emergences.

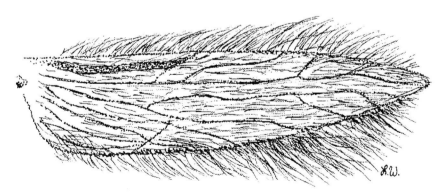

Figure 19: *Hydroptila hamata* adult forewing

SECTION 5: THE GREAT SEDGES AND GIANT SEDGES
(17MM TO 34 MM LONG)

Diagnostic verification of the families, the Limnephilidae, in this group have male maxillary palps 3 segmented and female maxillary palps 5 segmented, the Phryganeidae have male maxillary palps 4 segmented and female maxillary palps 5 segmented, the Hydropsychidae all have maxillary palps 5 segmented and segment 5 is more than twice as long as segment 4.

a. Length 19mm to 22mm; wings cinnamon brown with dark brown to black markings; body and legs cinnamon brown; distributed in the East, Appalachian South, Midwest, and West: Great Brown Autumn Sedge—Limnephilidae; Pycnopsyche lepida, P. guttifer, P. scabripennis.

b. Length 20mm to 22mm; cream and chocolate mottled wings; body dark yellow; distributed in the East, Appalachian South, and Midwest: **Chocolate and Cream Sedge—Limnephilidae;** *Platycentropus radiadus.*

c. Length 28mm to 34mm; wings light brown and cream with a Z pattern; body ginger; distributed in the East, Appalachian South, Midwest, and West: **Giant Cream Patterned Wing Sedge—Limnephilidae;** *Hydatophylax argus, H. hesperus.*

d. Length 21mm to 25mm; wing patterned gray, brown, and yellow; body reddish-brown; male maxillary palps 4 segmented; female maxillary palps 5 segmented (see figure 20); distributed in the East and Midwest: **Giant Rush Sedge—Phryganeidae;** *Phryganea cinera, P. sayi.*

e. Length 21mm to 25mm; wings reddish-brown with darker mottling; body reddish brown; male maxillary palps 4 segmented; females 5 segmented (figure 9); distributed in the East, Appalachian South, Midwest, and West: **Giant Rusty Sedge—Phryganeidae,** *Ptilostomis ocellifera, P. semifasciata.*

f. Length 25mm to 28mm; wings, legs and body ginger to brown; distributed in the West only: **Great Late Summer Sedge—Limnephilidae;** *Onocosmoecus frontalis, O. unicolor.*

g. Length: males 12mm to 15mm, females 16mm to 20mm; head, legs and body brown to brownish-yellow; wings mottled tan and brown; distributed in the East, Midwest, and West; from lakes. Called "Traveling Sedges" because the pupae swim to the surface to emerge, but adults run across the surface rather than fly off: **Traveling Sedges—Phryganeidae;** *Banksiola crotchi.*

h. Length 18mm to 34mm; wings gray with heavy veins; body orange; distributed in the West only: **Giant Orange Sedge: Limnephilidae;** *Dicosmoecus atripes, D. gilvipes, D. jucundus.*

i. Length *(H. designatus)* 17mm to 20mm; distributed in the East, Midwest, and West; Length *(H. incisus)* 30mm to 34mm; wings cream and light brown with a long silver stripe; body bright olive; distributed in

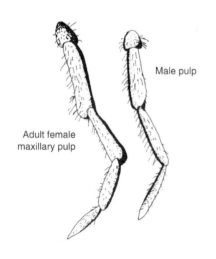

Male pulp

Adult female
maxillary pulp

Figure 20

the West only. These insects emerge from early July to early August on in the West. Egg laying is most important from morning to afternoon. **Silver Stripe Sedge** aka **Giant Golden Caddis: Limnephilidae;** *Hesperophylax designatus, H. incisus.*

j. Length 17mm to 20mm; wing dark gray with light spotting; body greenish-brown to olive; maxillary palp with segment 5 more than twice as long as segment 4; distributed in the Appalachian South and West: **Great Gray Spotted Sedge: Hydropsychidae;** *Arctopsyche grandis, A. irrorata.*

SECTION 6: THE GREEN SEDGES, LITTLE BLACK SHORT HORNED SEDGES, AND LITTLE TAN SHORT HORNED SEDGES

a. Segment 5 of maxillary palp is not much longer than segment 4 and segments 1 and 2 are short, much shorter than segments 3–4-5 (see figure 3); tibia of foreleg has apical and preapical spurs (see figure 14): **Green Caddis—Rhyacophilidae.**

> This family has one genus, *Rhyacophila.* These insects are from 8mm to 18mm long, have green or occasionally olive-brown bodies, and have brown wings with many lighter tan spots. There are many species found all over the country in clean, fast water.

b. Segment 5 of maxillary palp is not much longer than segment 4 and segments 1 and 2 are short, much shorter than segments 3–4-5 (see figure 3); tibia of foreleg lacks either apical or preapical spurs, or both, (see figure 13): **Little Black Short Horned Sedge** and **Little Tan Short Horned Sedge: Glossosomatidae.**

> This family has two genera which are important to fishermen, *Protophilia* (Pseudo-Microcaddis which we have all ready covered) and *Glossosoma* (Little Black Short Horned Sedge and Little Tan Short Horned Sedge). They range in size from 6mm to 10mm long; they are distributed in the East, Appalachian South, Midwest, and West. The tan species have greenish-brown bodies and tan to medium-brown wings.

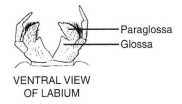

Paraglossa
Glossa

VENTRAL VIEW
OF LABIUM

Figure 1: Ventral view of labia

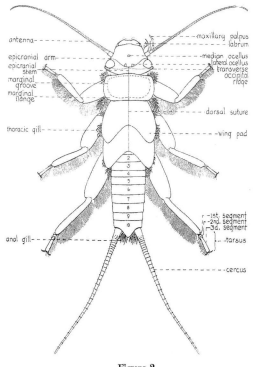

antenna
epicranial arm
epicranial stem
marginal groove
marginal flange
thoracic gill
anal gill

maxillary palpus
labrum
median ocellus
lateral ocellus
transverse occipital ridge
dorsal suture
wing pad

1st segment
2nd segment
3d. segment
tarsus
cercus

Figure 2

Keys to the Families
of Stoneflies

THE ANATOMY OF STONEFLIES
ADULT MALES AND FEMALES

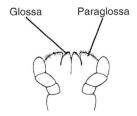

Glossa   Paraglossa

Figure 3: Ventral view of labia

1. Paraglossae and flossae of about equal length (figure 3) .... Go to **2**

   Paraglossae much longer than glossae (figure 1) .... Go to **7**

2. Anterior abdominal sterna with branched gill remnants (figure 4) anal area of forewings withtwo or more full rows of crossviens (figure 5) .... Pteronarcidae

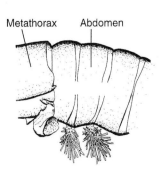

Metathorax   Abdomen

Figure 4

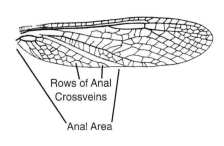

Rows of Anal Crossveins

Anal Area

Figure 5

Abdominal sterna without branched gill remnants; anal area of forewings without crossveins or with only one row . . . . Go to **3**

3. Ocelli two; form roachlike (figure 6); ten or more costal crosssveins in forewings . . . . .Peltoperlidae

   Ocelli three; form elongate (figure 7); Less than ten costal crossveins in forewings, except in Isocapnia, which may have ten or more . . . Go to **4**

4. Second tarsal segment much shorter than first (figure 8) . . . . . . Go to **5**

   Second tarsal segment at least as long as first (figure 9) . . . . Taeniopterygidae

5. General form stout and rather robust; x-shaped pattern present in forewings at cord (figure 10) . . . . Nemouridae

   General form thin and elongate (figure 7) except Megaleuctra, which is quite stout; x-shaped pattern absent from forewings at cord (figure 11) . . . . Go to **6**

6. Wings lying lat at rest (figure 7); cerci with four or more segments . . . . Capnidae

   Wings slightly rolled when at rest; cerci one segmented . . . . Leuctridae

7. Branched gill remnants present at lower angles of thorax . . . . . Perlidae

   Branched gill remnants absent from lower angles of thorax . . . . Go to **8**

8. External gill remnants entirely lacking; second anal vein of forewing not forked or forked beyond anal cell, except in Kathroperla, which has the fork at margin of cell or included in it (figure 12) . . . . . Chloroperlidae

   External gill remnants simple or absent; fork of second anal vein of forewing included in anal cell so that its branches leave cell separately (figure 13) . . . . Perlodidae

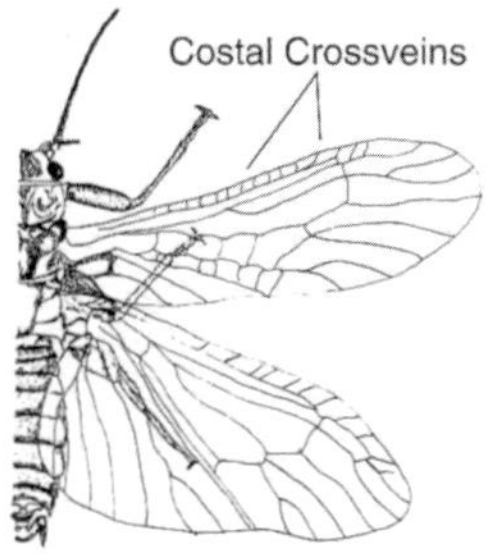

Figure 6

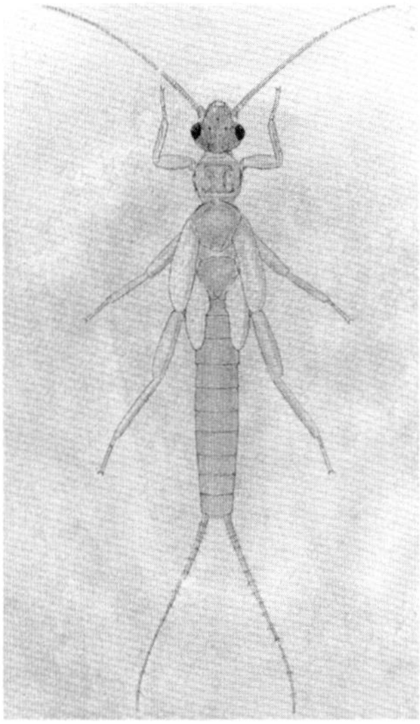

Figure 7

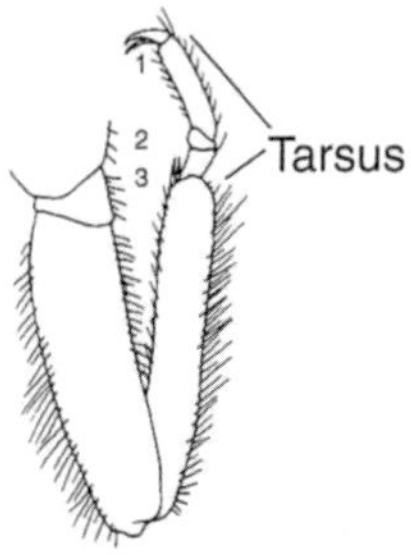

Figure 8

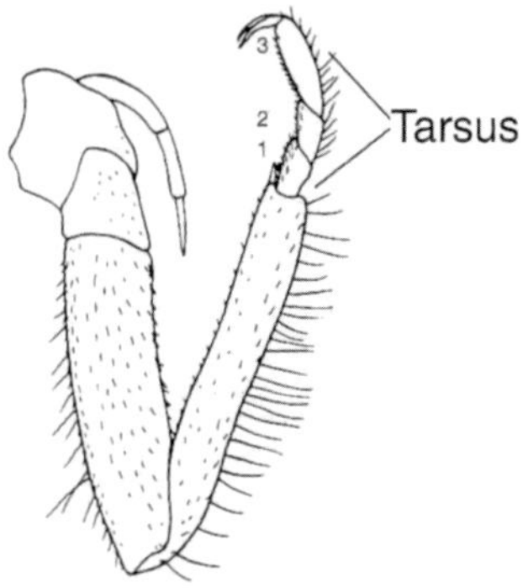

Figure 9

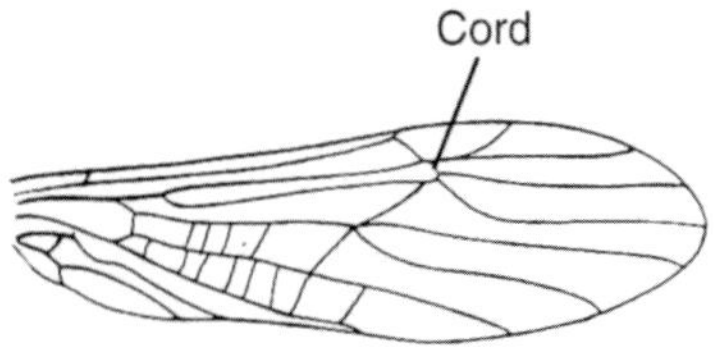

Figure 10

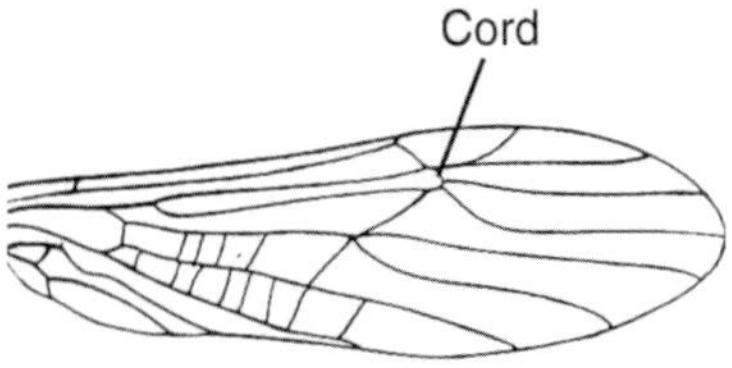

Figure 11

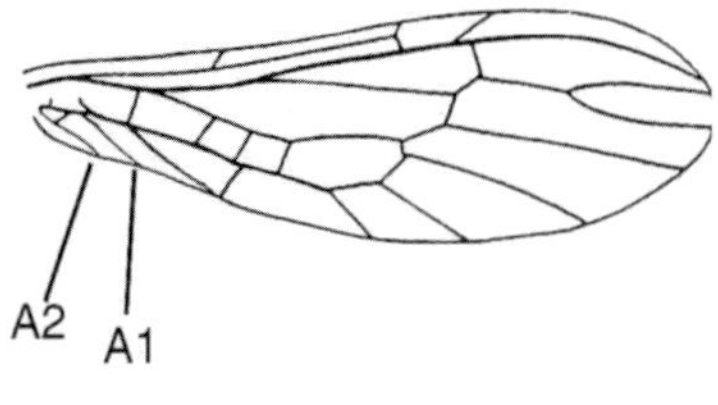

Figure 12

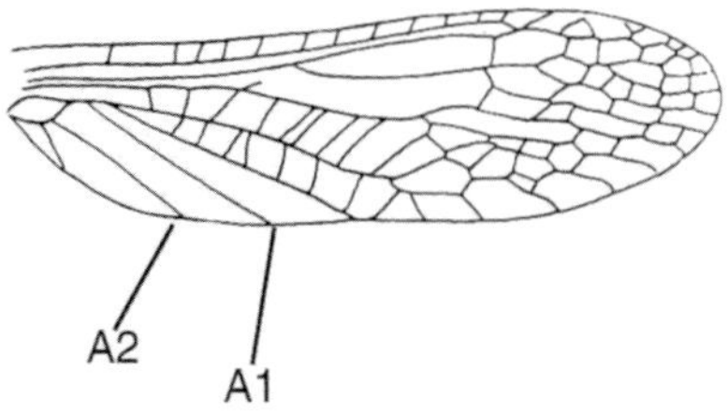

Figure 13

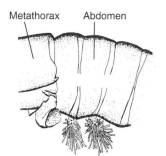

Metathorax Abdomen

Figure 14

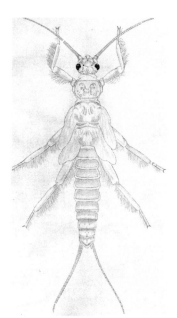

Figure 15

MATURE NYMPHS

1. Paraglossae and glossae of equal length (figure 3) . . . . Go to **2**

   Paraglossae much longer than glossae (figure 1) . . . . Go to **7**

2. Anterior abdominal sterna with branched gills
   (figure 14) . . . . Pteronarcidae

   Abdominal sterna without branched gills . . . . Go to **3**

3. Ocelli two; form roachlike (figure 15); thoracic sterna overlapping next
   segment . . . . Peltoperlidae

   Ocelli three; form elongate (figure 16); thoracic sterna not overlapping
   next segment . . . . Go to **4**

4. Second tarsal segment much shorter than first (figure 8) . . . . . . Go to **5**

   Second tarsal segment at least as longas first
   (figure 9) . . . . Taeniopterygidae

5. Form stout with hindwing pads strongly divergent from body axis
   (figure 17) . . . . Nemouridae

   Form elongate and cylindrical with hindwing pads nearly parallel
   (figure 16) . . . . Go to **6**

6. Notch on inner margins of hindwing pads located on anterior third; abdominal segments one to nine divided by a membranous fold laterally
   (figure 18) . . . . Capniidae

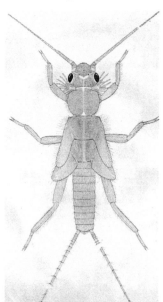

Figure 16

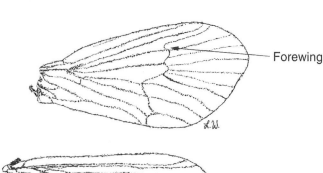

Forewing

Hind wing

Figure 17

Figure 18

Notch on inner margins of hindwing pad located on posterior third; at most only the first seven abdominal segments divided by a membranous fold (figure 19) .... Leuctridae

7. Branched gills present at lower angles of thorax; apex of glossae rounded .... Perlidae

   Branched gills absent from thorax; apex of glossae pointed .... Go to **8**

8. Dorsal surface usually pigmented in distinct pattern; cerci as long as or longer than abdomen; hindwing pads of mature nymphs diverging from body axis (figure 20 and figure 21) .... Perlodidae

   Dorsal surface concolorous; cerci not more than three fourths as long as abdomen; hindwing pads nearly parallel to body axis, except in Kathroperia, which has an elongate head (figure 21) ... Chloroperlidae

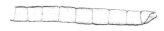

Figure 19

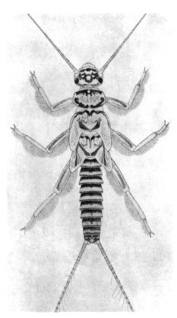

Figure 20

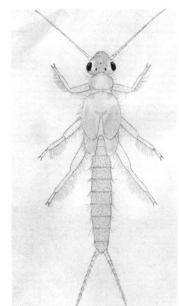

Figure 21

Index

Note: Flies are indexed under common and Latin names. Italicized page numbers refer to illustrations.